"NICE GUYS FINISH SEVENTH"

"NICE GUYS FINISH SEVENTH"

FALSE PHRASES, SPURIOUS SAYINGS, AND FAMILIAR MISQUOTATIONS

RALPH KEYES

HarperCollins*Publishers*

HarperCollins books may be purchased for educational, business, or sales promotional use. For information please write: Special Markets Department, HarperCollins Publishers, Inc., 10 East 53rd Street, New York, NY 10022.

FIRST EDITION

Designed by George J. McKeon

LIBRARY OF CONGRESS CATALOG CARD NUMBER 92-52539
ISBN 0-06-270020-0

92 93 94 95 96 CC/RRD 10 9 8 7 6 5 4 3 2 1

To my mother-in-law, Reba Gordon, for her interest and support

Contents

Acknowledgments

I would like to acknowledge help from the following people in writing this book: Peggy Anderson, Tony Bent, Ruth Bent, John Bibby, Dan Buck, Rich Bullock, Joe Cali, Bob Chieger, William Deminoff, Philomene D'Ursin, Jeff Evans, Louis Filler, Ed Fuller, Pat Gershwin, Virginia Gilmore, Dick Goldberg, Phil Goldberg, Reba Gordon, Dan Hotaling, Gene Keyes, Nicky Keyes, Scott Keyes, Steve Keyes, Janis Lee, Erik Lunde, Michael Medved, Jan Miller, Scot Morris, Donald Murray, Mark Neely, Pat O'Connor, Nick Proffitt, Suzanne Schulze, Enid Shomer, and Marta Vogel.

Bill Baker, Gay Courter, Bob Fogarty, Robert Ellis Smith, and Stanley Clarke Wyllie all gave me detailed, helpful responses to the manuscript.

Staffs of the following libraries were unusually helpful with my research: the Library of Congress; New York Public Library; Lincoln Center Theater Collection; Museum of Broadcasting; Philadelphia Free Library; Swarthmore Public Library; Swarthmore College Library;

Greene County (Ohio) District Library, Yellow Springs Branch; Antioch College Library.

My editor, Hugh Van Dusen, has been a fine source of support as has his assistant, Stephanie Gunning. The collaboration of my wife, Muriel, in every aspect of its preparation has made this a far better book than it would have been without her help.

Author's Note

I love quotations: love to use them, read them, and read about them. The frustrating thing is that so many of our most popular sayings can't be verified. What was actually said? Who said it first? How do we know?

This book is meant to answer such questions. Writing it took several years. With the indispensable help of my wife, Muriel, its preparation involved countless hours accessing databases, studying microfilms, examining archival material, reading books, making calls, and writing letters. Whenever possible I interviewed principals in person or by phone. Field trips took me to the Library of Congress, New York Public Library, many smaller collections, theater collections in New York and Philadelphia, the Museum of Broadcasting in New York City, movie studios, newspaper morgues, and various archives.

The fruits of this quest are gathered in *"Nice Guys Finish Seventh."* In it I've tried to take a fresh, skeptical look at familiar phrases, sayings, and quotations. Are the words on record what was actually said? What is their source? Is that source original or secondhand? If the words are accurate, who said them? What was the context? By trying to answer such questions, my hope has been to produce a book that is both interesting to read and useful as a work of reference.

Many of our best-known sayings and quotations turn out to be misworded, misattributed, and miscited in existing works of reference. This is why I've generally used such resources more as a starting than as a finishing point. As I worked on this project, a new edition of Bartlett's *Familiar Quotations* was being prepared. Its editor, Justin Kaplan, seemed to be making an energetic effort to broaden and confirm this book's contents. Since the fruits of his labor had not been published as I completed my own book, references to *Bartlett's* are primarily to its fifteenth edition (1980).

Although I have always reported the most accurate wording available of material in question, old English generally has been converted to modern, and British spellings to American. Whenever possible, I've tried to locate and cite original sources: a newspaper article, say, instead of another work's reference to that article. Source notes at the end of this book only cite an original source that I've actually examined. When this hasn't been possible, I've cited the secondary source consulted (along with *its* primary source, when one is given).

As hard as I've tried to make its contents accurate, this book undoubtedly includes mistakes and omissions. Additions and corrections will be gratefully—and, I hope, gracefully—received by the author, c/o HarperCollins, 10 East 53rd Street, New York, NY 10022.

Although it may not sound like it, working on this project has been fun. For a time, poring over books and magazines looking for clues became our typical evening's entertainment. Finding the actual wording or source of a disputed quotation was exhilarating. I hope reading the results is just as exhilarating. Verifying quotations is exciting, a detective game we all can play. In a more serious vein, it should be useful to have the results gathered in one book. I hope readers' eyes will be opened, as mine were, by the surprising number of popular phrases, sayings, and quotations that have been garbled in transmission, or moved from one mouth to another. This tells us something about ourselves. Why are so many of our most familiar sayings inaccurately worded or attributed? I hope *"Nice Guys Finish Seventh"* will answer that question.

1

Why Misquotes Drive Out Real Quotes

Quotation: The act of repeating erroneously the words of another. The words erroneously repeated.

AMBROSE BIERCE

Perish the man who said our good things before us.

AELIUS DONATUS

W. C. Fields's best remembered saying is **"Any man who hates dogs and children can't be all bad."** Fields didn't say it. These words were said *about* Fields, by Leo Rosten, as he introduced the comedian at a 1939 Masquers banquet in Los Angeles. Rosten, then a young social scientist studying the movie industry, found himself seated on the dais. He was invited to say a few words about the guest of honor. Unable to think of anything else, Rosten blurted out, "The only thing I can say about Mr. W. C. Fields, whom I have admired since the day he advanced upon Baby LeRoy with an ice pick, is this: Any man who hates babies and dogs can't be all bad." According to Rosten his quip brought down the house. He later called it "one of those happy 'ad libs' God sends you." Two weeks later Rosten's line was mentioned in *Time* magazine. At the time few people had heard of Leo Rosten. As a result, before long Rosten's words were put in a better-known mouth: that of Fields himself. They've stayed there ever since.

But Rosten deserves credit for this line, right? Well, not exactly. In November 1937—nearly two years before the Masquers banquet—

Harper's Monthly ran a column by Cedric Worth about a New York cocktail party which took place in 1930. This party was dominated by a man who had a case against dogs. After leaving, Worth found himself in an elevator with a *New York Times* reporter. As the elevator made its way to the ground, the reporter observed, "No man who hates dogs and children can be all bad."

To be accurate, therefore, reference books should attribute "No man who hates dogs and children can be all bad" to this *Times* reporter. His name was Byron Darnton. Byron who? That's just the point. Darnton was a metropolitan reporter and war correspondent who was killed early in World War II. Few remember his name. Yet most of us have heard of W. C. Fields. This is why Fields so often gets credit for someone else's words. He probably always will.

The case of W. C. Fields is surprisingly common. Even our most hallowed phrases are routinely misremembered. Many of history's best-known quotes have been inaccurately recorded, attributed to the wrong person, or both. In the course of this project I've discovered hundreds of examples of misquotation. For instance:

- **"Winning isn't everything, it's the only thing"** was the slogan of UCLA football coach Red Sanders, not Vince Lombardi.
- **"The opera ain't over till the fat lady sings"** was adapted from an older saying: "Church ain't out till the fat lady sings."
- **"Elementary, my dear Watson"** does not appear in any of Arthur Conan Doyle's books about Sherlock Holmes.
- Calvin Coolidge didn't say **"The business of America is business."**
- Leo Durocher never said **"Nice guys finish last."**

As long as there have been quotes, there have been misquotes. As a general rule, *Misquotes drive out real quotes.* This is the Immutable Law of Misquotation. Misquotation takes three basic forms: (1) putting the wrong words in the right mouth; (2) putting the right words in the wrong mouth; and (3) putting the wrong words in the wrong mouth.

During the Senate Judiciary Committee hearings about Clarence Thomas's Supreme Court nomination, Chairman Joseph Biden quoted Shakespeare as having said **"Hell hath no fury like a woman scorned."**

Senator Alan Simpson of Wyoming pointed out (correctly) that it was actually playwright William Congreve who wrote:

> Heaven has no rage, like love to hatred turned,
> Nor hell a fury like a woman scorned.

In the same play—*The Mourning Bride*—Congreve also wrote, **"Music has charms to soothe a savage *breast*,"** not "beast" as we often imagine.

Such alteration of quotations over time is surprisingly common. In his 1713 play *Cato,* Joseph Addison wrote, "The woman that deliberates is lost." Reflecting our changing values, history first revised this to "She who hesitates is lost," then **"He who hesitates is lost."**

Like ocean waves polishing pebbles, common usage tends to edit, smooth, and update original versions of popular sayings.

COMMON	ORIGINAL
Don't look a gift horse in the mouth.	Never inspect the teeth of a gift horse.
There is safety in numbers.	In the multitude of counsellors there is safety.
Necessity is the mother of invention.	. . . the true creator is necessity, who is the mother of our invention. . . .
If the shoe fits, wear it.	If any fool finds the Cap fit him, let him wear it.
You can't have your cake and eat it too.	Would you both eat your cake and have your cake?
To gild the lily.	To gild refined gold, to paint the lily . . .

The latter is from Shakespeare's *King John*. Shakespeare could be history's most misquoted figure. He wrote so many quotable lines that it's easy to attribute all manner of orphan comment to him—whatever *sounds* Shakespearean. Anyone quoted as often as the Bard is bound to be misquoted.

For example:

<u>POPULAR</u>	<u>ACTUAL</u>
Discretion is the better part of valor.	The better part of valor is discretion . . . (Henry IV)
There's method in his madness.	Though this be madness, yet there is method in't. (Hamlet)
Alas! poor Yorick. I knew him well.	Alas, poor Yorick! I knew him, Horatio. (Hamlet)

The reason we misquote Shakespeare so routinely is that we generally consult our memory for quotations. Memory alone is an undependable work of reference. Quoting from memory is like playing "Telephone," the game in which a comment passed from mouth to ear along a line of children ends up totally distorted by the end. This process can be seen at work in one of the most requoted sayings of our times: Andy Warhol's remark that in the future we all would be **famous for fifteen minutes.** Warhol's actual words, in the catalog of a 1968 exhibition, were, "In the future everybody will be world famous for fifteen minutes." Along the way something often got lost in transmission. Dozens of variations I've seen include:

"Now that everyone seems to have been famous for five minutes, as Andy Warhol predicted."

"You know what Warhol said about everybody in America being famous for ten minutes."

"What did Andy Warhol say—that everyone gets fifteen seconds of fame?"

"Andy Warhol's prediction—that everyone will be a celebrity for fifteen seconds—has come true with a vengeance."

" 'In the future,' the artist-seer Andy Warhol has promised, 'there won't be any more stars. TV will be so accessible that *everybody* will be a star for fifteen minutes.' "

"In art, everyone should be famous for fifteen minutes."

"Everybody is famous for fifteen minutes."

As Warhol's memory fades from our minds we tend to talk about "fifteen minutes of fame" and skip attribution altogether. That's how the pros do it. An axiom among public speakers is this: the first time you use a quote, introduce it by saying, "As Joe Doakes once said . . ." The second time say, "It's been said that . . ." The third time, "As I've often said . . ."

Think of this as Three-Step Quote Acquisition. Harry Truman was a master of the art. To explain his decision not to run for reelection in 1952, Truman quoted his old friend Harry Vaughan: **"If you can't stand the heat, get out of the kitchen."** A few months later Truman said in a speech, "The President gets a lot of hot potatoes from every direction and a man who can't handle them has no business on the job. That makes me think of a saying that I used to hear from my old friend and colleague on the Jackson County Court. He said, 'Harry, if you can't stand the heat you better get out of the kitchen.' " Eight years later Truman wrote in his autobiography, "I used to have a saying that applies here and I note that some people have picked it up: 'If you can't stand the heat, get out of the kitchen.' "

By now Harry Truman is generally considered the author of this familiar saying. He has also been credited with such quips as **"I don't care what they say about me as long as they spell my name right"** and **"It's a recession when your neighbor loses his job; it's a depression when you lose your own."** Both are old saws that were hardly original to Truman, if he ever said them at all. But because they *sound* like him, and he is well known to us, Truman's name routinely gets attached to words that weren't his. This is a common fate among public figures. For years I quoted Lincoln's apology for writing a long letter: He hadn't the time to write a short one. After undertaking this project I learned that it was actually French philosopher Blaise Pascal who said this. I also learned that Mark Twain never said the coldest winter he ever spent was a summer in San Francisco, as I'd always believed (and often said).

This is how misquotes get born and perpetuated: Someone wants to make a point during a conversation, in a speech, or in a piece of writing. That person recalls a quotation which illustrates the point perfectly. Not being sure of the exact wording, the quoter uses the closest remembered version. He or she may also not be sure exactly who said the words in question. But—because they sound like Truman or Twain or Lincoln or Churchill—the quoter puts the quote in the mouth of a plausible noted figure, whoever it most "sounds like." If the misquotation takes place in a public forum, the mistake is compounded.

While reviewing Mikhail Gorbachev's years in power, ABC-TV's Ted Koppel concluded, "All in all, Gorbachev personified John F. Kennedy's definition of courage: a man who showed **grace under pressure.**" You can see what the writer of Koppel's line must have been thinking: Courage; John Kennedy wrote a book on courage; the classic definition of that quality must have been his. It wasn't. Ernest Hemingway defined "guts" as "grace under pressure" in 1929, when John Kennedy was twelve years old.

This is the "sounds like" syndrome. Sayings of uncertain origin are routinely put in the mouth of the best-known person they most sound like. Comments having to do with shady showmanship, for example, are typically attributed to P. T. Barnum. **"There's a sucker born every minute"** is so commonly credited to him that it's entered the category of "everybody knows Barnum said it." He didn't. Barnum Museum curator Robert Pelton calls this "one of the few things he *didn't* say." No modern biographer of Barnum takes this attribution seriously. Among other things, the word *sucker* was not that common during the flamboyant showman's heyday. *Humbug* was. Barnum used that word frequently, once saying "the people like to be humbugged." Another early American term for a gullible hick was *jay*. A popular nineteenth century song included the line, "There's a new jay born every day." This could have inspired the modern version so commonly attributed to P. T. Barnum.

In his own search for the origins of "there's a sucker born every minute," Barnum biographer A. H. Saxon came up with two other possibilities. One was in an unpublished manuscript by Joseph McCaddon, the brother-in-law of James Bailey (of "Barnum & Bailey"), and no friend of Barnum's. Dismissing any thought that Barnum ever said a sucker was born every minute, this manuscript attributed that sentiment to a notorious con man of the early 1880s named Joseph Bessimer. According to McCaddon, a New York police inspector said Bessimer told him, "There is a sucker born every minute, but none of them die." This was the first time that the inspector had heard that expression. Alternatively, Barnum's rival Adam Forepaugh reportedly observed during a newspaper interview that a sucker was born every minute. Asked if he might be quoted, Forepaugh replied, "Just say it's one of

Barnum's slogans which I am borrowing for the occasion. It sounds more like him than it does me, anyway."

All of these leads probably include elements of the truth. "There's a sucker born every minute" most likely grew out of the earlier "jay born every day" saying. The new version undoubtedly was popular among late-nineteenth-century con men. After it showed up in print, the saying made its way to P. T. Barnum's lips, helped along by those who wished to imply he was a con man. Not that help was needed. These words sounded so much like Barnum that it was easy to assume he'd said them. It still is.

Similarly, who hasn't heard Sherlock Holmes's signature line: **"Elementary, my dear Watson"**? That phrase does not appear anywhere in the collected works of Holmes's creator, Sir Arthur Conan Doyle. In *The Crooked Man*, the narrator, Dr. Watson, does have this exchange with Holmes:

"Excellent!" I cried.

"Elementary," said he.

Where did the more familiar version come from? The year before Doyle died, this classic line made its debut in a movie: *The Return of Sherlock Holmes*. In that 1929 film, Clive Brook, playing Holmes, first said, "Elementary, my dear Watson, elementary." More than half a century later, it is still widely assumed that this phrase sprang from the pen of Arthur Conan Doyle.

One would think that in an age of film, videotape, audiotape, and computerized databanks, such misquotation would decline. It hasn't. Even where word-perfect records exist—of lines from movies, recorded television programs, taped interviews, or works in print—misquotation remains as common as ever. This is because our ability to find the exact wording and source of familiar quotations is beside the point. The more important point is to have things that need saying said by someone we've heard of. Accuracy is secondary. A pithy, pertinent misquote is preferred to one which is correct but tortured. Famous comments such as "Say it ain't so, Joe" or "Don't trust anyone over thirty" gain currency because they express so well a thought already on many minds. Whether such words were actually said, or by the person we thought said them, is beside the point.

When Muhammad Ali refused induction into the Army, he was widely quoted as saying, **"No Viet Cong ever called me nigger."** This was a perfect marriage of anti-war and anti-racist sentiment. Better yet, it came straight from the mouth of a mega-celebrity thought to possess primitive folk wisdom. But Ali never made this comment. "It wasn't really his mind-set to say something in that way," explained Ali biographer Thomas Hauser. "The companion thought of that comment is 'People call me nigger in this country every day.' I never heard Ali say 'White people in this country call me nigger.' He would attack racism. But he wouldn't personalize it." Despite extensive searching by himself and others, Hauser has never found the source of "No Viet Cong ever called me nigger." He concluded that it was just one of those sayings that got picked up and passed around in the sixties. We wanted Ali to say this so badly that we said it for him.

A similar fate befell General Motors President Charles E. Wilson. The comment for which we best remember Wilson is **"What's good for General Motors is good for the country."** That observation captured perfectly the smug arrogance of corporate titans. During General Motors's downsizing in the early 1990s, this fatuous remark was dusted to summarize GM's attitude in a sound bite. But that isn't what Wilson said. While testifying about his nomination as Secretary of Defense before the Senate Committee on Armed Services on January 15, 1953, Wilson was asked whether he could make a decision on behalf of the government which would adversely affect General Motors. "Yes, sir," Wilson replied, "I could. I cannot conceive of one because for years I thought what was good for our country was good for General Motors, and vice versa." This is similar to the more popular version, but not the same at all. We prefer the misquote, however, so that is the version which has stuck in the public mind. This version echoed a line from a corrupt banker in the 1939 movie *Stagecoach:* "And remember this: What's good for the bank is good for the country."

Wilson's familiar misquotation is a good test of quote collections. Many still include it. Others give varying reports of what they think Wilson said, and a wide range of dates and settings. Through its fifteenth edition in 1980, *Bartlett's Familiar Quotations* not only had Wilson's words wrong, but the year in which he said them and the setting, too. Their version of his words—"What is good for the country is good for General Motors, and what's good for General Motors is good for the country"—first appeared in *Bartlett's* 1955 edition, duplicating the version in Clifton Fadiman's *An American Treasury* which was published the year before.

Relying on quote collections for accurate wording and citation is problematic. Their compilers have so many thousands of entries to include that they can't possibly verify each one. In addition, quote compilers are promiscuous borrowers. As a result, errors wend their way from one collection to another. In one amusing example, the *Oxford Dictionary of Quotations* quoted Ulysses S. Grant as saying "I *purpose* to fight it out on this line if it takes all summer" (emphasis added). A few years later the *Macmillan Dictionary of Quotations* had Grant "purposing" to do the same thing. So did *The Bully Pulpit,* a compendium of quotes by American Presidents.

No book of quotations—including this one—can hope to be completely accurate. The best one can hope for is to minimize errors. Quote collectors are humble people. They must be. We usually start out planning to trace every entry back to its original source. It doesn't take long to realize that this is an impossible dream. While producing a quote collection for the Library of Congress, Suzy Platt said of verifying its contents, "It really opened my eyes to the fact that you can't be *totally* sure."

New York Times columnist William Safire devotes more effort than the average quotemonger to determining who actually said what. He too has concluded that one can never be certain. In his columns and books, Safire takes pains to point out that any attribution of a quote must be considered tentative. Among other reasons, the readers whom Safire calls his "gotcha gang" love nothing better than calling gaffes to his attention. Safire's British counterpart, Nigel Rees—host of a BBC radio program called *Quote . . . Unquote*—says his golden rule is this: "It is very dangerous ever to say that a particular person coined a phrase or that it came about in a definite way. There is almost always an example of earlier use. The furthest it is safe to go is to say that a certain person has popularized the phrase at a certain time."

Consider **"You can never be too rich or too thin."** This maxim is associated with any number of wealthy, skinny women. It has been attributed to Rose Kennedy, Diana Vreeland, the Duchess of Windsor, and Babe Paley. (The last two most often.) In the early 1970s the Duchess of Windsor had it inscribed on a throw pillow. No matter how rich and thin she may have been, the duchess was not particularly clever and is unlikely to have coined this phrase. Babe Paley is a more promising candidate. The second wife of CBS founder William Paley was known for her tart tongue. But no credible evidence exists that she coined this remark. The most likely candidate of all is one to whom the maxim is seldom attributed: Truman Capote. According to quote compiler Alec Lewis, Capote said he observed you can't be too rich or thin on *The David Susskind Show* in the late 1950s (probably 1959). Since kinescopes of Susskind's shows are tied up in litigation, this cannot be confirmed. Capote's biographer Gerald Clarke told me he has no evidence that the writer originated this phrase, but that he very well might have. Capote was close to Babe Paley and could have fed her the line.

As you can see, tracing quotes back to their original source is not easy. Harder yet is determining how a real quote became a misquote. Confirming that one person borrowed someone else's remark doesn't tell you whether that comment was original in the first place. It's also far easier to prove who *didn't* say something than to discover who *did*. "There are a surprisingly large number of Americanisms which never passed the lips of those to whom they are attributed," noted Suzy Platt of the Library of Congress. "How this manages to occur is always slightly inexplicable. The words do indeed strike a chord of truth with many of their audiences (regardless of who said them first), but without the cachet of the national figure, lose some of their impact in the dialogue."

Take **"You can't trust anyone over thirty."** Abbie Hoffman, right? Or was it Jerry Rubin? Mario Savio? Mark Rudd? All of them have been given credit for this clarion call of the 1960s' student revolt. None actually said it, at least not first. The man who first publicly advised his peers not to trust anyone over thirty was Jack Weinberg. Remember him? Hardly anyone does. That's why we so routinely put Weinberg's words in better known mouths.

Here is how his motto became part of the national discourse: As student protests heated up at the University of California in 1964, a *San Francisco Chronicle* reporter went to Berkeley to write a feature story about this new phenomenon. Jack Weinberg, then twenty-four, was one of the dissidents he interviewed. Weinberg got the impression that the reporter was trying to bait him, to get him to admit that revolt was part of a Communist conspiracy. To get under his skin, he said, "We have a saying in the movement that you can't trust anybody over thirty."

Twenty-six years later, now long past thirty himself, Weinberg told me that those words just occurred to him on the spot. He thought they were original to him. Calling them a "movement saying" was his way of trying to give them more zing. Weinberg got a far bigger response than he'd expected. After it appeared in the daily paper, his comment was repeated by *Chronicle* columnist Ralph Gleason. Soon it was buzzing all over the Bay Area, then around the country as a whole. Weinberg's generational redlining touched a nerve among over-thirties. It confirmed their worst fears about how they were perceived by their children. When student activists realized how much this motto bugged their elders, many began to chant "Don't trust anyone over thirty" in earnest. Before long this became the defining slogan of an era when surly youths were seen as rudely elbowing their parents aside. In Weinberg's words, "The phrase just resonated."

Among the few sixties rebels to stay active in social causes (Greenpeace, most recently), Weinberg was chagrined that his most lasting claim to fame is this puerile remark. "It's a bit disappointing," he has observed, "that the one event that puts me in the history books—the one thing people ask me to comment on—is an off-the-wall put-down I once made to a reporter." To make matters worse, the reporter he was trying to discredit as a reactionary turned out to be a veteran of progressive causes himself.

Once Weinberg's slogan caught on, more prominent movement members began to get credit for it. Weinberg thought that Abbie Hoffman encouraged this process, but doesn't think Jerry Rubin did. (In his book *Growing (Up) at 37* Rubin referred to himself as "someone who had helped popularize the slogan 'Don't Trust Anyone Over Thirty.' ") How did he feel about so seldom getting credit for his own catchphrase, juvenile as it might be?

"Amused?" said Weinberg. "It's certainly nothing I felt real possessive about," he added. "I felt some of the people who claimed it deserved it more. It was more meaningful to their lives. At the same time there's a certain sense of wanting to set the record straight. Even though it's not something that's central to my life, I guess there's some need to be remembered for something."

There are reasons that misquotation is so common. Certain things *need* to be said at certain times, and said by someone we've heard of. This is not a random process. Two axioms govern the process of misquotation. These axioms are:

1. Any quotation that can be altered will be.
2. Famous quotes need famous mouths.

2

The Rules of Misquotation

Axiom 1. *Any Quotation That Can Be Altered Will Be.*

As pressure mounted for him to become a presidential candidate in 1871, William Tecumseh Sherman wrote, "I hereby state, and mean all that I say, that I never have been and never will be a candidate for President; that if nominated by either party I should peremptorily decline; and even if unanimously elected I should decline to serve." Sherman-for-President fever revived in 1884. At one point the Civil War hero was wired from the Republican convention in Chicago that, like it or not, he was about to be nominated. Sherman's son Tom later recalled his father's response to this telegram: "Without taking his cigar from his mouth, without changing his expression, while I stood there trembling by his side, my father wrote the answer, 'I will not accept if nominated and will not serve if elected.'"

That response was pithy enough. But history's rewriters made Sherman's statement even pithier; the classic "Shermanesque" refusal: **"If nominated, I will not run. If elected, I will not serve."**

This is a recurring process. Quotations which start out too long, too clumsy and inharmonious end up shorter, more graceful and rhythmic

13

in the retelling. They are *euphonized*. One of the most requoted lines of modern times is Pogo's **"We have met the enemy and he is us."** The original expression of this thought, in Walt Kelly's 1953 introduction to *The Pogo Papers,* was, "Resolve then, that on this very ground, with small flags waving and tinny blasts on tiny trumpets, we shall meet the enemy, and not only may he be ours, he may be us."

It is a rare quote which can't be improved. Words are routinely added or subtracted or inverted to make good quotes even better. This is a basic axiom of misquotation. *Any quotation that can be altered will be.* This axiom has several corollaries.

COROLLARY 1A: VIVID WORDS HOOK MISQUOTES IN THE MIND.

On the eve of America's entry into World War I, a *Chicago Tribune* reporter pressed Henry Ford for the historical context of his pro-disarmament views. Ford reportedly said, "What do we care what they did 500 or 1,000 years ago? . . . History is more or less bunk. It's tradition. We don't want tradition. We want to live in the present and the only history that is worth a tinker's dam is the history we make today." This is the genesis of Ford's famous **"History is bunk"** comment. The full thought and his "more or less" qualifier were quickly cast aside. Copy desks and the public mind telescoped the crusty automaker's remark into one that was terser, less equivocal, more like what we imagined Henry Ford would say.

In the ensuing uproar, Ford said he'd been misquoted. He tried to shed the reputation of a know-nothing by suing the *Tribune* for libel (unsuccessfully), and by founding the "Greenfield Village" Museum to promote his kind of history. For all of that, Ford is still vividly remembered for having said "History is bunk." He had only himself to blame. *Bunk* proved to be a powerful hook word which caught this sentence in our collective memory. A single colorful word or phrase can have that effect. As we shall see, hook terms such as *mousetrap, iron curtain,* and *smoke-filled room* have secured many a misquotation in our minds.

COROLLARY 1B: NUMBERS ARE HARD TO KEEP STRAIGHT.

We've seen how many variations there are on Andy Warhol's "fifteen minutes of fame," especially regarding the amount of time we'll all be famous. Such number-based quotes are especially challenging to the memory. This is a common problem. Think of it as "numbernesia." Charles de Gaulle once said of the French, **"How can you govern a nation which has 246 kinds of cheese?"** Or was it 243? Or 265? The numbers vary in the retelling. Maybe de Gaulle himself wasn't quite sure how many cheeses were made in France. (By now it's over 400.)

Keeping amounts straight is a problem with any number-based quotation. Among many mots attributed to Alice Roosevelt Longworth was her observation that Franklin Roosevelt was **"one part mush and two parts Eleanor."** Requoters were more likely to agree about the idea than the proportions. Here is how some came out:

MUSH	ELEANOR	
90%	10%	*Newsweek*
80%	20%	Miriam Ringo, *Nobody Said it Better* (noting that percentages varied)
one part	two parts	*New York Daily News*
one part	three parts	Doris Fleeson (columnist)
⅓ (sap)	⅔	*New York Times*

To further complicate matters, Longworth—who was Eleanor Roosevelt's first cousin—vehemently denied saying any such thing. Whoever did may have been inspired by James Russell Lowell's 1848 depiction of Edgar Allan Poe:

> *There comes Poe with his raven like Barnaby Rudge,*
> *Three-fifths of him genius, and two fifths sheer fudge.*

COROLLARY 1C: SMALL CHANGES CAN HAVE A BIG IMPACT (OR: WHAT A DIFFERENCE AN A MAKES).

After landing on the moon on July 20, 1969, Neil Armstrong uttered the immortal words **"That's one small step for a man, one giant step for**

mankind." At least that's what Armstrong *meant* to say after taking man's first stroll on the moon. In fact, he forgot the *a*. Armstrong's actual words were, "That's one small step for man, one giant leap for mankind." This didn't make much sense. The National Aeronautics and Space Administration quickly explained that transmission problems clipped the *a* from their astronaut's words. Balderdash. Anyone who listens closely to the widely disseminated recording of Armstrong's broadcast can hear that there is no time between *for* and *man* for an *a*. Armstrong blew his line, pure and simple.

What was the press to do—report his actual words or those he meant to say? A computer search of major newspapers on the twentieth anniversary of Armstrong's stroll found that among fifty citations of his line during the two years preceding, nineteen quoted him as saying "a man" and thirty-one simply "man."

Another case of an added *a* involved writer Gertrude Stein. Stein's most famous line is **"A rose is a rose is a rose."** What she actually wrote, in her poem "Sacred Emily," was, "Rose is a rose is a rose is a rose." This line makes little sense. Does it refer to a flower or someone named Rose? (Stein collected paintings by Sir Francis Rose.) To make the words more coherent, we added an *A* to the beginning and pruned a blossom from the end. Eventually the poet herself adopted the popular version of her line.

COROLLARY 1D: IF NOTED FIGURES DON'T SAY WHAT NEEDS TO BE SAID, WE'LL SAY IT FOR THEM.

Our favorite all-time crime quotation is Willie Sutton's explanation of why he robbed banks: **"Because that's where the money is."** Sutton is supposed to have given this answer to a reporter who asked why he robbed banks. But in his autobiography Sutton denied ever saying the words for which he is famous. "The credit belongs to some enterprising reporter who apparently felt a need to fill out his copy," wrote Sutton. "I can't even remember when I first read it. It just seemed to appear one day, and then it was everywhere."

Sutton's colleague Meyer Lansky was the beneficiary of a similar misquote. While watching a 1962 television program on organized crime, the racketeer murmured something to his wife that might have been **"organized crime is bigger than U.S. Steel."** Unbeknownst to

Lansky, his hotel suite was being monitored by FBI microphones. The tape of what he said was later erased. Lansky biographer Robert Lacey discovered in FBI files that his subject's famous phrase existed only in the paraphrase of an agent reporting what he thought he'd heard. In time this paraphrase was made into a direct quote and given dramatic play in *Life, Time,* and many other publications. In *The Godfather II,* a Lansky-inspired character remarked, "Michael! We're bigger than U.S. Steel!" Lansky denied making the comment as quoted. Lacey thought it doubtful that he did. But those words were what we wanted to hear from Lansky. They became a quote that wouldn't die. When Meyer Lansky died in 1983, the *New York Times* reported: "In a moment of triumph, Mr. Lansky once boasted to an underworld associate, 'We're bigger than U.S. Steel.' "

COROLLARY 1E: JOURNALISTS ARE A LESS THAN DEPENDABLE SOURCE OF ACCURATE QUOTES.

Anyone who's ever been quoted in a newspaper knows this to be true. Nor is it necessarily the journalist's fault. The pressure of taking down thousands of words, then writing under deadline pressure, seldom permits complete accuracy. Furthermore, in many cases the cruelest thing a reporter can do is quote a subject accurately, including all the "uhs," "ums," "you knows," digressions, run-on sentences, and tortured syntax. While managing the inept New York Mets, an exasperated Casey Stengel once said, "Can't *anyone* play this here game?" After reporters cleaned up his grammar, **"Can't anyone here play this game?"** became one of Stengel's most famous lines. Similarly, when he got hit with a lemon meringue pie thrown by a protester, California tax crusader Howard Jarvis was quoted in the press as saying, "Don't worry folks. It doesn't bother me a bit." Videotape of the incident clearly showed that what Jarvis actually said was, "Don't worry folks. It don't bother me a bit." In such cases, cleaning up diction while preserving meaning is a service to reader and subject alike. Too often, however, reporters alter words for their own purposes: to get a pithier quote, illustrate a point they want made, or impress the person at the next desk.

One of Henry Kissinger's most famous observations is, **"I've always acted alone. Americans admire that enormously. Americans admire the cowboy leading the caravan alone on his horse, the cowboy**

entering a village or city alone on his horse." This comment—from an interview with Oriana Fallaci—created an uproar when it first appeared in late 1972. Kissinger rued the day he consented to talk with the Italian journalist, calling it "without doubt the single most disastrous conversation I ever had with any member of the press." The interview was conducted in English, translated into Italian by Fallaci, then translated back into English before appearing in *The New Republic*. The implication that he was a lone ranger drove Kissinger's boss—Richard Nixon— up the wall. Certainly as shrewd a man as Kissinger would have anticipated this. Kissinger denied saying any such thing during his lengthy conversation with Fallaci. He claimed that she put the words in his mouth. Fallaci denied the charge, but never let anyone check her tape. When Mike Wallace interviewed Fallaci for *60 Minutes,* she did let him and a producer listen briefly to an almost inaudible cassette of the interview. They could hear nothing about cowboys or anything like it. As so often happens, the authenticity of this familiar quotation depended solely on the word of a single witness.

COROLLARY 1F: FAMOUS DEAD PEOPLE MAKE EXCELLENT COMMENTATORS ON CURRENT EVENTS.

One of 1991–92's biggest bestsellers was *Brother Eagle, Sister Sky: A Message from Chief Seattle.* This children's book based its text on an eloquent statement by Chief Seattle of the Suquamish and Dowamish tribes. Seattle's statement (made as he was forced to sell tribal lands in the mid-nineteenth century) began: **"How can you buy the sky? How can you own the rain and the wind? My mother told me, every part of this earth is sacred to my people. Every pine needle. Every sandy shore. Every mist in the dark woods. Every meadow and humming insect. All are holy in the memory of our people."** By the time this book appeared, different versions of Seattle's words were already a commonplace in speeches, articles, and environmental tracts. Mythologist Joseph Campbell quoted them at length in his televised conversations with Bill Moyers. Though the man to whom they're attributed has been dead for well over a century, his reverence for the earth speaks to our times. The only problem is that Seattle's famous statement was written by screenwriter Ted Perry for a documentary on the environment in 1972. Unable to find any authentic speech by a prominent

Native American to argue for the earth's sanctity, Perry made one up and put it in Seattle's mouth (incorporating a few of the Indian's own words). Only when he watched the program did the writer realize that his name had been removed from its credits. When Perry complained, the show's producers explained that they felt doing this added authenticity to Seattle's words. The film was widely distributed with the name "Chief Seattle" listed in its writing credits. Perry's act of dramatic license thus became a sort of inadvertent hoax. As the screenwriter told KPLU-Radio reporter Paula Wissel, twenty years after the episode he is still upset, not just with the producers who deceived their viewers by denying him screenwriter credit, but with himself for presuming to become Chief Seattle's posthumous speechwriter. "I don't know what made me think I could be presumptuous enough to write a Native American speech," said Perry.

Think of this as retroquoting. It's a surprisingly common practice. Retroquotation takes two basic forms: (1) putting favorable comments in the mouth of a dead hero; (2) putting contemptible words in the mouth of a dead villain.

During the late 1960s, a thirty-five-year-old comment by Adolf Hitler drew widespread attention in America: **"The streets of our country are in turmoil. The universities are filled with students rebelling and rioting. Communists are seeking to destroy our country. Russia is threatening us with her might and the Republic is in danger. Yes, danger from within and from without. We need law and order. Yes, without law and order our nation cannot survive. Elect us and we shall restore law and order."** This statement was used by defenders of student rebels to imply that their critics were crypto-fascists. It was put in play by a liberal newsletter which said the sentences came from a 1932 speech Hitler made in Hamburg. In 1969, Jerome Beatty, Jr., used the quote in his *Saturday Review* column. When asked about its original source, he confessed ignorance. Beatty set out to find one. The editor of *The Dixon Line*—the California newsletter which originally reprinted Hitler's remarks—told Beatty that he'd gotten them from a professor at California State College in Long Beach. This professor said he'd been given the Nazi leader's speech by a colleague who'd seen it posted on a bulletin board somewhere. The professor couldn't remember where. Library of Congress researchers and others were no more successful than Beatty in trying to find an original source for Hitler's words.

Although the actual author of this quotation has never been found, it's unlikely that it was Adolf Hitler. Not that this mattered. Even after it had been debunked by Beatty and others, Maine Senator Edmund Muskie used Hitler's "quotation" in a speech. Supreme Court Justice William O. Douglas included it in a book. (Both later acknowledged their mistake.) *Parade* magazine excerpted Hitler's "speech" without a disclaimer, and Brown's graduating class of 1970 received their diplomas against the backdrop of a large poster quoting the Nazi leader on student rebellion and the need for law and order.

In a similar, more benign episode, the mayor of Amsterdam attributed this observation to Socrates: **"The children now love luxury; they have bad manners, contempt for authority; they show disrespect for elders and love chatter in place of exercise. Children are now tyrants, not the servants of their households. They no longer rise when elders enter the room. They contradict their parents, chatter before company, gobble up dainties at the table, cross their legs, and tyrannize their teachers."** This wisdom from the grave was subsequently reported in the *New York Times* and reprinted widely. After Malcolm Forbes included Socrates's words in a *Forbes* magazine editorial entitled "Youth," his research staff went crazy trying to prove their authenticity. They contacted a wide range of librarians, classicists, and other experts on Socrates. None knew of any source for the passage. The researchers finally called Amsterdam's mayor, Gijsbert van Hall. Van Hall said he'd seen the lines by Socrates in a Dutch book whose title he could not recall. There the search ended. "We suspect," *Forbes*'s researchers concluded, ". . . that Socrates never did make those cracks about Athenian youth."

Axiom 2. *Famous Quotes Need Famous Mouths.*

A widely repeated adage is: **"No one on his deathbed ever said, 'I wish I had spent more time on my business.'"** The only thing keeping this quotation from becoming more familiar is that no one's sure who said it. The comment was originally made by Arnold Zack, who included it in a letter to his friend Paul Tsongas. Tsongas was then a U.S. senator from Massachusetts recovering from lymphoma. He repeated his friend's insight in a 1984 book. Reviewers of this book often quoted Zack's line, though few mentioned his name. Hardly anyone attributes these words to Arnold Zack because few people have heard of him. Tsongas himself sometimes gets credit for the aphorism. Mostly it just floats around like a dandelion seed waiting for a famous name to land on. In time it will probably find one.

To become truly familiar, a quote must be attributed to a household name. Famous quotes need famous mouths. If words we like can't be credited to someone we've heard of, they might as well not have been said at all. Or, as commonly happens, they can be moved from an obscure mouth to a prominent one.

In 1851, Indiana Congressman Richard Thompson dropped in on John Babson Lane Soule, the young editor of the *Terre Haute Daily Express*. Thompson had just returned from a trip to Kansas. He was impressed with prospects west of the Mississippi. Thompson, who later became Secretary of the Navy, suggested that the young editor go west and grow up with the country. Barring that, perhaps he could write an editorial recommending that others do so. This sentiment was already being pushed vigorously by *New York Tribune* editor Horace Greeley. By one account, the Thompson-Soule conversation took this turn:

> THOMPSON: Why John, you could write an article that would be attributed to Horace Greeley if you tried.
>
> SOULE: No, I couldn't. I'll bet I couldn't.
>
> THOMPSON: I'll bet a barrel of flour you can, if you'll promise to try your best, the flour to go to some deserving poor person.
>
> SOULE: All right, I'll try.

Soule did just that. In an editorial exhorting others to migrate westward, he noted that Horace Greeley himself could not give a young man better advice than to "Go West, young man." Before long this admonition was credited to Greeley. Trying to correct the record, Greeley reprinted Soule's editorial. "The expression of this sentiment has been attributed to the editor of the *Tribune* erroneously," he commented about himself. "But so fully does he concur in the advice it gives that he endorses most heartily the epigrammatic advice of the Terre Haute *Express* and joins in saying, **'Go West, young man, go West.'** "

So that settled that, right? Hardly. This advice was something Americans wanted to hear as the frontier was pushed back, and Greeley was the man they wanted to hear it from. Who had ever heard of John Babson Lane Soule? The *Tribune*'s editor and Democratic candidate for President in 1872 was a prominent, tireless booster of westward migration. As Soule anticipated, "Go West, young man, go West" sounded like something Horace Greeley would say. Greeley spent years disavowing authorship of the line. Eventually he gave up, realizing that no one was interested. The quote demanded a marquee name. Greeley's was the best one available.

COROLLARY 2A: WELL-KNOWN MESSENGERS GET CREDIT FOR CLEVER COMMENTS THEY REPORT FROM LESS CELEBRATED MOUTHS.

Among the most hallowed truisms of feminism is, **"If men could get pregnant, abortion would be a sacrament."** This is usually attributed to radical lawyer Florynce Kennedy. Kennedy was so quoted in a compendium of her remarks which accompanied a 1973 *Ms.* profile of her by Gloria Steinem. Ten years after the quip was attributed to Kennedy, Steinem revealed that its actual source was an Irish cab driver, an elderly woman, who made this observation while ferrying her and Kennedy around Boston.

Alice Roosevelt Longworth's most famous remark was that Thomas Dewey resembled **the little man on a wedding cake**. Some thought the unsuccessful Republican candidate for President in 1944 never recovered from this devastating put-down. In the process Longworth's reputation as a tart-tongued king-breaker was enhanced. But Theodore Roosevelt's daughter didn't coin this phrase, and never claimed she had. A few years before her death in 1980, Longworth told William Safire that her friend Grace Hodgson Flandrau originally told her that Dewey looked like the bridegroom on a wedding cake. Longworth repeated the line so often that she eventually got credit for coining it. Others to whom this comment has been attributed include Franklin D. Roosevelt, Harold Ickes, Walter Winchell, Dorothy Parker, and Ethel Barrymore.

Mrs. Longworth was already famous for observing that Calvin Coolidge looked as though he'd been **"weaned on a pickle."** Once again, however, she was merely publicizing this quip. As Longworth later explained, during Coolidge's presidency, her doctor greeted her one day with a malicious grin. "The patient who has just left said something that I am sure will make you laugh," he said. "We were discussing the President, and he remarked, 'Though I yield to no one in my admiration for Mr. Coolidge, I do wish he did not look as if he had been weaned on a pickle.' Of course I shouted with pleasure and told everyone," Longworth reported, "always carefully giving credit to the unnamed originator, but in a very short time it was attributed to me."

COROLLARY 2B: PARTICULARLY QUOTABLE FIGURES RECEIVE MORE THAN THEIR SHARE OF QUOTABLE QUOTES.

The single most famous comment about television is Newton Minow's depiction of the medium as **"a vast wasteland."** *Wasteland* proved to be a powerful hook word which embedded that phrase in our memory. This 1961 observation has proved more enduring than the name of its author. As Minow's renown fades (he chaired the Federal Communications Commission for John Kennedy), I've begun to see his words attributed to Marshall McLuhan. Their originator may actually have been Minow's speechwriter, John Bartlow Martin. According to Martin, he originally coined the phrase "vaste wasteland of junk" for a magazine article on television, but included it in a Minow speech instead. "In editing the speech himself," wrote Martin, "Newt had the wit to cut 'of junk.' "

Another memorable put-down of television called it **"chewing gum for the eyes."** According to quote collector James Simpson, critic John Mason Brown made this comparison in a 1955 interview with him. But, as Simpson originally pointed out, Brown was actually passing along a comment made by a friend of his young son. In later collections Simpson attributed the comment to Brown himself. Fred Allen sometimes gets credit for the line. So does architect Frank Lloyd Wright, whose fame has proved more lasting than either Brown's or Allen's.

A quotable, caustic observer of contemporary life in his own right, Wright got credit for many things he didn't say (or at least didn't originate). Clifton Fadiman credited Wright with observing that **"Form and function are one,"** echoing Louis Sullivan's 1906 line, "Form ever follows function." **"Give me the luxuries of life and I will willingly do without the necessities"** has been credited to Wright by *Reader's Digest* and the *New York Times,* among others. In 1853, Oliver Wendell Holmes so quoted his friend John Lothrop Motley in *The Autocrat of the Breakfast Table.*

This is the "flypaper effect." Unclaimed comments floating about in their vicinity stick to famous quotable figures. "Certain writers have engendered so much wit that orphan quotations seem to gravitate towards them," noted Illinois reference librarian Charles Anderson. "If it's profound, it must be Camus or Confucius; if it's humorous and cynical, it must be Mark Twain, unless it's about politicians, in which case it could also be Will Rogers."

Think of such figures as "flypaper people." Others include Shakespeare, Voltaire, Emerson, Lincoln, Wilde, Shaw, Dorothy Parker, Samuel Goldwyn, Yogi Berra, and Winston Churchill. *New York Times* columnist Tom Wicker once credited Churchill with observing about nuclear war, **"The survivors will envy the dead."** Wicker subsequently admitted that he should have attributed this line to Soviet Premier Nikita Khrushchev (as John Kennedy did at a 1963 press conference). The Library of Congress couldn't find this phrase in Khrushchev's speeches or writings. Three years before Kennedy quoted the Soviet leader, Herman Kahn published a book on nuclear war in which he repeatedly asked, "Will the living envy the dead?"

COROLLARY 2C: COMMENTS MADE ABOUT SOMEONE MIGHT AS WELL HAVE BEEN SAID BY THEM.

Former presidential aide Charles Colson is best remembered for saying, **"I'd walk over my own grandmother if necessary to get Richard Nixon elected."** In fact, this was said *about* Colson, not by him. In a 1971 *Wall Street Journal* profile of Colson, a former aide to then-Senator Leverett Saltonstall observed that Nixon's henchman "would walk over his own grandmother if he had to." Before long the words ended up in Colson's own mouth. Despite Colson's vigorous attempts to deny he'd ever said this, that phrase remains his legacy. "I doubt that any statement never made by a person ever got so much publicity," reflected Colson in 1992, "and it does to this day."

Over a century earlier, Tammany boss William Marcy "Boss" Tweed, gained lasting notoriety for his arrogant response to those who questioned his political methods: **"As long as I count the votes, what are you going to do about it?"** By repetition alone this comment gained credibility. To this day it is cited routinely when Tweed's name comes up in history texts. The Tammany leader always denied making his famous retort, and with good reason. It was *Harper's Weekly* cartoonist Thomas Nast who put the words in his mouth. One showed Tweed's thumb resting heavily on New York City. Its caption read: "The Boss. 'Well, what are you going to do about it?' " Another showed a tiger ravaging innocents in a stadium as Tweed and his cronies—in Roman garb—enjoyed the spectacle. The caption of this cartoon was, "THE TAMMANY TIGER LOOSE—'What are you going to do about it?' " In time these words were assumed to be Tweed's by reporters, historians, and the public at large. Tweed biographer Leo Hershkowitz has tried to correct the record. Pointing out that the line is Nast's, not Tweed's, Hershkowitz asked, "what politician, especially in this country, would make such an asinine statement, no matter how sure he was of his position? It was certainly not Tweed's style. . . . It was never Tweed's question. It was all 'Boss,' all Nast and all nonsense."

COROLLARY 2D: WHO YOU THINK SAID SOMETHING MAY DEPEND ON WHERE YOU LIVE.

On this side of the Atlantic, newspaper columnist Franklin Pierce Adams was said to have been told that someone he despised was his own worst enemy. **"Not while I'm alive,"** was Adams's widely quoted response. In England, Labor Party leader Ernest Bevin is supposed to have said "Not while I'm alive, 'e ain't" when told that colleague and rival Aneurin Bevan was his own worst enemy.

In America, Oliver Wendell Holmes, Jr., is famous for saying **"Oh to be seventy again,"** when he saw a comely woman on his ninetieth birthday in 1931. A British quote collection credited French premiere Georges Clemenceau with saying the same thing on his eightieth birthday in 1921, as he ogled a pretty girl on the Champs-Élysées. Prussian Field Marshal Count Friedrich Heinrich Ernst von Wrangel is remembered in Germany for having remarked during his nineties (in the mid-1870s), "If only one were 80!"

As with nations, who gets credit for familiar quotations can depend on what group they belong to in a particular country. In the world of sports, Yogi Berra gets credit for saying, "If people don't want to come to the ballpark, how are you gonna stop them?" In American theater circles, producer Sol Hurok was reknowned for observing, **"If people don't want to come, nothing will stop them."** Show business types think **"I don't care what they say about me as long as they spell my name right"** was said by Sam Goldwyn, or George M. Cohan, or P. T. Barnum. Politicians attribute that adage to Harry Truman, or Boston mayor James Curley, or Tammany boss Timothy "Big Tim" Sullivan.

Representative Nicholas Longworth, the acerbic House speaker in the early part of this century (and husband of Alice Roosevelt), was known for his bald head and sharp tongue. A colleague was said to have run his hand over Longworth's smooth scalp and remarked, "It feels just like my wife's behind." Longworth reached back, rubbed his own head, and murmured, **"Why so it does."** Longworth is still remembered in Washington as much for this devastating squelch as for the House office building named after him. But in New York literary circles, the same exchange features bald playwright Marc Connelly and another regular at the Algonquin Round Table.

COROLLARY 2E: VINTAGE QUOTES ARE CONSIDERED TO BE IN THE PUBLIC DOMAIN.

When her husband retired as general manager of the New York Yankees in 1960, Mrs. George Weiss was not thrilled. **"I married him for better or worse,"** she explained, **"but not for lunch."** In England, The Duchess of Windsor once explained that she regularly ate out at midday because "I married the Duke for better or for worse, but not for lunch." This widely repeated mot turned out to be an old Australian saying.

In 1957, the Duke himself was quoted as saying, **"The thing that impresses me most about America is the way parents obey their children."** For a time this cheeky observation was requoted often, especially in the United States. Then it disappeared, only to reappear in 1991 in the *Wall Street Journal*'s European edition, where someone named Sam Ewing was quoted as saying, "One thing that really impresses people of other countries about the U.S. is the way parents obey their children."

Following the collapse of the 1991 Soviet coup attempt, a press spokesman for President Mikhail Gorbachev observed that the plotters "did something worse than treason; they committed a blunder." This comment echoed Dean Acheson's assessment of the Vietnam war: "It is worse than immoral, it's a mistake." Acheson, in turn, was inspired by a famous condemnation of the 1804 execution of the Duc d'Enghien in France—**"It's worse than a crime, it's a blunder!"**—which has been attributed to Talleyrand and others.

"Living well is the best revenge" has a modern sound. The saying is typically attributed to the Gatsby of the moment. Calvin Tomkins used it as the title of his 1971 biography about American expatriates Gerald and Sara Murphy, who were friends of Scott and Zelda Fitzgerald (and the model for Dick and Nicole Diver in *Tender Is the Night*). The Murphys had adopted this motto as their own. They thought it was a Spanish proverb. Scott and Zelda themselves are sometimes thought to have been its authors. In fact, the saying, in these exact words, is #524 of George Herbert's 1640 publication, *Outlandish Proverbs*. Herbert may have been inspired by Lyly's 1579 aphorism, "The greatest harm that you can do unto the envious, is to do well."

COROLLARY 2F: IN A PINCH, ANY ORPHAN QUOTE CAN BE CALLED A CHINESE PROVERB.

Author Gay Courter preceded one section of her novel *Flowers in the Blood* with this quote: **"The greatest pleasure in life is doing what people say you cannot do."** She called it a "Chinese Proverb." That's how this saying was identified in a book Courter read while researching her novel about opium traders in nineteenth century India. In fact, this line was part of an 1879 essay about Shakespeare written by Walter Bagehot.

Calling an orphan saying a Chinese proverb gives it cachet with very little risk that its actual source will be discovered. A deliberate exploitation of this syndrome involved the proverb **"One picture is worth a thousand words."** This saying first appeared in a 1921 ad in *Printer's Ink* which was written by publicist Frederick Barnard. Barnard headlined his ad "One look is worth a thousand words." He attributed this maxim to "a famous Japanese philosopher." Six years later Barnard revised the saying to read "One picture is worth ten thousand words," then republished it in the same magazine as a "Chinese proverb." Barnard thought this ploy would give his words added weight. He was right. For a time *Bartlett's* identified Barnard's line as "a Chinese proverb." Other sources attributed his proverb to Confucius. The *Macmillan Dictionary of Quotations* had it both ways. They cited Barnard as the maxim's author, adding, "Ascribed to Chinese origin."

These, then, are the laws of misquotation. All evolve from our basic need to have said what must be said, and by someone whose name we recognize.

Reflecting these laws, some terms that will be used during the rest of this book include:

flypaper people—prominent, quotable figures to whom more than their share of quotations stick.

sounds-like quotes—comments attributed to the prominent figure whom they most "sound like."

retroquotes—words placed posthumously in the mouth of a well-known dead person.

public domain quotes—remarks made so long ago that they can be safely claimed by whoever wishes to claim them.

orphans—unattributed quotes in search of a home.

bumper-sticker (verb)—compressing a longer statement to make it more quotable.

euphonize—making a clumsy quotation more harmonious.

requisitioning—attributing an old saying to someone famous.

lip syncing—mouthing someone else's words as if they were your own.

parenting—attributing authorship of one's own words to someone more prominent; the opposite of lip syncing.

hook words or phrases—colorful words or groups of words which make a quote easier to remember; often retrofitted.

modular sayings—multipurpose comments with blanks to be filled in (e.g., "If we can afford to go to the moon, we can afford to_____.").

numbernesia—getting the words right but the numbers wrong.

The many streams of miswording and misattribution eventually converge into a raging river of misquotation. As a result, even our most hallowed sayings are liable to be revised, requisitioned, and stolen outright.

3

Poor Richard's Plagiarism

The great writers of aphorisms read as if they had all known each other well.

ELIAS CANETTI

Two centuries after Benjamin Franklin published his last almanac, a graduate student named Robert Newcomb set out to explore the originality of its aphorisms. Many of the sayings that ran in *Poor Richard's Almanack* from 1733 to 1757 still appear in quotation collections under Franklin's name. Should they? This was the question Newcomb hoped to answer.

It had long been known that some of Poor Richard's sayings drew on the work of others. Almanac writers were notoriously sticky fingered, and Benjamin Franklin was no exception. He admitted as much himself. "Why should I give my Readers *bad lines* of my own," asked Franklin, "when *good ones* of other People's are so plenty?"

Franklin didn't even attempt to claim credit for **"An ounce of prevention is worth a pound of cure,"** an adage generally attributed to him. He called this "an old saying," or "an English proverb." In various forms, **"There are no gains without pains"** had already appeared in several proverb collections by the time Poor Richard got credit for it. Franklin borrowed **"A word to the wise is enough"** from a book of sayings, which in turn adapted it from a line written by the Roman playwright Plautus.

30

A few such petty plagiarisms were known to scholars. Nonetheless, they assumed that Franklin had made up most of Poor Richard's sayings, or at least adapted them from longer works by others. Evidence about his sources was skimpy, however. Short of combing through all of the source material available to Franklin when he published his almanacs, how could one develop such evidence?

This is exactly what Robert Newcomb proposed to do. First he recorded all of Poor Richard's thousands of sayings on note cards. Newcomb then composed a list of any conceivable source Franklin might have consulted for material. After that, the University of Maryland Ph.D. candidate spent years locating these sources and poring over their contents. What he discovered astounded him. It wasn't just *some* of Poor Richard's sayings that were unoriginal; *most* of them were. In one case after another Newcomb discovered Franklin's aphorisms in existing collections of sayings. "He went to the *Bartlett's Quotations* of his day," explained Newcomb, "and just used whatever was familiar."

In some cases Franklin's version improved on the original. A predecessor's "Success has blown up, and undone, many a man" became Poor Richard's **"Success has ruined many a Man."** Franklin compressed "A man in Passion rides a horse that runs away from him" into **"A Man in a Passion rides a mad Horse."** In a surprising number of cases, however, he was content to publish other men's work with little or no revision.

Newcomb found nearly four dozen lines that Franklin took virtually unchanged from George Herbert's proverb collection. These included:

FRANKLIN	HERBERT
For want of a Nail the Shoe is lost; for want of a Shoe the Horse is lost; for want of a Horse the Rider is lost.	For want of a nail the shoe is lost, for want of a shoe the horse is lost, for want of a horse the rider is lost.
Love your neighbor, yet don't pull down your hedge.	Love your neighbor, yet pull not down your hedge.
Marry your sons when you will; daughters when you can.	Marry your son when you will; your daughter when you can.
Nothing dries sooner than a tear.	Nothing dries sooner than a tear.

Franklin was especially partial to Herbert's work, as well as that of saying-compilers James Howell and Thomas Fuller. Poor Richard's **"At 20 years of age the Will reigns; at 30 the Wit; at 40 the Judgment"** is changed only in punctuation from the same line in a compilation by Fuller (who, in turn, adapted it from Herbert). **"Don't throw stones at your neighbors, if your own windows are glass"** was Franklin's revision of either Herbert's "Whose house is of glass, must not throw stones at another," or Howell's "Who hath glass-windows of his own, let him take heed how he throws stones at those of his neighbor." Where this thought originated is anyone's guess.

By the time Newcomb completed his research, he had located three quarters of Franklin's sayings in previously published compilations. Newcomb still chafes at the ones that eluded him. He is sure they could be found in books he couldn't locate. "I couldn't find the source of his Greek sayings," sighed the retired English professor. "I just know that somewhere out there is a book of Greek sayings that he used."

Throughout history, epigrammists have borrowed and loaned their work like busy librarians. The lending is usually involuntary, however, and the borrowing unacknowledged. In a rare exception, Thomas Fuller wrote about his 1732 collection of maxims, "It hath always been my Custom, that whenever I light upon a fine Passage in any Author, I take it and make it my own." Such borrowing was so routine among compilers of sayings that it's nearly impossible to tell which ones originated with whom. Just when you've determined that one aphorist plagiarized another, you discover that the predecessor took it from someone else, and God only knows who he got it from. In the process, words get changed, sometimes for better, sometimes for worse, sometimes for no reason other than to cover the borrower's tracks. In the reverse process, sayings have often been attributed to prominent aphorists that they didn't originate and never claimed. The result, when it comes to purveyors of epigrams, is near-total confusion about who actually said what.

Ralph Waldo Emerson

In a 1990 speech, Secretary of State James Baker quoted Emerson as having said, **"We do not inherit the earth from our ancestors, we**

borrow it from our children." That prompted more than one patron to ask a librarian about the source of this quote. For a time none could be found. Then a librarian at McGill University in Montreal discovered a 1990 article that identified the saying as a Haida Indian proverb. Then a Celestial Seasonings tea box turned up which said it was an Amish proverb. Neither attribution could be considered rock-solid. As *Newsweek* noted of this saying, "for public relations purposes, [environmentalists] often attribute it to the Indians, although that is probably wishful thinking." The same thing is undoubtedly true of its Amish heritage. Attributing the maxim to Emerson is even more fanciful.

As one of history's leading flypaper figures, Emerson drives library staffers crazy. The transcendental philosopher said many perceptive things, but not nearly as many as we think he did. America's reference librarians were once challenged to find the origins of another line attributed to him: **"A man is known by the books he reads, by the company he keeps, by the praise he gives. . . ."** After what was called "The Great Emerson Quotation Hunt," this observation was finally located in one of Emerson's journals. Looking further, however, one librarian discovered that a modern revision of William Law's 1726 book *Christian Perfection* included a similar line. Law's original words were, "We commonly say, that a man is known by his *Companions;* but it is certain, that a Man is much more known by the Books that he converses with." Thus ended the Great Emerson Quotation Hunt.

Ralph Waldo Emerson made so many observations about all manner of subjects that he lends himself to misquotation. **"Consistency is the hobgoblin of little minds,"** for example, is among his most popular aphorisms (especially among those caught doing something they said they wouldn't do). This is a bumper-stickered version of what Emerson actually wrote: "A foolish consistency is the hobgoblin of little minds, adored by little statesmen and philosophers and divines." In modern retellings the "foolish" tends to get dropped and the whole condensed, transforming a thoughtful observation into one that's rather simpleminded and doesn't make a whole lot of sense.

One of Emerson's best-remembered exchanges was said to have taken place in 1846 with Henry David Thoreau, who was in prison for refusing to pay poll taxes:

EMERSON: "Henry, why are you here?"

THOREAU: "Waldo, why are you *not* here?"

This tale originated in a book written by Thoreau's jailer. Various other versions exist. Thoreau didn't mention any visit from Emerson in his own account of his imprisonment. Library of Congress researchers have concluded that their legendary conversation never took place.

The best known of Emerson's lines is **"Build a better mousetrap and the world will beat a path to your door."** This maxim routinely appears in quote collections under his name. Emerson did once write, "If a man has good corn, or wood, or boards, or pigs to sell, or can make better chairs or knives, crucibles or church organs, than anybody else, you will find a broad hard-beaten road to his house, though it be in the woods." But no one has ever found a dependable source for the version of this thought featuring mousetraps (which proved to be a powerful hook word). Trying to discover who did compose this classic piece of folk wisdom ignited one of the biggest dust-ups in the history of quote attribution.

The mousetrap aphorism first won widespread attention in 1908 after it appeared under Emerson's name in a magazine called *The Fra*. Questions were raised about this saying's origins. Extensive searching by Emerson's son and others uncovered no such phrase in any of his published writing, letters, or journals.

When this became apparent, *The Fra*'s publisher—Elbert Hubbard—decided to reveal the saying's actual author. As his son reported, "after Emerson students failed to find it in his writings, Hubbard finally admitted that he wrote it himself." The 1911 book *A Thousand and One Epigrams by Elbert Hubbard* included the mousetrap quote shorn of Emerson's name. Those who worked for him explained that it had been Hubbard's practice to attribute some of his own sayings to better-known aphorists such as Emerson. "Mr. Hubbard," wrote a contributor to another of his magazines, "has a habit of writing something, and attributing it, thru modesty, to some one else." Of the mousetrap quote, this 1912 article added, "Always credited to Emerson, it has sent thousands hunting the *Essays,* never to find it—for 't was written by Elbert Hubbard."

Hubbard's claim to this line provoked a lot of controversy. Many believed him. Others thought his claim absurd. Considerable effort was devoted to discovering whether Emerson or Hubbard originated the maxim. Eventually this search turned up *Borrowings,* a collection of sayings published in 1889 by members of the First Unitarian Church in Oakland, California. *Borrowings* included several observations by Emerson. One of them was: "If a man can write a better book, preach a better sermon, or make a better mouse-trap, than his neighbor, though he builds his house in the woods, the world will make a beaten path to his door." In 1912, one of the book's compilers—Sarah S. B. Yule—stepped forward to say that she'd jotted this sentence in her notebook after hearing Emerson lecture in Oakland in the early 1870s. Emerson did speak in Oakland on May 18, 1871, about "Hospitality and How to Make Homes Happy." Whether he discussed mousetraps and beaten paths, we may never know. No written copy of his lecture exists, and press reports were sketchy. After conducting exhaustive research in the early 1930s, quote compiler Burton Stevenson concluded that Emerson probably did say the words that Mrs. Yule jotted in her notebook.

Following the rediscovery of *Borrowings,* Elbert Hubbard was asked how he could have originated a saying which appeared in print nineteen years before it ran in *The Fra,* and six years before he founded *The Philistine,* where his own writing was first published. Hubbard responded, "The fact that *The Philistine* was started in 1895 has nothing to do with the mousetrap quotation. I was born in 1856 and began writing hot stuff when I was four years old." Commented Burton Stevenson, "one can only wonder what happened to all the stuff he wrote between 1860 and 1893. Perhaps he kept it in a barrel and drew upon it in his later years, as need arose."

Biographer Freeman Champney dismisses any thought that Hubbard might have originated the phrase. Champney thought that Hubbard most likely found it in an 1894 epigram collection he was known to have read, which in turn lifted it from *Borrowings.* Today no one but Hubbard's lingering band of devotees gives any credence to his claim on the mousetrap saying. What's surprising is that anyone believed him in the first place. Who was Elbert Hubbard to have convinced so many that he, not Ralph Waldo Emerson, originated one of America's most familiar quotations?

Elbert Hubbard

Though he is barely remembered today, before World War I Elbert Hubbard was one of America's most prominent public personalities. With his long hair, flowing ties, and duster coats, Hubbard was a flamboyant writer, visionary, and pioneer of direct mail marketing. His communal Roycroft Printing Shop in East Aurora, New York, attracted visits from the likes of Alexander Woollcott, Frank Lloyd Wright, and Carl Sandburg. Roycroft produced handsomely printed books—many of them written by Hubbard—which were sold by mail to thousands of devoted customers. Hubbard's *A Message to Garcia* remains one of history's all-time best-sellers. Much of the material in his two magazines—including epigrams galore—appeared under their publisher's name. Elbert Hubbard's voluminous writing and avid audience made him one of the primary information disseminators of his time.

Before he went down on the torpedoed *Lusitania* in 1915, Hubbard was America's leading purveyor of maxims. To this day some quote collections include dozens of sayings attributed to him. In the case of Hubbard, however, the term "attributed" must be used with care. As a colleague once observed, Hubbard "never could acquire a due respect for quotation marks; never could see the iniquity and, in the long run, the suicidal error of purloining the fruit of another man's brain." Hubbard routinely borrowed other people's words without so much as an I.O.U. As recently as 1982, *Plain Truth* publisher Herbert W. Armstrong wrote that he recalled Hubbard telling him sixty-eight years earlier, **"Genius is one percent inspiration and ninety-nine percent perspiration."** This thought is generally credited to Thomas Edison.

Many of the epigrams which appeared in Hubbard's publications were unsigned, their readers free to conclude that he himself was their author. Among them were:

TOO MANY PEOPLE NOWADAYS KNOW THE PRICE OF EVERYTHING AND THE VALUE OF NOTHING.

This thought appeared in Hubbard's *Roycroft Dictionary and Book of Epigrams*. Thereafter it was sometimes credited to Hubbard. After his death, the Roycrofters produced *Elbert Hubbard's Scrap Book* ("Containing the inspired and inspiring selections gathered during a lifetime of discriminating reading for his own use"). In this compilation an earlier version of the line was correctly attributed to Oscar Wilde: "Nowadays people know the price of everything and the value of nothing."

NEVER EXPLAIN—YOUR FRIENDS DO NOT NEED IT AND YOUR ENEMIES WILL NOT BELIEVE YOU ANYWAY.

An embellishment of Disraeli's pithier "Never complain, never explain," this line recrossed the Atlantic when British politician Victor Grayson (1881–1920) was quoted as saying, "Never explain: your friends don't need it and your enemies won't believe it."

FOLKS WHO CAN, DO; THOSE WHO CAN'T, CHIN.

This, of course, is a degradation of Shaw's "He who can, does. He who cannot, teaches." ("Chin" was slang of the time for idle talk.)

THE REWARD OF A GOOD DEED IS TO HAVE DONE IT.

An echo of Emerson's "The reward of a thing well done is to have done it."

ANYTHING THAT HAS CHARMS TO SOOTHE THE SAVAGE BEAST.

Hubbard's definition of music; no mention of Congreve.

LIFE IS JUST ONE DAMN THING AFTER ANOTHER.

Also credited to *New York Sun* reporter Frank Ward O'Malley.

Like many who knew him, Carl Sandburg was ambivalent about Elbert Hubbard. After he visited Hubbard in East Aurora, the poet was impressed. "When the future generations weigh in the balance the life of Elbert Hubbard, they will pronounce him one of the greatest men the world ever saw," he wrote. Later, Sandburg revised his opinion of Hubbard. "As a poseur," he finally concluded, "he must be credited a genius."

Carl Sandburg

Inspired partly by Hubbard, Carl Sandburg himself became a purveyor of epigrams. In epic poems such as *Good Morning, America* (1928) and

The People, Yes (1936), Sandburg welded one maxim after another into proverbial verse. The sayings he cobbled into poetry included several discussed later in this book. Among them were "There are lies, dam lies and statistics," "Speak softly and carry a big stick," "War is hell," and "Never give a sucker an even break." Unlike Hubbard, Sandburg never claimed that these lines belonged to him or anyone else in particular.

The irony is that *The People, Yes* included a line which, in a different form, became one of America's all-time best-known slogans. That line was part of his portrayal of a little girl watching her first military parade. After being told who the marching soldiers were and what they did, the little girl grew pensive. Finally she said, "Sometime they'll give a war and nobody will come."

This passage didn't attract much attention when it first appeared, nor for many years thereafter. The time wasn't right. In 1961 *Scientific American* editor James R. Newman wrote a letter to the *Washington Post* in which he misremembered Sandburg's line as **"Suppose they gave a war and nobody came?"** My mother saw Newman's letter reprinted in a newsletter and filed it away for future reference. In 1966 she wrote an article for *McCall's* about my brother the war protester. For the title of that article she used Newman's misquotation of Sandburg. Her title soon appeared on a bumper sticker which David Brinkley held up on his nightly newscast. After that the saying caught fire. In time it became a key slogan of the anti-war movement. To this day it's among the best known of modern maxims. But Charlotte Keyes is rarely cited as the slogan's source, let alone Carl Sandburg. I've seen "Suppose they gave a war and nobody came?" attributed to Arlo Guthrie and Allen Ginsberg, among others. Like so many sayings of the 1960s and 1970s, this one simply floated from bumper stickers to buttons to picket signs and posters with little awareness and less interest in its heritage.

The Sages of Aquarius

The 1960s and 1970s were a golden age of warmed-over sayings passing for original insight. Among them were:

DO YOUR OWN THING.

After San Francisco's Haight-Ashbury district was taken over by heroin dealers and Jerry Rubin became a stockbroker, someone told me that this bedrock credo of the sixties first appeared in Emerson's "Essay on Self-Reliance." William Safire subsequently reported that Emerson's 1841 essay included this passage: "But do your thing, and I shall know you." In most Emerson collections, however, that line reads "But do your work, and I shall know you." This is because a creative editor changed the word *thing* to *work* in a 1903 edition of Emerson's essays. The change has been perpetuated ever since. Emerson may just have been cribbing Chaucer anyway. In *Canterbury Tales,* "The Clerke's Tale" includes this observation: "Ye been oure lord; dooth with youre owene thyng." Does that make Chaucer the original hippye?

TODAY IS THE FIRST DAY OF THE REST OF YOUR LIFE.

Back when a lot of things sounded more profound than they actually were, this saying received more than its share of "Far outs," and "Oh, wows." The cultish drug-rehab group Synanon claimed that their founder, Charles Dederich, first made this observation in a 1969 speech. Thomas Wolfe has also been credited with originating the maxim, as have Jean-Paul Sartre and Abbie Hoffman. Despite energetic searching by America's reference librarians, no dependable point of origin has ever been found for "Today is the first day. . . ." Maybe Dederich did make it up.

KEEP ON TRUCKIN'.

Popularized by hip cartoonist R. Crumb in the 1960s, this line originated in the Depression-era blues song "Truckin'." ("Keep on truckin', mama/ Truckin' my blues away.") The phrase became common during dance marathons of the 1930s. As far back as the 1890s "trucking it" referred to riding a train by holding on to the trucking hardware between its wheels. Lexicographer Stuart Berg Flexner thought this might have been where marathon jitterbuggers got the term. Another possibility is the term "trucking up" or "trucking back" used by early cinematographers.

YOU'RE EITHER PART OF THE PROBLEM OR PART OF THE SOLUTION.

In a 1968 speech Eldridge Cleaver said, "What we're saying today is that you're either part of the solution or you're part of the problem. There is no middle ground." As a result, Cleaver generally gets credit for this slogan. In a 1964, speech, however, New York's City College president Buell Gallagher told a graduating class, "Be part of the answer, not part of the problem, as the American revolution proceeds."

WE ARE THE PEOPLE OUR PARENTS WARNED US ABOUT.

This was a popular graffiti and poster slogan in the sixties and seventies. In 1968 journalist Nicholas Von Hoffman published a book about hippies called *We Are the People Our Parents Warned Us Against*. According to British quote maven Nigel Rees, this was a common observation between the wars in London, claimed as original by various literary and artistic figures.

LIFE IS WHAT HAPPENS TO YOU WHILE YOU'RE BUSY MAKING OTHER PLANS.

This line appeared in John Lennon's 1980 song "Beautiful Boy" and is sometimes attributed to him. Before Lennon recorded that song in 1980 it had already been attributed to such less well-known names as Thomas La Mance, Allen Saunders, and Betty Talmadge.

The Inarticulate Decade

Unlike the two decades preceding, the 1980s produced few memorable sayings. (Unless one considers "Go for the burn!" and "It's morning in America" memorable.) In fact, only one eighties slogan achieved quote-book status: **"The opera ain't over till the fat lady sings."** Where did this maxim come from? There is much confusion on that score. The most common opinion is that it sounds like Yogi Berra. I've also heard the saying attributed to W. C. Fields. Some associate it with the rotund Kate Smith, whose rendition of "God Bless America" was once the theme song of the Philadelphia Flyers hockey team. A New York lawyer said he thought the line referred to a woman of ample girth who sang "The Star Spangled Banner" *after* Dodgers games ended at Ebbets Field. His wife was sure she had read it in a J. D. Salinger short story.

Here is how that saying actually came into being: During 1978's National Basketball Association playoffs, the Washington Bullets took a commanding lead over the Philadelphia 76ers. Another victory would put them in the title game. Asked about their prospects, Bullets coach Dick Motta cautioned, "The opera ain't over till the fat lady sings."

The Bullets' coach never claimed to have coined this line. As Motta told reporters, after Washington had taken a 3–1 lead over the Spurs during an earlier series in San Antonio, he watched a late-night news story about the game on television. "This guy comes to the end of the story," Motta said with a laugh, "and he says on the sportscast, 'The opera ain't over until the fat lady sings.' " It didn't take long for this aphorism to make its way around the country. JR's daddy used the quip on *Dallas*. So did George Bush on the hustings, countless sportscasters, endless political commentators, and sundry secondhand wits. When attributed to anyone at all, the line was most often attributed to Dick Motta. But didn't the sportscaster he got it from deserve credit?

That sportscaster was *San Antonio Express-News* columnist Dan Cook. But few people outside of San Antonio have heard of Cook. Among basketball fans Dick Motta was a household name. When coaching in the playoffs he commanded national attention. This is why Motta so often was thought to have coined the fat lady line. But Dan Cook was his source (and already gets credit for the line in some quote collections.)

There's more to the story, however. Dan Cook may simply have been taking part in a great southern tradition: foisting off shopworn Dixieisms on unsuspecting Yankees as fresh merchandise. An obscure 1976 booklet called *Southern Words and Sayings* included this entry: "Church ain't out 'till the fat lady sings." Alvin Bethard of the Dupre Library in Lafayette, Louisiana, said that this was the way he'd always heard that saying while growing up in central Louisiana in the 1950s and 1960s. My poll of other longtime southerners confirmed that many were familiar with the saying long before Dick Motta gave it national exposure. San Antonio physician John Holcomb, forty-seven, said he'd heard variations on this theme for thirty years or more, usually as "It ain't over till the fat lady sings." Television newscaster Robert Inman of Charlotte, North Carolina, recalled hearing that version when he was press secretary to Alabama Governor Albert Brewer in the late 1960s. Political reporter Bob Ingraham said he first heard the "opera" version while with the *Montgomery* (Alabama) *Advertiser* in the 1950s. Ingraham said he never was quite sure what this saying referred to, but thought that it "was tied to the perception of those like me who don't know much about opera that when the fat lady sings, the opera's about to end."

As so often happens, this old saying needed receptive ears before it could become familiar. For some reason, "The opera ain't over till the fat lady sings" defined America's mood in the eighties. Perhaps we were more desperate beneath the surface than our Reaganite merrymaking suggested. Slogans can do that: define eras. When the right one doesn't appear spontaneously or isn't said by the best person, we're not above nudging the process along. This isn't a modern phenomenom. Rewording and misattributing quotations to better suit their times is a pastime with a long, long history.

4

Let Them Eat Brioche

. . . famous remarks are very seldom quoted correctly.

SIMEON STRUNSKY

Marie Antoinette, was renowned for her solution to the bread shortage among starving subjects: **"Let them eat cake."** This comment epitomized the flip insensitivity of France's royalty. The only problem is that it predated Marie Antoinette's 1770 arrival in France by at least a few years and possibly several centuries.

Rousseau's *Confessions*—which was written in the late 1760s and drew on journal entries made long before Marie Antoinette's 1755 birth, includes the passage, "Finally I remembered the way out suggested by a great princess when told that the peasants had no bread: 'Well let them eat cake.' " (It was not actually cake that this unnamed princess recommended, but the fancy pastry called *brioche*.) A French book published in 1760 credited the Duchess of Tuscany with offering the same advice. Louis XVIII later wrote that this comment's originator was actually Marie Therese, wife of Louis XIV. A 1959 letter to the *Times* of London reported that this observation could be found in the Latin letters of John Peckham, Archbishop of Canterbury during the late thirteenth century. Peckham, according to John Ward of London, did not attribute this sentiment to anyone in particular but noted that it was a proverbial example of indifference to the poor.

Conclusion: "Let them eat cake" is one more commonplace saying which gravitated to the best-known mouth. We may never know who said it first. We do know that it wasn't Marie Antoinette. She probably never said this at all.

A remarkable number of history's most familiar phrases have proved to be misattributed, misworded, or made up altogether. Under the pressure of war especially, the need for stirring slogans is far greater than the need for accuracy. Since so much of human history is the history of war, it's not surprising that so many historic quotations are spurious. In some cases, misquotation has served the purpose of writers who need pithy remarks to punch up their text. Accurate comments make rattling bad history. The most readable texts incorporate one misquote after another, many of them retrofitted by journalists, biographers, and historians.

Louis XIV is best remembered for exclaiming, **"I am the State!"** (*"L'état, c'est moi!"*) The teenage monarch was said to have made this claim in 1655 to a group of parliamentarians who were bent on reducing his power. It is a classic retroquote. Contemporary accounts of Louis XIV's confrontation with parliament mentioned no such oath. In an embellished history published a century later, Voltaire portrayed the young king confronting restive legislators in his hunting clothes, whip in hand, contemptuously rejecting their demands. Subsequent historians added their own touches to this scene: spurs on his boots, cushions beneath him, the petulant "I am the state!" on his lips. No modern historian gives any credence to this oath or the whole colorful scene. It owes far more to Voltaire than to Louis XIV.

Voltaire himself was the beneficiary of one of history's most enduring retroquotes: **"I disapprove of what you say, but will defend to the death your right to say it."** These eloquent words first appeared in a 1906 biography of the French philosopher written by Evelyn Beatrice Hall (using the pen name S. G. Tallentyre). Hall composed this sentence to characterize Voltaire's attitude toward a colleague's writing. To give it added weight, she put the comment in quotation marks. Three decades later, Hall's words appeared under Voltaire's name as a "Quotable Quote" in the June 1934 *Reader's Digest*. They've stayed there ever since. Hall herself seemed surprised by this turn of events. "I did not intend to imply that Voltaire used these words verbatim," she wrote in 1935, "and should be surprised if they are found in any of his works." To this day the words of Evelyn Beatrice Hall remain Voltaire's most familiar quotation.

Napoleon

One of Napoleon Bonaparte's most famous references was to **"two o'clock in the morning courage: I mean unprepared courage."** Nearly four decades after the French emperor made this observation, Thoreau wrote in *Walden* of "The three o'clock in the morning courage which Bonaparte thought was the rarest." In the inflationary 1980s, a character in Paul Theroux's novel *Mosquito Coast* twice referred to "four-o'clock-in-the-morning courage," though he never mentioned Napoleon.

During a conversation with one of his ambassadors following the Russian debacle of 1812, Napoleon kept repeating, **"From the sublime to the ridiculous there is but a step."** After this ambassador reported their conversation in a book, the mot was attributed to Bonaparte. It still is. But this thought was not original to him. In "Age of Reason" (1795), Thomas Paine wrote, "One step above the sublime makes the ridiculous, and one step above the ridiculous makes the sublime again."

Napoleon was the best known proponent of the view that **"The English are a nation of shopkeepers."** But he was merely publicizing a common expression. According to one historian, Louis XIV called Holland a nation of shopkeepers long before Napoleon said the same thing about England. In the late eighteenth century, English economists Josiah Tucker and Adam Smith both used this expression in their writings. In 1794 a French revolutionary called England "a shopkeeping nation," during a meeting attended by Napoleon. Clearly this put-down was common by the time Napoleon gave it the prestige of his name.

One of Napoleon's most lasting contributions to military science is the adage **"An army travels on its stomach."** His pithy comment remains an axiom of modern warfare. No one knows where it originated. Napoleon frequently discussed his concepts of war but never recorded them. An earlier saying—"An army, like a serpent, travels on its belly"—is credited to Frederick the Great, but probably was not original to him.

The Count and the Duke

Count Cambronne, who commanded France's Imperial Guards at Waterloo, was famous for his proud response to the English demand for their surrender: **"The guards die, but never surrender."** These heroic words put a balm on the French defeat. They were later inscribed on a statue of Cambronne in Nantes. He himself denied ever saying them. Since Cambronne was taken prisoner at Waterloo, the prima facie evidence supports his case. At an 1835 banquet in his honor, the count remarked, "In the first place, we did not die, and in the second, we did surrender." In *Les Miserables,* Victor Hugo incorporated what many think Camnbronne actually responded to the English: *"Merde!"* In France this became known as "le mot de Cambronne." The source of his more heroic response seems to have been a French reporter with a knack for making up stirring phrases who attributed this one to Cambronne the day after his defeat at Waterloo.

A second "guards" misquote has gone down in history from the same battle: **"Up, guards, and at 'em!"** This order was supposedly given at Waterloo by the Duke of Wellington. "What I must have said," the Duke later recalled, "and possibly did say, was, 'Stand up, guards!' and then gave the commanding officers the order to attack."

The Duke of Wellington (Arthur Wellesley) was even more famous for observing, **"The battle of Waterloo was won on the playing fields of Eton."** This was the perfect rationale for English private education. It was exactly what loyal Etonians wanted their distinguished alumnus to say. As the story went, Wellesley returned to his alma mater some years after whipping Napoleon. While watching students play cricket, he remarked, "The battle of Waterloo was won here." The longer version later gained wide circulation. Did the duke actually say this? Apparently not. His descendant, the seventh Duke of Wellington, pointed out that this phrase was not like others by Wellesley. It was more Gallic, almost Napoleonic in tone. Furthermore, the first duke was decidedly cool toward his alma mater. "Wellington's career at Eton was short and inglorious," wrote the seventh duke "and, unlike his older brother, he had no particular affection for the place." After his later triumphs the duke displayed little interest in his alma mater, and even spurned their fund appeals. He returned to Eton only twice: once to attend his brother's 1842 funeral, and two years later accompanying the queen and Louis Philippe. The first visit was brief, and the second—in the company of a French monarch—was hardly one in which he was likely to have discussed Waterloo.

So where did the "playing fields of Eton" remark originate? Apparently it first appeared in a French book on English politics which was published in 1856, three years after the Duke of Wellington's death. The book's author visited Eton while gathering material. Based on this visit he wrote, ". . . one understands the Duke of Wellington's mot when, revisiting during his declining years the beauteous scenes where he had been educated, remembering the games of his youth, and finding the same precocious vigor in the descendants of his comrades, he said aloud: 'It was here that the battle of Waterloo was won.' " In 1889, Sir William Fraser repeated this passage in his compilation *Words on Wellington*, but revised it a bit to read, "The battle of Waterloo was won in the playing fields of Eton."

"Quite apart from the fact that the authority for attributing the words to Wellington is of the flimsiest description," concluded the seventh duke, "to anyone who knows his turn of phrase they ring entirely false." No modern biographer of Wellington has disagreed.

The Iron Chancellor

During an 1862 debate in the Prussian Diet, Otto von Bismarck—Prussia's "Iron Chancellor"—uttered the words that became his epitaph: "Not by speeches and majorities will the great questions of the day be decided . . . but by iron and blood." Something about the word *blood* must addle memory synapses. As would later happen with Churchill's "Blood, toil, tears, and sweat," the order of Bismarck's words was quickly reversed in the popular mind, to **"Blood and iron."** Eventually Bismarck himself adopted the more popular form. Perhaps this was because in the first century Quintilian had observed, "Warfare seems to signify blood and iron."

The observation **"If you like laws and sausage, you should never watch either one being made"** is often attributed to Bismarck, but never with a source. There may not be one. The Library of Congress calls this Bismarckism "unverified." Betty Talmadge (the former wife of

Senator Herman Talmadge) has also been given credit for the line. In recent years an Ohio sausage maker and state legislator named Jim Buchy has made the motto his own.

Another well-known Bismarck remark was that a journalist is **"one who has missed his calling."** Bismarck actually said that the opposition press "consisted in great part of Jews and malcontents, people who had missed their vocation in life."

Dizzy

After meeting with Bismarck at the Congress of Berlin in 1878, British Prime Minister Benjamin Disraeli announced that "[Foreign Minister] Lord Salisbury and myself have brought you back peace—but a **peace,** I hope, **with honor.**" In his time Disraeli was celebrated for this eloquent phrase. Today it is more commonly associated with Neville Chamberlain. After his ill-fated 1938 meeting with Hitler in Munich, Prime Minister Chamberlain announced, "This is the second time in our history that there has come back from Germany to Downing Street peace with honor. I believe it is peace for [not *in*] our time." Many antecedents existed for this phrase. In an 1853 speech Lord John Russell said, "But while we endeavor to maintain peace, I certainly should be the last to forget that if peace cannot be maintained with honor, it is no longer peace." Prior to Russell's speech these words had appeared often in English literature. Samuel Pepys once observed of his wife, "With peace and honor I am willing to spare her anything. . . ." In *Memoirs of a Cavalier,* Daniel Defoe wrote of sending a military force "to procure peace with honor." And in Shakespeare's *Coriolanus,* Volumnia urged her son Coriolanus to

> *hold companionship in peace*
> *With honor, as in war, since that to both*
> *It stands in like request.*

Disraeli—whose nickname was "Dizzy"—is one of history's most quoted, and misquoted, figures. The British political leader, novelist, and wit was famous for his biting observations. Bennett Cerf offered this delightful example of the prime minister's gift for repartee: During one of their titanic exchanges, William Gladstone thundered in Parliament that Disraeli would meet his end either on the gallows or from some loathsome disease. **"That depends,"** responded his arch-rival, **"upon whether I embrace your principles or your mistress!"** Good anecdote. It certainly sounds like Disraeli. But most references to this exchange say it took place a century earlier, between the Earl of Sandwich and John Wilkes in 1768. (Sources differ on which type of disease was to kill Wilkes, venereal or the pox.)

Far more clever lines have been attributed to Disraeli than he ever uttered. In addition, many a Disraeli remark has been taken out on loan. The debt was mutual. Just as others borrowed his lines, he borrowed others'. Disraeli was little disposed to acknowledge such debts. He once said of Gladstone, **"I only wish that I could be as sure of anything as my opponent is of everything,"** without citing Lord Melbourne's earlier line: "I wish I was as cocksure of anything as Tom Macaulay is of everything." Disraeli later wrote, **"Everything comes if a man will only wait,"** echoing Rabelais's earlier observation, "Everything comes to him who knows how to wait." More than once Disraeli was caught in acts of blatant plagiarism. But Disraeli gave as much as he took. His famous 1837 riposte to an Irish opponent who taunted him about his Jewish heritage—**"Yes, I am a Jew, and when the ancestors of the Right Honorable Gentleman were brutal savages on an unknown island, mine were priests in the temple of Solomon"**—was adapted twenty years later by Louisiana Senator Judah P. Benjamin as a response to the anti-Semitic taunts of a German-American colleague: "The gentleman will please remember than when his half-civilized ancestors were hunting the wild boar in Silesia, mine were princes of the earth." More than a century later President Richard Nixon asked his top aides to resign so that the country might not be run by **"exhausted volcanoes."** Disraeli originally used this term to describe Prime Minister Gladstone's ministers. (Daniel Moynihan thought Nixon might have picked it up from a Disraeli biography he passed along to the President in 1972.)

In his autobiography, Mark Twain attributed the remark **"There are three kinds of lies: lies, damned lies, and statistics"** to Disraeli. This famous line now appears often in quote collections under Disraeli's name (and Twain's too, on occasion). "Lies, damned lies . . ." has also been attributed to Henry Labouchère, Abram Hewitt, and others. No one other than Twain is known to have credited Disraeli with making the comment. British statistician John Bibby once appealed to his colleagues for a reliable source of the saying. The best anyone could come up with was this 1896 comment by a member of the Royal Statistical Society: "We may quote to one another with a chuckle the words of the Wise Statesman, lies, damned lies, statistics . . ." After consulting a Disraeli biographer, Bibby concluded that he probably wasn't this Wise Statesman. Bibby is still trying to determine who was.

"Never complain, never explain" is Disraeli's most enduring contribution to the annals of misquotation. This adage, credited to him by Gladstone biographer John Morley, has lived on in the mouths of others. Disraeli's successor, Stanley Baldwin, revived the line in 1943 to characterize his own political credo. "Never complain and never apologize" was long a common saying among Royal Navy officers. In the 1949 movie *She Wore a Yellow Ribbon,* John Wayne said, "Never apologize and never explain—it's a sign of weakness." Disraeli's original version resurfaced in 1974 when Henry Ford II was arrested for drunk driving in Santa Barbara, California, accompanied by a young woman who was not his wife. Asked for an explanation, Ford said, "Never complain, never explain." This line was fed to the auto mogul by his British public relations adviser. After that, Ford himself often got credit for the words. In Elmore Leonard's novel *The Switch,* a character misattributed Disraeli's motto to Henry Kissinger. A companion corrected him. "It was Henry Ford the Second," said the companion, "the time he was arrested in California for drunk driving with another woman in the car."

Clemenceau

Following the Allied victory in World War I, French Premier Georges Clemenceau was said to have grumbled about Woodrow Wilson's Fourteen Points for peace, **"The good lord had only ten."** This was a common mot among Parisians, merely being publicized by Clemenceau.

Contentious and plainspoken, Clemenceau got credit for more than his share of quotable quotes. At times this was due to his own efforts. Some years after the fact, Clemenceau said he fed the line **"I accuse"** ("J'accuse") to Émile Zola when both were protesting the treason conviction of Alfred Dreyfus. The best-known comment attributed to Clemenceau is **"War is too important to be left to the military"** (sometimes "generals," or "soldiers"). British Prime Minister David Lloyd George said that Clemenceau's colleague Aristide Briand told him this during World War I, but may have been quoting Talleyrand. *Bartlett's* gave the nod to Clemenceau in 1968, Briand in 1980.

Along with Oscar Wilde, Henry James, H. L. Mencken, and John O'Hara, Clemenceau has been credited with observing, **"America is the only nation in history which miraculously has gone directly from barbarism to degeneration without the usual interval of civilization."** In a 1945 magazine article called "Merry Christmas, America!" Danish writer Hans Bendix reported that his aunt told him Clemenceau said this. Bendix's article seems to be the only source for the Clemenceau attribution, which now appears in *Bartlett's* and other quote collections. Based on France's often stormy alliance with America during and after World War I, Clemenceau certainly might have made such an observation. It sounds like him. However, as a young man, the French leader spent several years in the United States, met his wife there, and called America his "second country."

An orphan quote sometimes attributed to Clemenceau is **"Any man who is not a socialist at age twenty has no heart. Any man who is still a socialist at age forty has no head."** The most likely reason is that Bennett Cerf once reported Clemenceau's response to a visitor's alarm about his son being a Communist: "Monsieur, my son is twenty-two years old. If he had not become a Communist at twenty-two, I would have disowned him. If he is *still* a Communist at thirty, I will do it then." George Seldes later quoted Lloyd George as having said, "A young man who isn't a socialist hasn't got a heart; an old man who is a socialist hasn't got a head." The earliest known version of this observation is attributed to mid-nineteenth century historian and statesman François Guizot: "Not to be a republican at twenty is proof of want of heart; to be one at thirty is proof of want of head." Variations on this theme were later attributed to Disraeli, Shaw, Churchill, and Bertrand Russell. (I misquoted Churchill to this effect for years.)

Churchill

Since Winston Churchill said so many quotable things in his long lifetime, it's understandable that he would be involved in repeated episodes of misquotation. Anyone that quotable will be routinely misquoted.

Countless anecdotes involving Churchill's gift for repartee were bruited about during his lifetime. In one of the most famous, an out-raged member of Parliament named Bessie Braddock accused him of being drunk at a dinner party. Churchill responded, **"And you, madam, are ugly. But I shall be sober tomorrow."** No evidence exists that this exchange ever took place. On the other hand, we do have a record of this dialogue in a W. C. Fields movie:

INJURED PARTY: You're drunk.

FIELDS: You're crazy.

INJURED PARTY: You're drunk.

FIELDS: All right, but tomorrow morning I'll be sober and you'll still be crazy.

In another legendary exchange, Lady Nancy Astor was said to have told Churchill, "If I were your wife I'd put poison in your coffee." Churchill responded, **"If I were your husband I'd drink it."** George Thayer, who helped Randolph Churchill research a biography of his father, discounted this rejoinder as totally uncharacteristic of the rather Victorian prime minister. The anecdote actually has a rather long history and changing cast of characters. An earlier version involved this exchange between Lloyd George and a female heckler:

HECKLER: "If you were my husband I would give you poison."

LLOYD GEORGE: "Dear lady, if you were my wife I would take it."

In America, Bennett Cerf thought this story involved St. Louis Cardinals pitcher Dizzy Dean and a baiting woman spectator during the 1934 World Series with Detroit. According to Cerf the woman yelled "If I was your wife I'd give you poison." Dean yelled back, "If I wuz your husband, I'd take it!"

During World War II, Churchill supposedly said of Sir Stafford Cripps, **"There but for the grace of God, goes God."** Some time before that, screenwriter Herman Mankiewicz said the same thing about Orson Welles as they filmed *Citizen Kane*.

After the war, Churchill was famous for noting of his Labor party rival, **"[Clement] Atlee is a very modest man . . . who has much to be**

modest about." Churchill denied ever saying this, not the least reason being that he didn't consider Atlee to be at all modest. Churchill was also said to have said to have called the mild-mannered Atlee **"A sheep in sheep's clothing."** When political scientist D. W. Brogan asked him about that one, Churchill said it was based on a more pointed remark he'd once made about someone else. Quote monger Nigel Rees thought the comment might have originated with newspaper columnist J. B. Morton in the 1930s.

Although generally considered one of the most elegant stylists in English history, Churchill borrowed more of his best material than is generally recognized. He alluded to this fact in observing about himself: "It is a good thing for an uneducated man to read books of quotations. Bartlett's *Familiar Quotations* is an admirable work, and I studied it intently. The quotations when engraved upon the memory give you good thoughts."

One of Churchill's most renowned observations was his definition of democracy. But this definition was not new to him. As he himself noted during a speech in Parliament, *"It has been said that democracy is the worst form of government except all those other forms that have been tried from time to time"* (emphasis added). In this case Churchill was simply in the second stage of Three-Step Quote Acquisition. Information about his source died with him.

Churchill's most famous single phrase is **"blood, sweat, and tears."** Before our ears edited and rearranged his words Churchill actually said during his first speech as prime minister in 1940, "I have nothing to offer but blood, toil, tears, and sweat." This phrase has a distinguished history. In 1611, John Donne wrote:

> That 'tis in vaine to dew, or mollifie
> It with thy Teares, or Sweat, or Bloud. . . .

More than two centuries later Byron included these words in a poem:

> Year after year they voted cent. per cent.
> Blood, sweat, and tear-wrung millions—why?—for rent!

In 1919, Lord Alfred Douglas wrote that poetry is "forged slowly and painfully, and link by link with sweat and blood and tears." An 1896 poem by Douglas included the lines:

But he would have none of my soul
That was stained with blood and with tears

According to Paul Boller and John George in *They Never Said It,* someone once pointed out to Churchill that Henry James wrote in his 1886 novel *The Bostonians,* "The sacrifices, the blood, the tears, the terrors were theirs." Churchill said he'd never read the novel and was sure he'd originated the phrase himself. In his 1931 book *The Unknown War,* Churchill wrote about Russian soldiers: "Their sweat, their tears, their blood bedewed the endless plain." Obviously this form was so common by the time Churchill tattooed it on our collective memory that it's futile to consider it original to anyone modern. Based on earliest use alone, Donne's claim is the most valid. Churchill deserved more credit for publicizing than for originating the phrase "blood, toil, tears, and sweat."

The same thing is true of **"iron curtain."** In his March 5, 1946 speech at Fulton, Missouri, Churchill said of the emerging political map, "From Stettin in the Baltic to Trieste in the Adriatic, an iron curtain has descended across the continent." That sentence thrust the term "iron curtain" into public discourse, where it stayed for nearly half a century. This is a classic case of a publicist receiving credit for a phrase of long standing.

"Iron curtain" originally referred to the fireproof metallic curtains introduced to theaters in the late eighteenth century. As early as 1819, an Englishman traveling in India used them metaphorically when he wrote, "As if an iron curtain had dropped between us and the Avenging Angel, the deaths diminished." Four years later, Metternich's contemporary, the Abbé de Pradt, wrote, "Beyond the Vistula a curtain descends which makes it difficult to find out what goes on within the Russian empire." In his 1904 novel *The Food of the Gods,* H. G. Wells noted of one character, "an iron curtain had dropped between him and the outer world." On the eve of World War I, Belgium's Bavarian-born Queen Elizabeth said of the invading Germans, "Between them and me there is now a bloody iron curtain which has descended forever!" A year later, in his 1915 book *A Mechanistic View of War and Peace,* George Crile asked Americans to imagine how they would react if Mexico "were a rich, cultured, and brave nation of forty million with a deep-rooted grievance, and an iron curtain at its frontier."

After the successful Bolshevik Revolution, Russian author Vasily Rozanov wrote, "With a clang, thud, and bang the iron curtain is dropping down on Russian history." In 1920, a British visitor named Ethel Snowden said of her arrival in the Soviet Union: "We were behind the 'iron curtain' at last!" One year later an American magazine article reported, "Bolshevik Russia lay concealed behind an iron curtain." During the 1930s, Soviet leaders themselves repeatedly warned that the West was trying to seal itself off from the Communist world with an iron curtain of contempt.

All of this suggests that the term "iron curtain" was commonly used to refer to the Soviet Union long before Churchill lent the phrase his prestige. Three years before Churchill's Fulton speech, Nazi propagandist Joseph Goebbels warned that if Russia defeated Germany, "behind an iron curtain mass butcheries of people would begin." On the eve of Germany's defeat, Foreign Minister Count Lutz Schwerin von Krosigk talked of Bolshevism's "Iron Curtain." The speech in which von Krosigk used this term was reported by the *Times* of London on May 3, 1945. Nine days later Churchill cabled Harry Truman: "An iron curtain is drawn down over their [the Russian's] front. We do not know what is going on behind. There seems little doubt that the whole of the region east of the line Luebeck-trieste-Corfu will soon be completely in their hands . . . and then the curtain will descend." On October 21, 1945, London's *Sunday Empire News* ran an article headlined "An Iron Curtain Across Europe." One year later Churchill ran this phrase up the flagpole in Fulton. The time was right, the speaker famous, and we've assumed ever since that "iron curtain" originated with him.

Improving and reassigning ringing phrases is clearly part of a long international tradition. Colonists carried this tradition with them to the New World. Like most things American, the dissemination of spurious sayings took on unusual urgency as the founders of a new country invented a legacy which incorporated one false phrase after another.

5

Founding False Phrases

In late May 1765, a young lawyer named Patrick Henry rose in Virginia's House of Burgesses to denounce the Stamp Act and defend the colonies' right to tax themselves. That speech is famous for its dramatic conclusion: "Caesar had his Brutus, Charles the First his Cromwell, and George the Third—"

"Treason!" interrupted the speaker of the House.

"—may profit by their example. **If *this* be treason make the most of it!**"

Henry spoke without notes. There were no press accounts of his speech. This account was reconstructed half a century later by biographer William Wirt. To do so, Wirt consulted the memory of some who were present, including John Tyler and Thomas Jefferson. Wirt was an adoring biographer and florid writer. In the absence of better evidence, his reconstruction of Henry's speech remained the accepted version for over a century. In 1921, however, a journal kept by a Frenchman who toured America during the mid-1760s was discovered in an obscure Paris archive. On May 30, 1765, this unnamed tourist—who may have been a French spy—visited Williamsburg. There he witnessed a debate held in Virginia's House of Burgesses. The Frenchman wrote of the debate (misspellings and all):

> Shortly after I Came in one of the members stood up and said he had read that in former times tarquin and Julus had their Brutus, Charles had his Cromwell, and he Did not Doubt but soje good americans would stand up in favour of his Country, but (says he) in a more moderate manner, and was going to Continue, when the speaker of the house rose and Said, he, the last that stood up had spoke traison, and was sorey to see that not one of the members of the house was loyal Enough to stop him, before he had gone so far, upon which the Same member stood up again (his name is henery) and said that if he had afronted the speaker, or the house, he was ready to ask pardon, and he should shew his loyalty to his majresty King G. the third, at the Expence of the last Drop of his blood, but what he had said must be attributed to the Interest of his Countrys Dying liberty which he had at heart, and the heat of passin might have lead him to have said something more than he intended, but, again, if he said any thing wrong, he beged the speaker and the houses pardon. some other Members stood up and backed him, on which that afaire was droped.

Take your pick. Based on the decades-old memory of some distinguished early Americans, Patrick Henry was blunt, fiery, and fearless in his 1765 oratory. Or, based on an eyewitness account recorded at the time by an anonymous Frenchman, he was abject, apologetic, and obsequious. In his monumental biography of George Washington, Douglas Southall Freeman gave more credence to the latter version. Noting that Henry had apologized for his hotheadedness in a previous episode, Freeman concluded that the version recorded by the Frenchman was "in character" for him; more so than the one reconstructed by William Wirt.

Wirt was also the source of Patrick Henry's most famous oration, the one he made to the second Virginia Convention in March 1775 which concluded: "Is life so dear or peace so sweet as to be purchased at the price of chains and slavery? Forbid it, Almighty God, I know not what course others may take, but as for me, **give me liberty or give me death!**" We like to think that this stirring call to action was instrumental in getting the revolution under way. But these words were also reconstructed decades later by Wirt, based primarily on the recollection of John Tyler and St. George Tucker. Both Washington and Jefferson were present at Henry's oration, but neither found it worth mentioning in their own writing. In his biography of Washington, Douglas Southall Freeman wrote that it was again his "thankless duty" to conclude that Henry's historic oath most likely was apocryphal. In Freeman's judgment, his famous phrase was "probably far more Tucker, Tyler and Wirt, chiefly Wirt, than Henry."

As they built a new nation, Americans were hungry for stirring calls to action. Many things begged to be said in a country lacking traditions. Its people needed historic sayings, and they needed them fast. If no one actually said some, it was done for them. Or else eloquent statements were moved from obscure mouths to famous ones.

According to historian Daniel Boorstin, such legend-making typified a people "so hungry for resounding utterances that they relived their past in counterfeit orations." According to the historian, "many of the most influential, longest remembered, and most popularly memorized of these were actually not delivered at all on their supposed occasion. Of many of the most famous and widely quoted, we possess texts which are no more than apocryphal. Some were grossly revised and improved versions; others were the work of posthumous ghostwriters, fabrications out of whole cloth."

Among the more familiar misquotations in American history are:

TAXATION WITHOUT REPRESENTATION IS TYRANNY.

This revolutionary call was said to have been made by firebrand lawyer James Otis during a 1761 trial in Boston. No one recorded any such declaration by Otis at the time, however. Some sketchy notes John Adams took at the trial did not include this sentence. It didn't become part of American lore until an 1823 biography said Otis issued this call to arms. That biography, by William Tudor, relied on John Adams's memory. In an 1818 letter to Tudor, Adams recalled that at the 1761 trial, Otis denounced "the tyranny of taxation without representation." This letter did not make it clear whether these were Otis's actual words or Adams's paraphrase. In fact, taxation was not a major bone of contention at the time, nor was it germane to the trial at which Otis spoke. Nonetheless, based on Adams's six-decade-old memory, Tudor wrote of Otis, "From the energy with which he urged this position, that taxation without representation is tyranny, it came to be a common maxim in the mouth of everyone." If this maxim wasn't common before, it certainly was after Tudor's biography put it in the mouth of James Otis. In time it became a cornerstone of America's revolutionary history. Modern historians don't take it seriously.

WHERE THERE IS LIBERTY, THERE IS MY COUNTRY.

According to *Bartlett's* this was James Otis's motto. The Library of Congress has been unable to find the motto in any writing by or about Otis. Others think it originated with Benjamin Franklin. In his 1941 quote collection, H. L. Mencken said Franklin used this phrase in a March 14, 1783 letter to Benjamin Vaughan. The editors of Franklin's papers can find no such letter. A tradition among biographers of Thomas Paine is that Franklin once told him, "Where liberty is, there is my country." Paine responded, "Where liberty is not, there is mine." This unlikely exchange was first reported in an 1819 book which never actually said that the two men were together when they took their stands. According to Paine biographer Alfred Owen Aldridge, "the story must be written off as apocryphal."

ETERNAL VIGILANCE IS THE PRICE OF LIBERTY.

This sounds like an axiom of the American revolution. It is routinely attributed to one or another of its luminaries: Jefferson, Henry, Paine, etc. The first recorded use of anything like this phrase was in a 1790 speech by Irish statesman John Philpot Curran: "The condition upon which God hath given liberty to man is eternal vigilance." In 1852, abolitionist Wendell Phillips said "Eternal vigilance is the price of liberty." Phillips later wrote that he believed this phrase was original to him. No one has proved otherwise.

DON'T FIRE UNTIL YOU SEE THE WHITES OF THEIR EYES!

By tradition this is what Colonel William Prescott told his men at the Battle of Bunker Hill. Others attribute the words to Prescott's colleague General Israel ("Old Put") Putnam. An 1849 history of the battle simply listed this as one of several commands given by American officers without crediting anyone in particular. (One participant did say he'd heard Putnam use these words.) If such an order was given at Bunker Hill, there was ample precedent:

SILENT TILL YOU SEE THE WHITES OF THEIR EYES.

Prince Charles of Prussia, 1745

BY PUSH OF BAYONETS, NO FIRING TILL YOU SEE THE WHITES OF THEIR EYES.

Frederick the Great, 1757

THERE, I GUESS KING GEORGE WILL BE ABLE TO READ THAT!

According to biographer William M. Fowler, Jr., the legendary tale of John Hancock defiantly signing his name extra large on the Declaration of Independence is a myth. Hancock's signature had taken this exaggerated form for years. Legend and paintings to the contrary, there was no dramatic group signing of the Declaration on July 4, 1776. Those who put their names to the declaration did so over several days' time. Various accounts have been given of what, if anything, Hancock said as he wrote his ornate signature. Since no colleague joined him on the day he signed the Declaration, most likely Hancock said nothing at all.

WE MUST ALL HANG TOGETHER, OR MOST ASSUREDLY WE SHALL ALL HANG SEPARATELY.

This is what Ben Franklin was said to have said when he signed the Declaration of Independence (responding to Hancock's remark, "We must be unanimous. There must be no pulling different ways; we must all hang together.") Since Hancock signed alone, there is a prima facie case against its authenticity. For over half a century after 1776, this comment was attributed to Richard Penn. In 1839, a joke book put the words in Ben Franklin's mouth. An 1840 biography followed suit. They've stayed there ever since.

I ONLY REGRET THAT I HAVE BUT ONE LIFE TO GIVE FOR MY COUNTRY.

Nathan Hale may have said something eloquent before being hanged as a spy in 1776, but it probably wasn't this. A British officer who witnessed Hale's execution wrote that day in his diary: "He behaved with great composure and resolution, saying he thought it the duty of every good Officer to obey any orders given him by his Commander-in-Chief; and desired the Spectators to be at all times prepared to meet death in whatever shape it might appear." Some months later, a Massachusetts newspaper reported, "At the gallows he made a sensible and spirited speech; among other things, told them they were shedding the blood of the innocent, and that if he had ten thousand lives, he would lay them all down, if called to it, in defence of his injured, bleeding country." Hale's more famous final words were first reported in the memoirs of General William Hull (1848). Hull, a friend of Hale's, wasn't present at his hanging but said he heard about it from a British officer who was. If these were the young patriot's last words, they almost certainly were inspired by Joseph Addison. Hale was known to be familiar with the works of this popular playwright. Addison's 1713 play *Cato* included the line, "What pity is it/That we can die but once to serve our country!"

I HAVE NOT YET BEGUN TO FIGHT!

The defiant words attributed to America's first naval hero are a patriotic staple. Did John Paul Jones really give this response to a request for surrender as his ship—the *Bonhomme Richard*—took in water during a 1779 battle? It's not clear. Jones's retort was first reported by an eyewitness, First Lieutenant Richard Dale, nearly half a century later. Ten days after the engagement, Jones himself described the battle in a letter to Benjamin Franklin. In this letter Jones said he responded to the English surrender request "in the most determined negative," but didn't report his actual words. Two decades later, Benjamin Rush recalled that a couple of years after the battle Jones told him he'd said, "No, Sir, I will not [surrender], we have had but a small fight as yet." A sailor on the *Bonhomme Richard* later said that when one of his own men pleaded with him to strike, Jones responded, "No, I will sink, I will never strike!"

MILLIONS FOR DEFENSE BUT NOT ONE CENT FOR TRIBUTE!

This is supposed to have been the contemptuous response of American envoy General Charles Cotesworth Pinckney to French leaders who asked for a substantial bribe to stop attacking American ships. Some years later, Pinckney discussed the 1797 incident with Thomas S. Grimké in his native Charleston, South Carolina:

> GRIMKÉ: General, we would like to know if the French Directory ever actually proposed anything like tribute from the United States to you, when Minister?
>
> PINCKNEY: They did, sir. The question was, What will the United States pay for certain political purposes, etc.?
>
> GRIMKÉ: What was your answer, General?
>
> PINCKNEY: Not a sixpence, sir.
>
> GRIMKÉ: Did you say anything else, General?
>
> PINCKNEY: Not a word, sir.
>
> GRIMKÉ: Was there nothing about millions for defense, but not a cent for tribute?
>
> PINCKNEY: I never used any such expression, sir. Mr. Robert Goodloe Harper did at a public meeting. I never did.

Robert Goodloe Harper was a Maryland congressman whose most lasting claim to fame is that he coined the name "Liberia" for that African country. At a 1798 dinner honoring John Marshall, the returning U.S. ambassador to France, Harper offered one of sixteen toasts. The next day a newspaper reported that Harper's toast was: "Millions for Defense but not a cent for Tribute." At the same banquet, Charles Pinckney's toast to Marshall was: " 'Tis not in mortals to command success. He has done more—deserved it." It didn't take long for Harper's words to get put in Pinckney's mouth, where they hung on like a bone in a hungry dog's teeth. When Grimke asked Pinckney if he'd ever tried to correct the record, Pinckney replied, "No, sir. The nation adopted the expression, and I always thought there would have been more ostentation in denying than in submitting to the report."

DON'T GIVE UP THE SHIP!

By legend these were the dying words of Captain James Lawrence as his frigate *Chesapeake* battled its British counterpart *Shannon* off the Massachusetts coast during the War of 1812. This slogan became an American rallying cry. It first appeared in the report of Lawrence's attending physician. According to him, Lawrence "ordered me to go on deck, and tell the men to fire faster, and not to give up the ship." During a 1776 engagement with the British in Boston Harbor, Captain James Mugford's dying words were said to have been, "Don't give up the ship! You will beat them off." Regarding the later attribution of this slogan to Lawrence, the daughter of *Boston Centinel* editor Benjamin Russell once told this anecdote about her father: Before the *Chesapeake* was captured by the British, a sailor made his way from that ship to Boston. There he went to the *Centinel* office to report the news of Lawrence's death. Russell asked the sailor what his captain's last words were. The sailor said he didn't know. "Didn't he say, 'Don't give up the ship'?" asked the editor. "Don't know," repeated the sailor. "Oh, he did," said Russell. "I'll make him say it."

The War Between the Statements

DAMN THE TORPEDOES—FULL SPEED AHEAD!

Rear Admiral David Farragut's legendary command was made as he led a U.S. Navy fleet through Mobile Bay during the Civil War. The lead ship was apparently hit by a Confederate torpedo causing another ship to halt, holding up the line. When told that this ship had stopped from fear of being torpedoed, Farragut's actual words were a bit less snappy: "Damn the torpedoes! Four bells! Captain Drayton, go ahead. Jouett, full speed."

SHOOT IF YOU MUST THIS OLD GRAY HEAD, BUT SPARE YOUR COUN-
TRY'S FLAG.

Early in the Civil War, a story concerning an old widow named Barbara
Frietchie made Yankee rounds. According to this story, Frietchie refused
Stonewall Jackson's command to lower her Stars and Stripes after his
troops occupied Frederick, Maryland. Instead she defiantly waved the
American flag from her upstairs window as Jackson's troops rode by.
Relayed to John Greenleaf Whittier, the story of Barbara Frietchie
appeared in his famous 1863 poem by that name. Its best-known line
was, "Shoot if you must this old gray head, but spare your country's
flag." As told to Whittier, Mrs. Frietchie's actual words were said to
have been, "Fire at this old head, then, boys; it is not more venerable
than your flag!" When the poet's embellished version appeared in the
Atlantic, other Frederick residents pointed out that the ninety-seven-
year-old Mrs. Frietchie was bedridden when the Confederates occupied
their town, and in no condition to wave a flag. At least one other
resident claimed to have been the actual subject of this legend. Whittier
responded that there was an old woman named Barbara Frietchie in
Frederick, that some said she had waved a flag out her attic window, and
that if the details of his poem about her weren't accurate, they ought
to be.

HOLD THE FORT! I AM COMING!

This is exactly what a determined William Tecumseh Sherman should
have wired the beleaguered defenders of a Union supply depot in
Georgia's Allatoona Pass. What General Sherman actually semaphored
from Kennesaw Mountain was more mundane. According to one report
he signaled, "Hold out; relief is coming." Another said his message was,
"Sherman says hold fast. We are coming." Popular retelling dramatized
these words. The improved version was cemented in popular lore when
it became the first line of a postwar hymn:

> *"Hold the fort, for I am coming."*
> *Jesus signals still;*
> *Wave the answer back to heaven,*
> *"By the grace we will."*

WAR IS HELL.

Sherman certainly believed that war was hell. He made a number of remarks to that effect. During the siege of Atlanta, Sherman wrote that city's mayor, "War is cruelty, and you cannot refine it." During an earlier battle he reportedly said, "War is barbarism." In an 1880 speech at the Ohio State Fair, Sherman told several thousand listeners, "There is many a boy here today who looks on war as all glory, but, boys, it is all hell." Historians have concluded that "War is hell" is an edited version of these remarks.

GET THAR FUSTEST WITH THE MOSTEST.

Confederate General Nathan Bedford Forrest is best remembered for this bit of military philosophy. Since he was an ill-educated former slave trader from southern Tennessee, these words sounded about right—to Northern ears especially. Isn't that the way they talk down there? Apparently not, at least not in this case. Memoirs written by officers from both sides who talked with Forrest reported these versions of his credo:

I ALWAYS MAKE IT A RULE TO GET THERE FIRST WITH THE MOST MEN.

I JUST TOOK THE SHORT CUT AND GOT THERE FIRST WITH THE MOST MEN.

I GOT THERE FIRST WITH THE MOST MEN.

While admitting that he was hardly an intellectual, colleagues of Forrest objected to the cracker-sounding version that later became popular. According to biographer Ralph Selph Henry, "Forrest would have been totally incapable of so obvious and self-conscious a piece of literary carpentry."

How did the Confederate's syntax get revised in the first place? As Henry admitted, given the diction of the time, Forrest's pronunciation might have been, "Git thar fust with the most men." This motto first appeared in print (as "I got there first with the most men") in a Confederate general's memoir published two years after Forrest's 1877 death. Over time his words were gussied up, first with "mostest," then with "fustest." ("The mostest" was a spoofy term popular in the post–Civil War period.) By World War I, the embellished version had so taken hold that when a British correspondent quoted Forrest's actual words in a 1918 dispatch, the *New York Tribune* chided him for sissifying the Confederate's earthy talk. The *Times* then took its competitor to task, pointing out that the popular version of Forrest's epigram was "not dialect but 'baby talk.' The truth is, that somebody who was trying to make Forrest talk what he imagined to be Southern dialect evolved that incredible phraseology, and [it] has been followed slavishly ever since."

Have we finally learned our lesson, in the South anyway? Mississippi's Shelby Foote used the correct wording during Ken Burns's Civil War series on PBS. *Bartlett's* has it right. So do many other quote collections. Early in this project, however, I was discussing another topic with a friend from Alabama. "Well," observed my friend, "as [Confederate General] J. E. B. Stuart used to say, 'You should always git thar fustest with the mostest.' "

THE ONLY GOOD INDIAN IS A DEAD INDIAN.

In January 1869, General Philip Sheridan received a delegation of Indians at Fort Cobb in Oklahoma Territory. A Comanche chief reportedly introduced himself by saying, "Me Toch-a-way; me good Indian." According to a member of Sheridan's staff, "A quizzical smile lit up the General's face as he set those standing by in a roar by saying: 'The only good Indians I ever saw were dead.' " This comment raced around the country, euphonized to "The only good Indian is a dead Indian." Sheridan denied saying any such thing. Michael Sheridan later wrote that the attribution came from a "fool friend" of his brother, "and though he immediately disavowed the inhuman epigram, his assailants continued to ring the changes on it for months."

White Americans needed *someone* to voice this widespread sentiment as they opened up the West. Who fit the bill better than Fightin' Phil Sheridan? Like Sherman, Sheridan was a plainspoken man. (His second best known comment was, "If I owned Texas and Hell, I would rather rent out Texas and live in Hell.") Whether Sheridan actually said that the only good Indians were dead has never been determined. Ken Burns thought he did. So do many quote collections. "It has the ring of typical Sheridan rhetoric," wrote biographer Paul Hutton. But even if

Sheridan did say that the only good Indians were dead, he wasn't the first to do so. On May 28, 1868—some months before Fightin' Phil was supposed to have made this remark—Montana Congressman J. M. Cavanaugh said on the floor of the House, "I have never in my life seen a good Indian (and I have seen thousands) except when I have seen a dead Indian." A 1926 history of postwar America reported that in the 1865–1868 period, "the proverb that the only good Indian was a dead one was subscribed to in every ranch house, military post, overland stage station and mining gulch in the Western states and territories."

YOU FURNISH THE PICTURES AND I'LL FURNISH THE WAR.

On the eve of the Spanish-American war, newspaper publisher William Randolph Hearst sent artist Frederic Remington to record the hostilities in revolutionary Cuba. After spending a few days in Cuba, Remington wired that he could find no hostilities to record. The artist wanted to come home. In an infamous response, Hearst is supposed to have wired back, "Please remain. You furnish the pictures and I'll furnish the war." This response is central to the conviction that "yellow journalists" such as Hearst instigated the Spanish-American War. There is no reliable evidence that Hearst ever sent such a telegram. He himself denied having done so. The telegram in question has never been found. Hearst biographer John K. Winkler pointed out that such an inflammatory message would never have got past Spanish censors. So where did this legend originate? The source of Hearst's pithy wire seems to have been a 1901 memoir by journalist James Creelman. Creelman was a Hearst admirer who reported his exchange of telegrams with Remington without giving a source. Based on this single dubious report, the exchange was repeatedly included in histories of the Spanish-American War and biographies of William Randolph Hearst. Orson Welles made sure we'd never forget the legendary telegram when he included a version in *Citizen Kane*. In this classic 1941 movie, Charles Foster Kane, the newspaper publisher modeled after Hearst, wires a reporter in Cuba, "You provide the prose poems, I'll provide the war."

Word Wars

THE WAR TO END ALL WARS.

Although he never used those exact words, Woodrow Wilson is generally credited with calling World War I "the war to end all wars." On the eve of that conflict, H. G. Wells published a book called *The War that Will End War* (1914). Wells discussed his prior claim to this slogan when he wrote in 1934, "I launched the phrase 'The War to End War'— and that was not the least of my crimes."

LAFAYETTE, WE ARE HERE.

After American troops landed in France in 1917, General John J. Pershing was celebrated for honoring the Marquis de Lafayette with this eloquent remark. He himself knew better. "Many have attributed this striking utterance to me," Pershing wrote thirteen years after the armistice, "and I have often wished that it could have been mine. But I have no recollection of saying anything so splendid. I am sure that those words were spoken by Colonel Stanton and to him must go the credit for coining so happy and felicitous a phrase." Col. Charles E. Stanton was the chief disbursing officer of the American Expeditionary Force. Historians generally credit him with saying "Lafayette, we are here" at Lafayette's tomb on July 4, 1917. *Bartlett's* raises this reservation, however: American correspondent Naboth Hedin, who was present at the July 4 ceremony, later reported that he heard Pershing say "Lafayette, we are here" three weeks earlier. In *The Dictionary of Misinformation*, Tom Burnam suggested that this remark was current at the time our forces arrived in France and was probably not original to either man.

ONLY THOSE ARE FIT TO LIVE WHO ARE NOT AFRAID TO DIE.

So said Douglas MacArthur at a 1935 reunion of combat veterans from the 42nd Infantry Division. A few decades earlier Theodore Roosevelt wrote, "Only those are fit to live who do not fear to die."

I SHALL RETURN.

MacArthur's vow to return after the Japanese drove his forces from the Philippines was suggested to him by Carlos Romulo. The Office of War

Information in Washington strongly urged the American commander to pluralize the first word and say, "We shall return." Romulo, at the time a Filipino journalist, argued that his countrymen trusted MacArthur personally more than they trusted Americans in general. MacArthur took Romulo's advice and stuck to the singular. Among his troops, this egotistical vow became a standing joke (e.g., "I'm going to the latrine, but I shall return.)"

IN WAR . . . THERE CAN BE NO SUBSTITUTE FOR VICTORY.

On April 19, 1951, MacArthur told a joint session of Congress: "In war, indeed, there can be no substitute for victory." Nearly seven years earlier General Dwight D. Eisenhower wrote his wife Mamie, "In war there is no substitute for victory." It is unlikely that Douglas MacArthur was reading Mamie's mail. It is likely that this phrase was common among military men during World War II. Although he is indelibly associated with the saying, MacArthur was merely its publicist.

OLD SOLDIERS NEVER DIE. THEY JUST FADE AWAY.

MacArthur concluded his 1951 speech to Congress by saying, "I still remember the refrain of one of the most popular barrack ballads of that day [early in the century], which proclaimed most proudly, that 'Old soldiers never die. They just fade away.' " The song he referred to was a parody of the hymn, "Kind Words Can Never Die." That parody, "Old Soldiers Never Die," included these lines: "Old soldiers never die,/ They simply fade away." After citing this song, MacArthur closed his speech by saying, "And like the old soldier in that ballad, I now close my military career and just fade away, an old soldier who tried to do his duty as God gave him the sight to see that duty." As William Safire pointed out, MacArthur's words brought to mind a passage from Lincoln's second inaugural address: "with firmness in the right, as God gives us to see the right."

Post-Wars

WE'RE EYEBALL TO EYEBALL, AND I THINK THE OTHER FELLOW JUST BLINKED.

This was Secretary of State Dean Rusk's successful bid for *Bartlett's*—his depiction of the Cuban missile crisis. Former Army Chief of Staff Howard Johnson told Safire that Rusk's catchphrase was well known in the military at the time he used it. According to Johnson the phrase originated early in the Korean War when the 24th Infantry Regiment was confronted by a furious enemy attack. MacArthur's headquarters asked if they'd had contact with the enemy. Their widely reported reply was that they were "eyeball to eyeball."

LIGHT AT THE END OF THE TUNNEL.

This assessment of our early prospects in Vietnam is usually credited to Dean Rusk, Robert McNamara, William Westmoreland, or any other prominent figure whom we'd like to blame for leading us into that quagmire. In fact it was John Kennedy who said during a 1962 press conference, "So we don't see the end of the tunnel, but I must say I don't think it is darker than it was a year ago, and in some ways lighter." This probably was the first application of the tunnel simile to American involvement in Indochina. But it wasn't the first time the phrase was applied to that conflict. On the eve of the 1954 French debacle at Dien Bien Phu, French General Eugene-Henri Navarre said, "A year ago none of us could see victory. There wasn't a prayer. Now we can see it clearly—like light at the end of a tunnel." According to the *Oxford English Dictionary*, the phrase "light at the end of the tunnel" dates back at least to 1922. British politicians saw this light often during the twenties and thirties. After World War II British and French leaders alike made frequent use of the term.

A SECRET PLAN TO END THE WAR.

In a 1968 campaign speech Richard Nixon said he would end the war in Vietnam, but couldn't be specific about how he would do so for fear of undercutting President Lyndon Johnson. In the lead to his report of that speech, a wire reporter characterized Nixon's approach as a "secret plan." This hook phrase hung on to Nixon himself as if he himself had said it. In time it became part of common wisdom that Richard Nixon once said, "I have a secret plan to end the war." When PBS did an elaborate history of the Vietnam conflict, its producer spent a lot of money and effort searching for a tape recording of Nixon saying he had a secret plan to end the war. "Since he never said it," noted former Associated Press executive Walter Mears, "they never found it, but the producer apparently wouldn't take his staff's no for an answer and insisted that they keep hunting."

GUNS AND BUTTER

Lyndon Johnson's attempt to prosecute the war in Vietnam without sacrificing domestic programs was widely called the "guns and butter" approach. That phrase is generally associated with Johnson. In 1936 Nazi Field Marshal Hermann Göring said, "Guns will make us powerful; butter will only make us fat."

Johnson had little need for other people's words. He was an eminently quotable politician. Nonetheless, as with most politicians, closer examination sometimes proved that LBJ's better lines were not always his own. When he was majority leader of the Senate, Johnson said he was more the type to give ulcers than get them. That line had been used by Hollywood moguls for years. During a railway labor dispute in 1964, a member of the management team told the President that he was just an 'ole country boy. "Hold it," said Johnson. "Stop right there. When I hear that around this town, I put my hand on my billfold. Don't start that with me." This crack made Bill Adler's *The Johnson Humor*. According to LBJ's Press Secretary Bill Moyers, ostentatiously protecting your wallet when someone tells you they're "just an 'ole country boy" is an old Texas tradition.

In general it's an old tradition for political figures to borrow material wherever they find it. Politicians often complain about other people putting words in their mouths. More often it's the other way around. More often politicians put other people's words in their own mouths.

6

Lip-Sync Politics

The political subdivision of the English language has been in business too long for almost any phrase to be totally original. . . .

WILLIAM SAFIRE

n the late summer of 1983, Congresswoman Patricia Schroeder was fixing eggs for her family's breakfast. As she pulled out a nonstick frying pan, her mind turned, as it often did, to Ronald Reagan. What kept this bumbler from being penalized for his mistakes? Reagan was just like . . . like—she looked at the pan—like Teflon. Nothing stuck to him.

Later that day, Schroeder and her administrative assistant, Dan Buck, worked on a speech about Reagan for her to make in Congress. Buck suggested that she compare the president to *Mad* magazine's Alfred E. Newman by saying, "Ronald E. Reagan has replaced 'The Buck Stops Here' with 'What, me worry?' " Schroeder thought that sounded forced. The congresswoman said she'd come up with something on her way to the House floor. She did. The *Congressional Record* for August 2, 1983 included these comments by Pat Schroeder:

> Mr. Speaker, after carefully watching Ronald Reagan, he is attempting a great break-through in political technology—he has been perfecting the Teflon coated Presidency.

72

He sees to it that nothing sticks to him. He is responsible for nothing—civil rights, Central America, the Middle East, the economy, the environment—he is just the master of ceremonies at someone else's dinner.

"Oh, *that* naval exercise." "Oh, *that* Interior Secretary." "Oh, *that* Middle East." "Oh, *that* acid rain." "Oh, *that* unemployment."

Harry Truman had a sign on his desk emblazoned with his motto: 'The buck stops here.' It has obviously been removed and Reagan's desk has been Teflon coated. . . .

A week later the *New York Times* included Schroeder's first two paragraphs in their "Required Reading" section. Its headline was **"The Teflon Presidency."** In their August 22, 1983 issue, *People* magazine excerpted the paragraph which concluded, "Reagan's desk has been Teflon coated."

During the 1984 presidential campaign "Teflon-coated" became a cliché description of Ronald Reagan's ability to dodge political bullets. In the process, Schroeder's phrase took many forms. According to the most popular version, she'd called Reagan "the Teflon President." Others preferred "the Teflon candidate." Some thought Reagan had been called "Teflon coated." Vice President George Bush reported that his boss had been called "the man in the Teflon suit" by "whatshername from Colorado." Others had no idea who'd said it first. In an amazingly brief period of time Pat Schroeder's bit of political wit became public domain. Far more people discussed Reagan's "Teflon" quality than knew who'd hung the tag on him.

How did Schroeder herself feel about hearing so many colleagues lip-sync her line? Philosophical. "There's a rule in Washington that the first time you are supposed to attribute [a line to its author]," she said, "the second time you attribute it generically, and from then on it's yours. So I've always operated that that's the law of the land and not paid much attention to it."

The average politician is quite unoriginal and utterly shameless about borrowing material from those who are original. Much of the time they have no idea where their material came from in the first place. During a debate with Ronald Reagan in 1984, Walter Mondale quipped, "Well,

I guess I'm reminded a little bit of what Will Rogers once said about Hoover. He said, **'It's not what he doesn't know that bothers me, it's what he knows for sure that just ain't so.'** " When reporters asked where this quote came from, Mondale's aides said the candidate got it from a campaign worker who'd read it in a Salt Lake City newspaper. The director of the Will Rogers Memorial said that in twenty years' time she'd read all two million of the humorist's published words but had never seen these. A 1940 joke book recorded as a "Negro saying": "It ain't the things you don't know what gets you into trouble; it's the things you know for sure what ain't so." Other sources credit a similar thought to nineteenth century humorist Artemus Ward. That is probably because the introduction to Ward's collected works included this line: "You'd better not know so much, than know so many things that ain't so." But that remark is clearly attributed to Ward's colleague Josh Billings. Billings's own collected works included: "I honestly believe it iz better tew know nothing than two know what ain't so." Elsewhere Billings used variations on this theme, always ending with the words "ain't so." The line probably originated with him. Library of Congress researchers discovered that twentieth century humorist Frank Hubbard later wrote, "Taint what a man don't know that hurts him; it's what he knows that just ain't so." No such observation was ever found in Will Rogers's corpus. It just *sounds* like Rogers, and was more conveniently put in his well-known mouth for Mondale's national audience than in those of Josh Billings, Artemus Ward, or Frank Hubbard.

During an earlier debate, Mondale had challenged Gary Hart about his "new ideas." **"Where's the beef?"** asked Mondale. That line came from commercials for Wendy's hamburgers which were popular at the time. When campaign manager Bob Beckel advised Mondale to pose this question, the candidate said he'd never heard it before. Beckel pleaded with him to do so anyway. Mondale rehearsed the phrase a few times, then sprung it on Hart. It is still the best-remembered line of an unmemorable campaign. Two campaigns later a political commentator said Nebraska Senator Bob Kerrey would have to answer the same question that stumped Gary Hart: "Where's the beef?"

The case of Walter Mondale is utterly typical. When it comes to oratory, *original* and *politician* are oxymoronic. Politicians are human sponges, soaking up whatever proves useful: positions, ideas, quotes. This does not make them bad leaders, unscrupulous orators, or mediocre intellects. These are men and women of action. They seldom have the time or inclination to read or reflect. Political figures have assistants for that sort of thing. "They are dependent upon hasty briefings from aides who scurry alongside as they dash about the Capitol," noted longtime Washington reporter Samuel Shaffer. As a result, "Literary references in congressional speeches are few, repetitive, and most often inaccurate."

According to Shaffer, Senator Everett McKinley Dirksen once told his colleagues, "As Don Byrne said, 'No man is an island unto himself.' " When a reporter reminded him that it was John Donne, not Don Byrne, who said no man is an island, Dirksen murmured, "Oh, my God," and dashed off to correct the *Congressional Record*.

During his long career in politics, Dirksen's fellow Illinoisan Adlai Stevenson developed a reputation for erudition. But that reputation was not as deserved as it appeared to be. Those who worked closely with Stevenson, and admired him, quickly discovered that the two-time presidential nominee wasn't much of a reader. Although he was proud of his reputation as an original thinker (Stevenson's speechwriters were called "researchers"), this reputation was more apparent than real. "He did not so much create ideas as synthesize the ideas of others," noted Stevenson's aide and biographer John Bartlow Martin.

Shortly before he died in 1965, Stevenson was interviewed by Leon Harris for his book on *The Fine Art of Political Wit*. During their conversation Illinois's former governor showed Harris the notebooks he'd kept for over forty years. In them was a jumble of his own ideas, quotations from others, and political bon mots. As with others who give many speeches, the origins of phrases which Adlai liked to use were often lost in transmission.

While running for President in 1952, Stevenson said of his Republican opponents, **"If they will stop telling lies about the Democrats, we will stop telling the truth about them."** This was thought to be a cracking good example of Adlai's sharp wit. Nearly half a century earlier, while running against Charles Evans Hughes for governor of New York in 1906, William Randolph Hearst said, "If Mr. Hughes will stop lying about me, I will stop telling the truth about him." Chauncey Depew, who was a Republican senator from New York from 1899 to 1911, often said, "If you will refrain from telling any lies about the Republican Party, I'll promise not to tell the truth about the Democrats." This line probably antedates both Hearst and Depew (to say nothing of Stevenson).

As part of his "let's talk sense to the American people" campaign in 1952, Stevenson often reminded audiences that **"there are no gains without pains."** Stevenson borrowed this thought from Benjamin Franklin, who in turn took it from Thomas Fuller. We have no idea where Fuller got it.

James Reston of the *New York Times* used to enjoy quoting this quip from his friend Adlai: **"An editor is one who separates the wheat from the chaff and prints the chaff."** Many others followed suit (I used to attribute that quote to Stevenson myself). In a eulogy to reporter Peter Kihss, journalist Sydney Schanberg credited his colleague with saying the same thing. But in *1001 Epigrams*—which was published two years before Kihss was born, and when Adlai Stevenson was eleven—Elbert Hubbard defined an editor as "A person employed on a newspaper, whose business it is to separate the wheat from the chaff, and to see that the chaff is printed." Since Hubbard was such a chronic thief of other people's lines, it's unlikely that this thought began with him. But it certainly did not begin with Adlai.

Some quote collections credit Stevenson with saying, **"A politician is a person who approaches every subject with an open mouth."** This line has also been attributed to Oscar Wilde and Arthur Goldberg. Nigel Rees called it "another of those quotations which floats continually in search of a definite source." When asked whether the term **"brinkmanship"** could properly be credited to him (as it often was), Stevenson himself said, "I am not sure whether I read it or heard it or dreamed it up. I am reasonably sure I did not invent it." Another phrase popularized by Stevenson—**"quality of life"**—originated with journalist Eric Sevareid.

When Eleanor Roosevelt died in 1962, Stevenson observed that the former First Lady **"would rather light a candle than curse the darkness."** At first he was widely praised for this bit of eloquence. It turned out, however, that Adlai's tribute to Franklin Roosevelt's widow came from the longtime motto of the Christopher Society: "It is better to light one candle than to curse the darkness." The Christophers, in turn, say their motto was originally a Chinese proverb.

Eleanor Roosevelt seemed to bring out the banality in her admirers. **"No woman has ever so comforted the distressed—or so distressed**

the comfortable," is the way Clare Booth Luce introduced her at a 1950 dinner. This is an old saw usually used to describe the proper role of a newspaper. It is sometimes attributed to Mr. Dooley. In his 1941 quote collection, H. L. Mencken credited the saying to "Author unidentified."

Such petty pilfering is seldom noted by political commentators. Wholesale theft is another matter. Senator Joseph Biden was forced out of the 1988 presidential primaries when it was shown that he'd repeated almost verbatim a heartrending speech made by British Labor party leader Neil Kinnock about his family's struggle to escape the coal mines. Biden's knuckles were rapped smartly for this blatant plagiarism. But the Delaware senator was exceptional only in the degree and brazenness of his literary embezzlement. Disraeli—a rare politician who actually displayed original wit—was caught more than once in similar acts of plagiarism, the evidence running side by side in newspapers just as it was with Biden.

And how about Neil Kinnock, the injured party in this caper? As Nigel Rees reported, Kinnock once said that were he to walk across the Thames, the next day's headline would read, "NEIL KINNOCK FAILS TO SWIM RIVER." Some years earlier Lyndon Johnson quipped that if he strolled across the Potomac one morning, that afternoon's headline would read, "PRESIDENT CAN'T SWIM." A few months after Kinnock recycled LBJ's quip, Archbishop Desmond Tutu of South Africa said that if he and then–South African President P. W. Botha were in a boat which got caught in a storm on Table Bay and he walked across the water to get help, the next day's headline would read, "TUTU CAN'T SWIM."

Such cases are more the rule than the exception in politics. When a politician "gets off a good one," you can almost be sure that he or she didn't make it up. Former Congressman Morris Udall, who was celebrated as a wit during three decades in Congress, freely admitted that much of his material was second-hand. According to Udall any good line over twenty-four hours old is in the public domain. "Jokes are public, not private property," he explained, "and you can't be prosecuted for borrowing them." Consider the evidence:

• After Harry Truman died in 1972, he was recalled fondly for having observed of his early days in the Senate: **"For the first six months, you wonder how the hell you ever got here. For the next six**

months you wonder how the hell the rest of them ever got here." When Truman first made that droll observation, he said it was something Illinois Senator Ham Lewis told him in the mid-1930s. This actually is an old saw that has made the rounds of Congress for a century or more. An 1899 article in the *Saturday Evening Post* noted, "One of the standing jokes of Congress is that the new Congressman always spends the first week wondering how he got there and the rest of the time wondering how the other members got there." Seventy years later, in 1969, Ohio Senator William Saxbe said, "The first six months, I kept wondering how I got here. After that I started wondering how all of them did."

• One of Robert Kennedy's best quips was always thought to be, **"My views on birth control are somewhat distorted by the fact that I was the seventh of nine children."** Several decades before Kennedy made this rueful observation, Clarence Darrow wrote, "Whenever I hear people discussing birth control, I always remember that I was the fifth."

• In 1984, Republican politician Anne Burford called Washington, D.C., **"Too small to be a state but too large to be an asylum for the mentally deranged."** On the eve of the Civil War, a South Carolinian named James Petigru called his state "too small for a republic and too large for an insane asylum."

• During the 1992 New Hampshire primary, Pat Buchanan said, **"I admire Ted Kennedy. How many fifty-nine-year-olds do you know who still go to Florida for spring break?"** Jay Leno pointed out that he had already used this line on *The Tonight Show* several months earlier. Leno called Buchanan "the Joe Biden of the Republican Party." When Dan Quayle later caused an uproar by criticizing the decision of TV character Murphy Brown to become a single parent, Leno told his audience that—unlike Quayle—Brown at least knew she'd be back in the fall. One month later, the Vice-President said in a speech, "Actually, I'm a little bit envious of Murphy Brown. At least she's guaranteed to come back this fall."

During the 1988 primaries, Democratic contender Bruce Babbitt often remarked, **"George Bush reminds every woman of her first husband."** That quip appeared under Jane O'Reilly's byline in the November 1984 issue of *GQ*. Ann Richards later scored a hit in her keynote address to the Democratic convention by saying, **"Poor George . . . he can't help it—he was born with a silver foot in his mouth."** Richards said this line came to her via Lily Tomlin's writing partner Jane Wagner. Two weeks before the Democratic convention, Citizen's Action president Heather Booth used that line in a speech. Over two decades earlier the same observation was made about Newbold Morris, New York's patrician Commissioner of Parks (who once recommended Central Park as a good place for homeless people to spend the night). The *New York Times'* 1966 obituary of Morris credited its own reporter Paul Crowell with observing, "Newbold was born with a silver foot in his mouth."

In her 1988 keynote, Ann Richards also got laughs with, **"Ginger Rogers did everything that Fred Astaire did. She just did it backward and in high heels."** This is an old feminist saw that Richards had been using for years. She thought television journalist Linda Ellerbee fed her the line. Ellerbee said she might have gotten it from someone on an airplane. The same gag has been attributed to Republican politician Faith Whittlesey.

Even when they do try to cite their sources, politicians get in trouble. New York Congressman Stephen Solarz once quoted Camus as saying, **"Nothing so wonderfully concentrates a man's mind as the imminent thought of execution."** (Samuel Johnson's exact words were, "Depend on it, Sir, when a man knows he is to be hanged in a fortnight, it concentrates his mind wonderfully.") In 1990, an aide to then-Congressman William Gray of Pennsylvania told a reporter, "Like Dante said, **'The hottest place is in hell and for those who do not speak out in times of moral crisis.'** " Nearly two decades earlier, John F. Kennedy said Dante's words were, "The hottest places in hell are reserved for those who in a period of moral crisis maintain their neutrality." Dante did say some things about hell, but this wasn't among them. The closest passage the Library of Congress could find in Dante's *Inferno* was, "They are mixed with that repulsive choir of angels . . . undecided in neutrality. Heaven, to keep its beauty, cast them out, but even Hell itself would not receive them for fear the wicked there might glory over them."

As long as politicians have quoted, they have misquoted. The practice is bipartisan, and has a rich history. The mangling of quotes is hardly modern. Nor is it always benign, or simply a matter of not looking things up. The calculated or semi-calculated misquote has been a staple of political combat for a long, long time.

The Misquote Tradition in Politics

EVERY MAN HAS HIS PRICE.

British Prime Minister Sir Robert Walpole (1676–1745) is best remembered for saying, "Every man has his price." What Walpole actually said (about some nemeses) was, "All those men have their price." The more sweeping, cynical version was put in Walpole's mouth by political enemies. It stuck.

YOUR PEOPLE, SIR, IS A GREAT BEAST.

Alexander Hamilton is still remembered for calling the people "a great beast." Historian Barbara Tuchman thought he said this during an argument with Jefferson. The more common assumption is that Hamilton called the people beastly at a New York dinner party. This anecdote was first reported in Theophilus Parsons's 1859 memoir, fifty-five years after Alexander Hamilton was killed by Aaron Burr. According to Parsons, a friend told him that a guest at this party said he heard Hamilton call the people a great beast. No historian has ever been able to verify this fourth-hand report.

How did an unconfirmed rumor in an obscure memoir become the source of Alexander Hamilton's most familiar quotation? Historian William Ander Smith pinned the blame on Henry Adams. In his monumental *History of the United States* (1891) Adams referred twice to Hamilton's portrayal of the people as beastly. Although he was generally fastidious about citing sources, Adams gave none for this oath. Smith concluded that it could only have been the memoir of Theophilus Parsons (who was John Adams's attorney general). Adams must have known this source was dubious but wanted to use the Hamilton remark so badly that he did so anyway.

Henry Adams had a well-known antipathy toward Hamilton dating back to this man's conflicts with his great-grandfather, John Adams. Reporting that Hamilton thought of the people as a great beast hung him posthumously with his own words. By repetition alone, Hamilton's slur on democracy became his legacy. No evidence other than a vague rumor exists that he ever called the people beastly. Did anyone? Comparing the people to a beast dates back at least to Horace. In 1513, Nicollò Machiavelli wrote in *The Prince,* "The masses of the people resemble a wild beast." More than two centuries later, Alexander Pope said, "The people are a many-headed beast." In the course of his research, William Ander Smith discovered an 1867 letter in which Henry Adams wrote to his brother Charles about the pressure of public opinion on writers. "It is the public which controls us," concluded Adams, "and in the long run we must obey the beast."

RUM, ROMANISM, AND REBELLION

In 1884 this slogan was thought to be a slander of the Democrat's credo by Republican presidential candidate James G. Blaine. The resulting uproar was instrumental in Blaine's defeat. These words were actually those of a supporter, the Reverend Samuel Burchard. A month before the election, Burchard said at a Blaine reception, "We are Republicans, and don't propose to have our party identify ourselves with the party whose antecedents have been rum, Romanism and rebellion." The last part of this statement caught the public's ear. Before long it was as if Blaine had said it himself, or so the Democrats successfully persuaded American voters. Their candidate, Grover Cleveland, won the presidency. Many historians credit the misattribution of Burchard's words to Blaine for turning the tide of this election.

PUBLIC OFFICE IS A PUBLIC TRUST.

Grover Cleveland's credo was meant to present him in a statesmanlike light. Many took credit for suggesting this phrase. The most credible claim was that of former political reporter and campaign aide William C. Hudson. Unable to find a proper slogan for the title page of Cleveland's first campaign document, Hudson approached the matter as if he were writing a newspaper headline. "PUBLIC OFFICE IS A PUBLIC TRUST," is what Hudson came up with. When a proof sheet of Cleveland's pamphlet was shown to the Democratic candidate, he pointed to its title and asked, "Where the deuce did I say that?" Hudson persuaded Cleveland that this was a precis of views he'd often expressed. The candidate's aide then wrote "G. Cleveland" under the headline, and sent it off to the printer and the history books.

Successful as it proved to be, Cleveland's 1884 slogan was hardly original. In 1829 Henry Clay said, "Government is a trust." Six years later John C. Calhoun noted, "The very essence of a free government consists in considering offices as public trusts." In 1867 President Andrew Johnson told Congress, "It is not the theory of this government that public offices are the property of those who hold them. They are given merely as a trust for the public benefit." Five years later Senator Charles Sumner observed, "The phrase, 'public office is a public trust,' has of late become common property." In his memoirs, William Hudson denied any conscious awareness that the slogan he suggested to Cleveland had been around for years. Nonetheless, Hudson conceded, "It is quite among the possibilities that I had met with the phrase in my earlier readings; that it made its impression and remained in my mind until the requirements brought it to the surface, when it appeared to me as an original conception."

May We Quote You? (The Press Lends a Hand)

SMOKE-FILLED ROOM

It's a given that Warren Harding's 1920 nomination for President was engineered in a **smoke-filled room**. This is because some weeks before the Republicans convened in Chicago, Harding's cohort Harry Daugherty predicted that toward the end of a dead-locked convention—at about 2:11 A.M.—a small group of men "in a smoke-filled room" would pick Warren Harding as their party's nominee. Since that seemed to describe what actually happened, Daugherty's prophecy caught the public's fancy. To this day "smoke-filled room" is synonymous with political machinations behind closed doors.

When he tried to reconstruct the birth of this phrase, however, journalist-historian Mark Sullivan came up dry. After interviewing some of those involved, Sullivan finally concluded that what happened was this: While packing his bags in a hotel room, Daugherty was confronted by two reporters intent on interviewing him. Harding's campaign manager said he had no time. One of the reporters followed him down the hall asking questions anyway. Trying to get a rise out of Daugherty, he speculated that Harding's only chance for the nomination would be one engineered by hot, exhausted delegates in a smoke-filled room at two in the morning. "Make it two-eleven," Daugherty snapped. Thus was born his epitaph.

While conceding that Harry Daugherty was a candid fellow with a gift for pungent language (about his discovery of the photogenic Harding at a county convention in Ohio, Daugherty said, "I found him sunning himself like a turtle on a log, and I pushed him into the water"), Sullivan concluded that Daugherty himself had never said "smoke-filled room" or anything like it. That phrase was put in his mouth. It proved so compelling that we've used it ever since.

ARE YOU AWARE THAT CLAUDE PEPPER IS KNOWN ALL OVER WASHINGTON AS A SHAMELESS EXTROVERT? (etc.)

During his successful 1950 senatorial race, George Smathers ran a particularly brutal campaign against incumbent Claude Pepper. Some of Smathers's allegations about his opponent shocked audiences in rural Florida. The annals of political history include this especially memorable charge:

> Are you aware that Claude Pepper is known all over Washington as a shameless extrovert? Not only that, but this man is reliably reported to practice nepotism with his sister-in-law, and he has a sister who was once a thespian in wicked New York. Worst of all, it is an established fact that Mr. Pepper before his marriage habitually practiced celibacy.

Smathers's diatribe is still considered an amusing low point in American politics. It was first reported nationally by *Time* magazine in 1950 and has been repeated often since. Smathers once offered $10,000 to anyone who could prove that he'd actually said these words. No one could. *Time* itself admitted in its original account that the allegation was of dubious authenticity. But they did so in a way that implied it might be authentic anyway:

> Smathers was capable of going to any length in campaigning, but he indignantly denied that he had gone as far as a story printed in northern newspapers. The story wouldn't die, nonetheless, and it deserved not to. According to the yarn, Smathers had a little speech for cracker voters, who were presumed not to know what the words

meant except that they must be something bad. The speech went like this: 'Are you aware . . . [etc.]' "

Smathers claimed that this spoof was one of several that reporters made up to amuse themselves (and sometimes showed him). A Pepper aide recalled the same thing. One of Smathers's assistants admitted that after the joke went public they used it to hold Pepper up to ridicule. It is still reported as fact. A 1988 *TV Guide* article quoted from the hoax allegation as if it were gospel. So did *Newsweek*'s Samuel Shaffer in a 1980 memoir about his three decades as a political reporter. William Buckley at first perpetuated the legend in his book *McCarthy and His Enemies,* then corrected himself in later editions. Few followed suit. We all love a good campaign yarn and are loath to give up one this good, even when it's so easily debunked.

WHERE FRATERNITIES ARE NOT ALLOWED, COMMUNISM FLOUR-ISHES.

Among various silly statements attributed to Barry Goldwater over the years, this was the silliest. As Edwin McDowell pointed out in a biography of the Arizona Senator, Goldwater said no such thing. During a speech to the National Inter-Fraternity Council in 1962, Goldwater did observe that fraternity-free Harvard was a bastion of Keynesianism. In the same speech he said that fraternities produce leaders. The next day a wire reporter put this together as, "Where fraternities are not allowed, Communism flourishes." At Goldwater's behest, the reporter's bureau chief agreed to review a tape of his speech. Sure enough, it was "Keynesianism" that Goldwater had referred to. When asked about his account, the reporter admitted that he'd confused Keynesianism with Communism. The wire service sent out a correction. Nonetheless, for years thereafter Goldwater got credit for the uncorrected version.

THE VICE PRESIDENCY ISN'T WORTH A PITCHER OF WARM SPIT.

Long after leaving office, John Nance Garner—Franklin Roosevelt's first running mate—became famous for observing that the vice presidency "wasn't worth a pitcher of warm spit." This remains one of the most widely quoted assessments of that office. What Garner actually said, however, was that the vice presidency "wasn't worth a pitcher of warm piss." *Time*'s Hugh Sidey told me that this was the version he passed along to his editors in a memo. But piss got changed to spit in *Time* and other publications, and spit it's been ever since. Before he died in 1967, Garner complained that "those pantywaist writers wouldn't print it the way I said it."

JERRY FORD IS SO DUMB THAT HE CAN'T WALK AND CHEW GUM AT THE SAME TIME.

Before the copy desk gave him a hand, what Lyndon Johnson actually said was that Ford couldn't fart and chew gum at the same time.

INOPERATIVE

On April 17, 1973, Richard Nixon promised "major developments" in the Watergate case. His press secretary, Ronald Ziegler, told reporters that this was the president's "operative" statement. R. W. Apple of the *New York Times* asked whether it would be fair to infer that because "the other statement is no longer operative, that it is now inoperative." After fencing with Apple for a time, Ziegler relented and said, "The President refers to the fact that there is new material; therefore, this is the operative statement. The others are inoperative." This comment made headlines the next day. *Inoperative* proved to be a powerful hook word. In time it became Ron Ziegler's legacy. Ziegler did use that word, but it was at Apple's behest. The *Times* reporter deserved at least a collaborator's credit.

Getting By With a Little Help from Their Aides

When he was Richard Nixon's counsel, a plaque hanging on Charles Colson's wall read, **"If you've got them by the balls, their hearts and minds will follow."** Although he never claimed authorship of the slogan, it was widely associated with Nixon's hard-bitten aide. Colson said the plaque was given to him by a former member of the Green Berets. Many members of the Special Forces thought this slogan characterized their mission in Vietnam. Some Teamsters were also partial to the motto. Where did it originate? One possibility is suggested by Morris Udall. During a Vietnam-era congressional debate, a liberal Democrat pleaded for programs designed to "win the hearts and minds of the downtrodden." Hawkish Congressman Mendel Rivers responded, "I say get 'em by the balls and their hearts and minds will follow." Given the reluctance of politicians to cite their sources, it's doubtful that this rejoinder began with Rivers. It certainly didn't begin with Charles Colson.

Richard Nixon's White House was a hotbed of old phrases passing for new. **"The Big Enchilada"**—a nickname Nixon's aides hung on John Mitchell—was in common use on the West Coast in the 1940s as "the whole enchilada." Mitchell himself was fond of saying, **"When the going gets tough, the tough get going."** This slogan was sometimes attributed to him, as it's been to Knute Rockne and Joseph Kennedy. That maxim has papered locker room walls for decades—centuries, even. (I first heard it during a pep talk by my high school's cross country coach in 1959.) **"Deep six,"** what John Dean said John Erlichman suggested he do with incriminating Watergate documents (i.e., drop them into the Potomac River), drew on naval jargon. This was also the title of a 1958 Alan Ladd–William Bendix movie about submariners.

Political aides play an important, ill-appreciated role in generating misquotes. The best ones pick up material from a wide range of sources to enhance whatever point their boss needs to make. If such material sounds original, or suggests erudition, more's the better. But on closer examination, what's assumed to be a fresh or erudite comment by a politician seldom is. The most famous phrase in Barry Goldwater's speech accepting the 1964 presidential nomination was **"Extremism in the defense of liberty is no vice. And . . . moderation in the pursuit of justice is no virtue."** Credit for this memorable phrase was generally given to speechwriter Karl Hess. Hess said it drew on Lincoln's "House divided" speech. Goldwater thought it might have come from Cicero. A more likely source was Thomas Paine's, "Moderation in temper is always a virtue; moderation in principle is always a vice."

During part of his career as a congressman and senator from New York, Kenneth Keating enjoyed a reputation as a phrasemaker. Keating's main claim to wit was his observation that **"Roosevelt proved a man could be President for life; Truman proved anybody could be President; and Eisenhower proved you don't need a President."** When Leon Harris interviewed Keating for *The Fine Art of Political Wit,* however, Keating denied ever saying this, showed no sense of humor, and pleaded with Harris not to consider his funny lines part of the public record. Harris concluded that it wasn't the senator himself but an aide—Hugh Morrow, it turned out—who was responsible for the senator's reputation as a wit. When New York Governor Nelson Rockefeller hired Morrow away from Keating, that reputation went with him.

Morrow himself may not have been all that original. Earlier in the century, Clarence Darrow was credited with observing, "When I was a boy I was told that anybody could become President; I'm beginning to believe it." I recall hearing Keating's version as a pass-around gag in the fifties. Whoever said it first, many are still repeating the basic theme. After ascending to the presidency, former Vice President Gerald Ford observed ruefully, "I guess it proves that in America anyone can be President." In 1990 humorist Dave Barry dedicated a book to "Dan Quayle, who proved to my generation that, frankly, *anybody* can make it."

"We're all just repeating folk wisdoms," admitted Dan Buck, Pat Schroeder's administrative assistant. "You drink a few beers, start spouting this and that. I'm convinced that several people at the same time will say the same thing in different parts of the country. Certain things come out of the woodwork." Buck has worked for Schroeder since she was first elected to Congress in 1972. He is typical of the breed: a well-informed veteran of political wars, part of whose job is to brighten his boss's speeches. In a tiny office lined with books Buck discussed that aspect of his work. "I go through these things"—he waved at a set of quote books—"find something that I think is funny, rework it, yellow it in, then drop it into a Schroeder speech or something. Then I keep my own notebook and just jam things in wherever I think they might work." Buck showed me his notebook. It was a secretary's pad full of taped-in clippings, scrawled ideas, and quotations. Some had citations, others didn't. George Orwell is there for "There is always room for one more custard pie." The observation that "Imagination is more important than technology" appears under Albert Einstein's name. No name is listed for "Making policy means making decisions" or "If a man starts out to make himself President, he hardly ever arrives." This potpourri is probably typical of an aide's notebook, perhaps even richer. Using the contents of such a notebook can lead to problems, however, even when sources are scribbled in. Buck recalled once using a Jefferson quote about the danger of being a nation that pays its plumbers more than its teachers. "A Jefferson scholar called us on it," he recalled. "There were no plumbers then. We had to research it. It turned out that Kennedy had used the quote, saying it was from Jefferson."

Buck was not the first aide to have trouble with a quotation used by John Kennedy. Kennedy was our most quoting modern President. He was also the most likely to misquote.

7

All the President's Misquotes

For years librarians struggled unsuccessfully to find out who said **"The only thing necessary for the triumph of evil is that good men do nothing."** That quotation became popular after John Kennedy began to use it in speeches. Kennedy attributed the thought to Edmund Burke. By now it's among our most familiar quotations. Advertising agency Young & Rubicam used to feature Burke's remark in public service ads. When George Seldes asked about their source, however, no one at the agency could supply one. Their source might have been Seldes's own 1960 book *Great Quotations,* which attributed this idea to Burke without a citation. Through its 1968 edition, *Bartlett's* reported that the line originated in a 1795 letter Burke wrote to William Smith. When William Safire used this citation to verify the quote, one of his gotcha gang (Hamilton Long of Philadelphia) pointed out that *Bartlett's* was in error. Burke said nothing about good men and evil's triumph in a letter to Smith. Determined to redeem himself and *Bartlett's,* Safire contacted the British Library. They could find no source for Burke's famous observation. In her introduction to the *Bartlett's* 1980 edition, editor Emily Morison Beck reported that she'd been unable to determine who, if anyone, originally said that the only thing necessary for evil's triumph was that good men do nothing. The quotation was dropped. In his 1985 book *The Great Thoughts,* George Seldes admitted that he couldn't find a credible source for the sentence he'd once attributed to Burke. Seldes dropped it too. To this day we have no idea where John Kennedy got the quote.

Long after his brother put this comment in play, Ted Kennedy moved the confusion to a new venue when he told a 1979 audience, "Thomas Jefferson said all that is necessary for evil to strive over good was for good to remain silent."

John Kennedy and his brothers had a reputation for being eloquent, well-informed orators. Some of this reputation was deserved, some not. Like all modern Presidents, JFK depended on speechwriters, Theodore Sorensen in particular. Kennedy also drew on the intellect and scholarship of such aides as Arthur Schlesinger, Jr., John Kenneth Galbraith, and Richard Goodwin. The president didn't just tap their supply of quotable quotes but turned often to ones he'd been jotting down since college. Kennedy was a wealth of unrecorded, half-remembered quotations which his own staff and that of the Library of Congress continually struggled to confirm. Until his wife Jacqueline corrected him, Kennedy sometimes combined Emerson and Frost to say,

> *I'll hitch my wagon to a star*
> *But I have promises to keep*
> *And miles to go before I sleep*

As a result of this haphazard approach to quotation, John Kennedy was not always as erudite as he sounded. Even his most famous, original-sounding phrases had longer pedigrees than we realized.

THE NEW FRONTIER

In his speech accepting the 1960 nomination, Kennedy said, "We stand today on the edge of a new frontier." This became the defining slogan of his brief administration. By one account this phrase was suggested to Kennedy independently by aide Walt Rostow and Max Freedman of the *Manchester Guardian.* "The New Frontier" was the title of a chapter in Alf Landon's 1936 book *America at the Crossroads.* Landon used the term often during his campaign against Franklin Roosevelt that year. He may have borrowed it from Roosevelt's 1940 running mate Henry Wallace, whose book *New Frontiers* was published in 1934. In the years to come many other political figures—especially conservative Republicans—made this phrase part of their repertoire. It was fairly common by 1960, the year that Kennedy ran for President and the U.S. Chamber of Commerce appointed a Committee on New Frontiers in Technology.

ASK NOT WHAT YOUR COUNTRY CAN DO FOR YOU; ASK WHAT YOU CAN DO FOR YOUR COUNTRY.

The most stirring line in Kennedy's inaugural address has a rich history. In 1884, Oliver Wendell Holmes, Jr. asked an audience to "recall what our country has done for each of us, and to ask ourselves what we can do for our country in return." Warren Harding anticipated Kennedy by almost half a century when he told the 1916 Republican convention, "we must have a citizenship less concerned about what the government can do for it and more anxious about what it can do for the nation." That line is on display in Harding's own handwriting at his Marion, Ohio home. Kennedy's heirs don't have much to say about Harding's earlier use of this concept, just as they are mum on the Alf Landon–New Frontier connection. Acknowledging a debt to Burke or Jefferson is one thing; citing Harding or Landon quite another. While admitting that the "ask not" line had antecedents, Arthur Schlesinger, Jr. argued that this thought was the President's own. Schlesinger thought it took root in 1945 when Kennedy recorded a quotation from Rousseau in his notebook: "As soon as any man says of the affairs of the state, What does it matter to me? the state may be given up as lost." I'll go with Holmes and Harding.

VICTORY HAS A HUNDRED FATHERS AND DEFEAT IS AN ORPHAN.

This was Kennedy's rueful remark after he accepted blame for the Bay of Pigs fiasco. He called it "an old saying." When Schlesinger asked the President where he'd heard this old saying, Kennedy said he couldn't recall. Schlesinger checked with Emily Morison Beck. Beck said that during many years of editing *Bartlett's* she'd never come across this line. Kennedy most likely picked it up from a 1951 movie called *The Desert Fox*, in which a Nazi officer repeated the saying. Its scriptwriter's probable source was the diary of Count Galeazzo Ciano, Mussolini's son-in-law and foreign minister, which was published in 1947. As the Italian army suffered serious reverses in 1942, Ciano wrote on September 9, "As always, victory finds a hundred fathers, but defeat is an orphan." Presumably this was an Italian proverb. By now, via JFK, it's global. In a typical inflationary spiral the line has evolved into "Victory has a *thousand* fathers." In 1991 *Parade* magazine made the proverb gender-neutral when they suggested that former Ford executive Lee Iacocca took credit for the Mustang but not the Pinto because "Success has a thousand parents. Failure is an orphan."

WASHINGTON IS A CITY OF NORTHERN CHARM AND SOUTHERN EFFICIENCY.

William Manchester credited this witticism to Kennedy in his book *Portrait of a President*. So did Arthur Schlesinger, Jr., in *A Thousand Days*. To this day it's considered a fine example of JFK's native wit. But as the President himself alluded in a 1961 speech, the line wasn't his. In that speech Kennedy reached the second phase of Three-Step Quote Acquisition when he remarked: "Somebody once said that Washington was a city of Northern charm and Southern efficiency."

YOU SEE THINGS AND YOU SAY, "WHY?" BUT I DREAM THINGS THAT NEVER WERE; AND I SAY: "WHY NOT?"

In a 1963 speech, John Kennedy correctly attributed these words to George Bernard Shaw. His brother Robert subsequently used them as the theme for his 1968 presidential campaign. Shaw's authorship was soon forgotten. By the time W. P. Kinsella used a revised version of his comment ("Some men see things as they are, and say why, I dream of things that never were, and say why not") in his 1982 novel *Shoeless Joe*—which inspired the movie *Field of Dreams*—he attributed this thought to "Bobby Kennedy."

As the Kennedy case illustrates, among many powers bestowed upon U.S. presidents (and their kin) is the power to misquote on a grand scale. All American presidents have engaged in the give and take of misquotation, and some more than others.

Thomas Jefferson

PEACE, COMMERCE, AND HONEST FRIENDSHIP FOR ALL NATIONS, ENTANGLING ALLIANCES WITH NONE.

For some reason the phrase "entangling alliances" is more associated with George Washington than Thomas Jefferson. But it was Jefferson who used that term in his first inaugural address (see above). Washington said in his farewell address "It is our true policy to steer clear of permanent alliance with any portion of the foreign world" and "Why, by interweaving our destiny with that of any part of Europe, entangle our peace and prosperity in the toils of European ambition, rivalship, interest, humor or caprice?" But he referred to "entangling alliances" only in our memories. This hook phrase made it easier for us to recall Washington's warning, even though the words belonged to Jefferson.

THAT GOVERNMENT IS BEST WHICH GOVERNS LEAST.

Our third President is sometimes cited for observing, "That government is best which governs least." As Boller and George noted in *They Never Said It,* even the erudite William Buckley misattributed this observation to Jefferson. Jefferson didn't say it. This credo became a common part of public discourse when Thoreau quoted the sentence without attribution in his 1849 essay "Civil Disobedience." Its original author may have been John L. O'Sullivan who edited *The United States Magazine and Democratic Review.* This publication was founded in 1837 to propound the view that, "The best government is that which governs least."

FEW DIE AND NONE RESIGN.

This is a bumper-stickered version of Jefferson's actual complaint about entrenched officeholders: "If a due participation of office is a matter of right, how are vacancies to be obtained? Those by death are few, by resignation none."

Andrew Jackson

JOHN MARSHALL HAS MADE HIS DECISION. NOW LET HIM EN-
FORCE IT!

These words may represent Andrew Jackson's attitude toward an 1832
Supreme Court decision barring the relocation of Cherokee Indians
from Georgia. No credible evidence exists that he said them, however.
This oath was put on the record two decades after Jackson's death.
Horace Greeley first reported his contemptuous retort to the chief justice in an 1864 book. Greeley said that a former congressman told him
of hearing about Old Hickory's challenge to Marshall when he was in
Washington during Jackson's presidency. A quotation this familiar deserves a more dependable source.

ONE MAN WITH COURAGE MAKES A MAJORITY.

When he nominated Robert Bork to the Supreme Court in 1987, Ronald
Reagan noted, "Andrew Jackson once said that one man with courage
makes a majority. Obviously, Bob Bork has that courage." No reliable
source has ever been found for this quotation. In his foreword to a
young people's edition of *Profiles in Courage,* Robert Kennedy so
quoted Jackson, but without a citation. An 1888 biography quoted
Jackson as saying, "Desperate courage makes one a majority." This
actually is a modular quotation with many ancestors and relatives. An
inscription on the Reformation Monument in Geneva credits John Knox
with saying, "A man with God is always in the majority." Since then a
variety of alternatives to "God" have been used in that quotation: the
law, courage, etc. Andrew Jackson is no less likely than anyone else to
have jumped on this rhetorical bandwagon, but we have no proof that
he did.

Considered a boor by the better bred, Jackson was the Yogi Berra
of his day, commonly given credit for inane remarks. A British collection quoted him as saying during the battle of New Orleans, "Elevate
them guns a little lower." That's about what the descendants of Old
Hickory's vanquished foes would like to think such an uncouth barbar-
ian might say. According to a story which delighted northern intellectuals for decades, when Jackson was given an honorary degree by Harvard
in 1833, he tried to impress those present by reciting the only Latin he

knew: *"E pluribus unum,* my friends, *sine qua non."* According to Jackson biographer John William Ward, this story was still being repeated at Harvard in the 1950s. By most accounts Jackson actually received his degree in silence. Ward thinks the Latin parody was made up by detractors to ridicule the president.

Abraham Lincoln

Most of the presidents after Jackson were not quotable enough to be misquoted. Then we get to Abraham Lincoln. Even before his death in 1865, a pertinent remark from the Great Emancipator clinched many an argument. Lincoln is the most misquoted president largely because he's the one who is most quoted. The fact that America's sixteenth president didn't say much of what speakers and authors want him to have said hasn't stopped them from quoting him anyway. During the past century spurious Lincoln quotes have been used by management, labor, free traders, protectionists, wets, drys, and sundry others to prop up their causes.

Much apocryphal Lincolniana takes the form of retroquotes. But even when he was alive, the president himself estimated that half of the anecdotes involving him were either spurious or misattributed. Since he did his own share of borrowing, misquotations fly in all directions when it comes to Abraham Lincoln.

APOCRYPHAL LINCOLNISMS

YOU CAN FOOL ALL OF THE PEOPLE SOME OF THE TIME; YOU CAN EVEN FOOL SOME OF THE PEOPLE ALL OF THE TIME; BUT YOU CAN'T FOOL ALL OF THE PEOPLE ALL OF THE TIME.

By tradition Lincoln made this observation on September 2 or September 8, 1858, in a speech at Clinton, Illinois. Other sources say he said it in Bloomington, Illinois on May 29, 1856. Or it might have been at some unknown location in 1862. Or was it 1863 in Washington? No one is quite sure. These words do not appear in any of Lincoln's published works. No newspaper account of the various speeches in which they might have been used report this observation. Our only evidence that Lincoln said you can fool all the people, etc., is the memory of those who think they heard him say so, usually long after his death. This saying gained widest circulation in a 1904 book called *Abe Lincoln's Yarns and Stories*. According to its author, Pennsylvania Republican leader Alexander K. McClure, the President discussed fooling the people during a conversation with a visitor. Lincoln scholars don't give much credence to this citation or any other.

TELL ME WHAT BRAND GRANT DRINKS. I'LL SEND A BARREL TO MY OTHER GENERALS. (wording varies)

This is a favorite Lincoln chuckle, his alleged response to complaints that Ulysses S. Grant drank too much whiskey. Since this fanciful story circulated during Lincoln's lifetime, he was able to debunk it personally. Lincoln thought the anecdote was inspired by an earlier one in which George II of England said of the allegation that General James Wolfe was mad: "If General Wolfe is mad I hope he bites some of my other generals."

(1) YOU CANNOT BRING ABOUT PROSPERITY BY DISCOURAGING THRIFT. (2) YOU CANNOT STRENGTHEN THE WEAK BY WEAKENING THE STRONG. (etc.; 10 points defending conservative free enterprise principles)

This list of maxims is beloved by free enterprise zealots. For decades they plastered it on wall hangings, calendars, pamphlets, and advertisements. As recently as 1976 Tiffany's ran "Lincoln's" ten points in an ad, then had to take the heat when reminded that these sayings were actually written by the Reverend William J. H. Boetcker in 1916. In this case we have clear evidence of how the misattribution originated. In 1942 a group called the Committee for Constitutional Government distributed a leaflet called "Lincoln on Limitations." One side had an authentic Lincoln remark. The other side had the ten points, attributed to the "Inspiration of Wm. J. H. Boetcker." In time Boetcker's name was forgotten and authorship of the ten points was reassigned to his better known leaflet-mate. When *Look* magazine published this apocryphal Lincolnism in 1950, *Time* took its sister publication to task. "In printing what Lincoln hadn't said," *Time* snickered, "nobody had felt the need to print something that he did say, 'You can fool all the people . . . [etc.].'"

LINCOLN'S BORROWING

GOVERNMENT OF THE PEOPLE, BY THE PEOPLE, FOR THE PEOPLE

Thirty-three years before Abraham Lincoln used this phrase in his Gettysburg Address, Daniel Webster spoke of "people's government, made for the people, made by the people and answerable to the people." In the 1850s, clergyman Theodore Parker used various versions of this credo in many anti-slavery speeches. Lincoln's law partner William Herndon later gave him a copy of Parker's published speeches. According to Herndon, before composing his Gettysburg Address Lincoln marked the words "democracy is direct self-government, over all the people, by all the people, for all the people" in an 1858 Parker sermon.

WITH MALICE TOWARD NONE, WITH CHARITY FOR ALL

In his 1838 response to an invitation to attend a celebration of slavery's abolition in the British West Indies, John Quincy Adams wrote, "In charity to all mankind, bearing no malice or ill-will to any human being, and even compassionating those who hold in bondage their fellow-men, not knowing what they do." Lincoln said it better, but Adams said it first.

HE REMINDS ME OF THE MAN WHO KILLED HIS PARENTS, THEN PLEADED FOR MERCY BECAUSE HE WAS AN ORPHAN.

Lincoln is one of many to whom this quip is credited. Truman's vice president, Alben Barkley, also liked this simile. So did William Howard Taft. Leo Rosten calls it the classic definition of "chutzpah." The gag seems to have originated in a much longer yarn called "A Hard Case," which was written in the early 1860s by Lincoln's favorite humorist, Artemus Ward.

"I remember a good story when I hear it," Lincoln once admitted, "but I never invented anything original. I am only a retail dealer."

MANGLED LINCOLNISMS

While running for President in 1988, George Bush told an audience, "As Abraham Lincoln said, **'Here I stand, warts and all.'** " Lincoln was full of physical imperfections, but no evidence exists that he made such an observation. More than two centuries before Lincoln's presidency, Oliver Cromwell admonished a portrait painter to "use all your skill to paint my picture truly like me, and not flatter me at all; but remark all these roughnesses, pimples, warts and everything as you see me, otherwise I will never pay a farthing for it." (William Safire got a Bush speechwriter to take the fall for goofing up this one.) Bush needn't have felt too bad. A Jimmy Carter television spot once quoted Lincoln as saying, **"A statesman thinks of the future generations, while a politician thinks of the coming election."** This was actually said by nineteenth century clergyman James Freeman Clarke. On another occasion a Carter speechwriter altered Lincoln's **"last best hope of earth"** to "last best hope *on* earth," thinking no one would notice. Someone did. Writer Richard Hanser, who makes a hobby of catching misquotes, immediately spotted the error and alerted William Safire. Ronald Reagan subsequently embellished Carter's altered version. In his own speeches Reagan frequently used the phrase "last best hope of man on earth," without mentioning either Carter or Lincoln. George Bush, in turn, used the phrase "last great hope of man on earth" during the 1988 presidential campaign.

Theodore Roosevelt

Theodore Roosevelt was more quotable than the average president, and more inventive, to boot. The many phrases he contributed to our language include "hat in the ring," "pussyfooting," and "lunatic fringe." For all of his originality, TR was no less likely than any other politician to requisition existing material. Long before he got credit for coining it, the term "weasel word," had appeared in a magazine article. "Muckraker"—from Roosevelt's 1906 description of overzealous journalists as **"raking the muck"**—drew on John Bunyan's "the Man With the Muck Rake" in *Pilgrim's Progress* (1678). Thirty-five years before Roosevelt applied the term to journalists, an American politician had already been described as raking in muck.

Roosevelt was fond of spinal similes. He once said about Oliver Wendell Holmes, Jr., "I could carve out of a banana a justice with more backbone than that." Of his predecessor, Roosevelt is supposed to have said, **"[William] McKinley has no more backbone than a chocolate eclair."** During TR's lifetime, one commentator called this "a favorite saying of his." The line was also attributed to House Speaker Thomas Reed. In fact, like "one man with_____makes a majority," the backbone simile is a modular quotation of long standing. Several decades before Teddy Roosevelt filled in the blank with bananas and chocolate eclairs, Ulysses S. Grant reportedly said about his successor as president, "Garfield has shown that he is not possessed of the backbone of an angleworm."

During a 1901 speech at the Minnesota State Fair, Roosevelt came out for a **"square deal."** This was a gambling term he probably picked up during his cowboy days out West. (In *Life on the Mississippi,* a Mark Twain character said, "Thought I'd better give him a square deal.") During the same speech in which Roosevelt promised the American people a square deal, he also used the adage that became his best known:

SPEAK SOFTLY, AND CARRY A BIG STICK.

According to the *Minneapolis Tribune,* this is how TR publicly introduced what became his signature line: "A good many of you are probably acquainted with the old proverb, 'Speak softly and carry a big stick—you will go far.'" During a subsequent speech in Chicago, Roosevelt called this saying "a homely old adage." In a 1900 letter to a friend, he'd said it was a "West African proverb." In *The People, Yes,* Carl Sandburg called TR's favorite maxim "A Spanish proverb first Americanized by Theodore Roosevelt." Whatever its origins, this saying clearly was not original to Roosevelt and was probably well known by the time he requisitioned it.

Calvin Coolidge

Calvin Coolidge—"Silent Cal"—is best remembered for the things he didn't say. In his time, however, the thirtieth President was considered something of a wit. His effervescent wife Grace did what she could to promote this reputation. So did a popular 1933 book called *Coolidge Wit and Wisdom,* which combined authentic and spurious material in equal measure. As with most of those who have a reputation for being witty, far more quips were attributed to Calvin Coolidge than he ever actually uttered. This is true in general of Silent Cal's best-remembered comments.

THE BUSINESS OF AMERICA IS BUSINESS.

Calvin Coolidge's most famous observation is worded this way in most reference books, including *The Oxford Dictionary of Quotations*. What Coolidge actually said, during a January 17, 1925 speech to the Society of American Newspaper Editors, was "After all, the chief business of the American people is business." *Bartlett's* is one of the few collections to quote this line correctly from Coolidge's speech (although they omitted "After all"). His actual words are similar to the ones for which Coolidge is best remembered, but not the same at all.

THEY HIRED THE MONEY, DIDN'T THEY?

President Coolidge's legendary rationale for denying debt relief to nations who owed America money after World War I was said to have been made during a press conference. It was the perfect illustration of a skinflint's approach to international affairs. Coolidge biographer Claude Fuess reviewed transcripts of all of his press conferences and other sources as well, but could find no such statement. Grace Coolidge told Fuess that she had no idea whether or not her husband actually said it. The biographer concluded that these words were apocryphal. Perhaps recognizing the political value of a tightfisted reputation, Coolidge himself never tried to correct the record.

YOU LOSE.

This is Calvin Coolidge's famous response to a woman who sat beside him at dinner and told him about her bet that she could get the President to say more than two words. A few months after Coolidge died, his widow wrote that she'd heard he once said something like this, though she wasn't present at the time. What Mrs. Coolidge heard was that her husband responded this way to a dinner companion who described her bet that she could engage the President in at least five minutes of conversation.

HE WAS AGAINST IT.

These four words were the punch line of a widely circulated anecdote about the President's Sunday morning in church. In this story, Grace asked Calvin what the sermon had been about. "Sin," he replied. When Mrs. Coolidge asked what the minister said about sin, her husband replied, "He was against it." This story never failed to get a laugh. Grace Coolidge said she was present the first time it was told in her husband's presence. According to her, the President guffawed, then observed that the story would be even funnier if it were true.

TELL MRS. COOLIDGE THERE IS MORE THAN ONE HEN.

Calvin Coolidge is supposed to have said this after his wife preceded him to a chicken farm, was impressed by a rooster who did a lot of copulating, and asked that the rooster be pointed out to her husband. Based on this story, some sexologists call the aphrodisiac effect of sexual variety "The Coolidge Effect." It's a good yarn with no basis in fact. Coolidge was too inhibited a Yankee to have said any such thing.

WHEN MORE AND MORE PEOPLE ARE THROWN OUT OF WORK, UNEMPLOYMENT RESULTS.

Liberals love to hang lines like these on conservatives whom they consider stupid. Coolidge has long been credited with this one. No reliable evidence exists that he actually said it. As a newspaper reporter, James Thurber used to make up inane Coolidgisms, then report them as authentic. One was: "A man who does not pray is not a praying man." Perhaps this was another.

Herbert Hoover

RUGGED INDIVIDUALISM

Herbert Hoover himself disclaimed authorship of the phrase so often associated with him. "While I can make no claim for having introduced the term 'rugged individualism,' " he wrote in 1934, "I should be proud to have invented it."

A NOBLE EXPERIMENT

Herbert Hoover is supposed to have endorsed Prohibition with this phrase. In fact it is a distortion of what he actually said while accepting the Republican presidential nomination in 1928: "Our country has deliberately undertaken a great social and economic experiment, noble in motive and far-reaching in purpose." Hoover's carefully worded waffle was bumper-stickered by newspapers and Democrats alike. The short version is the one we remember. Hoover later complained that "this phrase, a great 'social experiment noble in motive,' was distorted into a 'noble experiment' which, of course, was not at all what I said or intended to say."

A CHICKEN (or two) IN EVERY POT

Although the Republican party used this slogan in some of their 1928 advertising (at times adding "a car in every garage"), Herbert Hoover himself made no such promise. Hoover's secretary told George Seldes in 1958 that no reference to a chicken in every pot or a car in every garage could be found in the President's speeches and writing. The culinary part of that thought originated with King Henry IV of France, who said, "I desire that every laborer in my realm should be able to put a fowl in the pot on Sundays."

PROSPERITY IS JUST AROUND THE CORNER.

A generation of Democratic orators notwithstanding, Hoover never said this after the stock market crash of 1929. In the early years of the Depression, this phrase was used generically to ridicule business and government leaders who kept making optimistic economic forecasts. Hoover himself made a lot of reassuring sounds about better times ahead, but this wasn't one of them.

Franklin Roosevelt

A NEW DEAL

"A new deal for the American people" was the keystone phrase of Roosevelt's speech accepting the Democratic presidential nomination in

1932. "New deal" itself became the shorthand for his anti-Depression program. Two of Roosevelt's speechwriters, Samuel Rosenman and Raymond Moley, claimed credit for coining the slogan. Like "square deal," "new deal" had traditionally been a gambler's term. ("Hurrah for a new deal," wrote an 1849 novelist of some card players.) In 1863, Senator John Sherman gave this term a political spin when he wrote of seeing little chance that the Civil War would end "until we have a new deal." A few years after that Senator Carl Schurz referred to "the prospect of 'a new deal.'" Two decades later, Woodrow Wilson observed in a 1910 speech, "If it is reorganization, a new deal and change you are seeking, it is Hobson's choice." Lloyd George's 1919 campaign for the British Parliament promised "A New Deal for Everyone." A number of other politicians and commentators used this term prior to 1932. As with Kennedy's "new frontier," the phrase "new deal" was making the rounds long before Franklin Roosevelt laid claim to it.

THE ONLY THING WE HAVE TO FEAR IS FEAR ITSELF.

This memorable line in Franklin Roosevelt's first inaugural address had a distinguished pedigree:

THE THING OF WHICH I HAVE MOST FEAR IS FEAR.
                              Montaigne, 1580

NOTHING IS TERRIBLE EXCEPT FEAR ITSELF.
                              Francis Bacon, 1623

THE ONLY THING I AM AFRAID OF IS FEAR.
                    Duke of Wellington, ca. 1832

NOTHING IS SO MUCH TO BE FEARED AS FEAR.
                              Thoreau, 1851

Shortly before his inauguration someone gave FDR a collection of Thoreau's writings. This volume was in his hotel suite as he worked on the inaugural address. Samuel Rosenman thought that Thoreau was the probable source of FDR's line on fear. Raymond Moley had a more prosaic explanation. Moley said Roosevelt got the sentence from his campaign manager, Louis Howe, who had seen it in a department store ad.

I SEE ONE-THIRD OF A NATION ILL-HOUSED, ILL-CLAD, ILL-NOURISHED.

This line in FDR's second inaugural address brought to mind a passage from H. G. Wells's 1906 novel *In the Days of the Comet:* "I was ill clothed, ill fed, ill housed, ill educated and ill trained."

WE . . . WOULD RATHER DIE ON OUR FEET THAN LIVE ON OUR KNEES.

Roosevelt made this vow while accepting an honorary degree from Oxford University in 1941. He probably got the line from Dolores Ibarruri ("La Pasionaria") who used it repeatedly during the 1936–1939 Spanish Civil War. Ibarruri, in turn, may have been inspired by Emiliano Zapata, who reportedly said during the Mexican revolution two decades earlier, "Better to die on your feet than live on your knees." During bicentennial observances at Independence Hall in Philadelphia, President Gerald Ford echoed Roosevelt/Ibarruri/Zapata when he said, "We would rather die on our feet than live on our knees."

Ronald Reagan

In manner, if not politics, Ronald Reagan reminded many of Franklin Roosevelt. Both were blessed with a jaunty manner, a gift for gab, and an ability to enlist existing material on their own behalf. Even more than FDR, Reagan had a vast storehouse of lines he'd read or heard and drew upon as if they were written especially for him. Whether he thought such words were his own, had forgotten their source, or simply didn't care was never clear (even to his aides).

I PAID FOR THIS MICROPHONE, MR. GREEN!

Reagan made this angry rebuke to *Nashua Telegraph* editor Jon Breen (not Green) who tried to turn off his microphone in the midst of a debate during the New Hampshire primary. It brought to mind Spencer Tracy's

1948 portrayal of a presidential candidate in *State of the Union*. When a radio producer tried to cut him off in that movie, Tracy protested, "Don't you shut me off. I paid for this broadcast!" Reagan's reuse of that line was a put-up job. Although Breen didn't know it, the debate's sound technician was working for Reagan and was not about to turn off his microphone.

A RECESSION IS WHEN YOUR NEIGHBOR LOSES HIS JOB. A DEPRESSION IS WHEN YOU LOSE YOURS.

This line was pretty stale by the time Ronald Reagan revived it during the 1980 campaign (adding the tag line, "And recovery is when Jimmy Carter loses his"). Harry Truman used to say this back in the fifties. So did Teamster president Dave Beck.

IF NOT US, WHO? IF NOT NOW, WHEN?

When he uttered these fairly eloquent words in 1981, Reagan failed to note (and may not even have known) that Rabbi Hillel was reknowned for having said some twenty centuries earlier:

> *If I am not for myself, who is for me?*
> *And when I am for myself what am I?*
> *And if not now, when?*

THERE IS NO GREATER HAPPINESS FOR A MAN THAN APPROACHING A DOOR AT THE END OF THE DAY KNOWING SOMEONE ON THE OTHER SIDE OF THE DOOR IS WAITING FOR THE SOUND OF HIS FOOTSTEPS.

The President made this heartwarming observation in a letter to his son Michael. It drew heavily on a thought attributed earlier to Clark Gable: "The most important thing a man can know is that, as he approaches his own door, someone on the other side is listening for the sound of his footsteps."

HONEY, I FORGOT TO DUCK.

Reagan's endearing comment to his wife Nancy after he survived John Hinckley's 1981 assassination attempt, was the same one Jack Dempsey made to *his* wife after losing the heavyweight title to Gene Tunney on September 23, 1926.

GO AHEAD AND MAKE MY DAY.

Reagan's 1985 dare to Congress to send him a tax increase to veto came from Clint Eastwood's taunt of a criminal in the 1983 movie *Sudden Impact*. Though Eastwood gave it his own spin, the phrase itself had been floating around for years.

WHERE DO WE FIND SUCH MEN?

This was part of the President's stirring tribute to American soldiers on the fortieth anniversary of D-day. In previous speeches Reagan credited the line to an admiral in James Michener's novel *Bridges at Toko-Ri*. He then began saying an actual admiral had used these words. Finally, in the last phase of Three-Step Quote Acquisition, Reagan took possession of the words.

THERE IS NOTHING BETTER FOR THE INSIDE OF A MAN THAN THE OUTSIDE OF A HORSE.

When the President made this observation in late 1987, many horse lovers thought it sounded familiar. They had lots of reasons to feel that way. Early this century Lord Palmerston was quoted as saying, "There's nothing so good for the inside of a man as the outside of a horse." That comment had also been attributed to a Dr. John Abernethy and Oliver Wendell Holmes. Woodrow Wilson's physician, Dr. Cary Grayson, later remarked, "The outside of a horse is good for the inside of a man." In 1946, M. C. Self wrote in *Horseman's Encyclopedia,* "There is something about the outside of a horse which is good for the inside of a man." California educator Sherman Thacher was also quoted as having said, "There's something about the outside of a horse that's good for the inside of a boy." Obviously this thought had occurred to quite a few others before it dawned on Ronald Reagan. Be that as it may, the saying was said to be one of his favorites.

George Bush

A THOUSAND POINTS OF LIGHT

Speechwriter Peggy Noonan put these words in George Bush's mouth. Although Noonan assumed they were original to her, she subsequently discovered that this was a risky assumption. In 1955, C. S. Lewis wrote in *The Magician's Nephew,* "One moment there had been nothing but darkness, next moment a thousand points of light leaped out—single stars, constellations, and planets, brighter and bigger than any in our world." Thomas Wolfe used the phrase "a thousand points of friendly light" in his 1939 novel *The Web and the Rock.* After Bush was elected President, William Safire sent Noonan a speech by a turn-of-the-century engineer urging the electrification of Venice so that it might be filled with "a thousand points of light." Bush's speechwriter said she had no conscious awareness of drawing on any of these sources. Noonan did recall reading *The Web and the Rock* as a teenager and admitted that its thousand points of friendly light might have burrowed dimly in her consciousness just waiting for an opportunity to shine through.

A KINDER, GENTLER NATION

Peggy Noonan's other key contribution to the annals of political oratory also had a familiar sound when she served it up for Bush to use in accepting the Republicans' 1988 nomination. (In her memoir, *What I Saw at the Revolution,* Noonan implied that Bush himself added "gentler" to her "kinder.") In his 1932 autobiography, Clarence Darrow said of America's premiere socialist, "There may have lived somewhere a kindlier, gentler, more generous man than Eugene Debs, but I have not known him." Eight years later, in *The Great Dictator,* Charlie Chaplin played a Jewish barber masquerading as a Hitler-like leader who said at the movie's climax, "more than cleverness, we need kindness and gentleness." In his 1978 memoir, *A Childhood,* writer Harry Crews wrote of his stepfather, "The stronger the smell of whiskey on him, though, the kinder and gentler he was with me and my brother." New York Governor Mario Cuomo subsequently urged Barnard's class of 1983 to "be wiser than we are, kinder, gentler, more caring." Two years after that singer Roy Orbison observed that Elvis Presley had "made gentler and kinder souls of us all." Three years later Peggy Noonan suggested

George Bush follow in the footsteps of Roy Orbison, Mario Cuomo, Harry Crews, Charlie Chaplin, and Clarence Darrow in articulating his vision for America.

READ MY LIPS.

This saying had been around on the street for years by the time Bush used it repeatedly in his 1988 campaign to emphasize that he would never, ever raise taxes.

George Bush is a rhetorical slummer. The patrician President likes to downscale his prep-talk with street phrases such as "kick ass." He is one among many who repeatedly said "The opera ain't over till the fat lady sings." Bush has also frequently quoted Woody Allen's line "Ninety percent of life is just showing up." Due to numbernesia this one can be problematic. *In Search of Excellence* authors Thomas Peters and Robert Waterman thought that Allen had said "Eighty percent of success is showing up." Other figures have also been quoted. "People throw in new numbers," said Woody Allen's biographer Eric Lax. "They can't seem to remember the right one. *I* can't remember the right one." When William Safire inquired, Woody Allen recalled that in the midst of an interview he did once say that **"Eighty percent of success is showing up."**

"The figure seems high to me today," Allen added, "but I know it was more than sixty and the extra syllable in seventy ruins the rhythm of the quote, so I think we should let it stand at eighty."

That's how it goes with bon mots. If humorists themselves have this much trouble remembering their own lines, imagine how much risk the rest of us run when we borrow them.

8

The Twain Syndrome

Any honest celebrity who subscribes to a clipping service, will admit that he learns about some of his cleverest punch-lines for the first time when he reads that he has delivered them.

The curators of Mark Twain's papers at the University of California are often called upon to verify his quotes. Did Twain say "Don't go to sleep, so many people die there"? How about "There's nothing so annoying as to have two people go right on talking when you're interrupting"? Or "Better to keep your mouth shut and appear stupid than to open it and remove all doubt."

No, no, and no.

These are just a few of the many witticisms misattributed to Twain. Any orphan line with even a hint of drollness is subject to being put in his mouth. Did Twain say **"So I became a newspaperman. I hated to do it, but I couldn't find honest employment"?** Many think he did. Curators of the Twain papers can't find that one. Nor can they find **"The only way for a newspaperman to look at a politician is *down,"*** which has also been attributed to Twain. According to H. L. Mencken, that should be credited to twentieth century journalist Frank Simonds. How about **"For every problem there is always a solution that is simple, obvious, and wrong"?** Sounds like Twain. Representative

Gerry Studds quoted him to that effect during a 1991 congressional hearing. Mencken himself is the more likely source, having written, "There is always an easy solution to every human problem—neat, plausible, and wrong."

Some apocryphal Twainisms are easier to debunk than others. Ed Bradley of CBS once credited Twain with Will Rogers's observation that he belonged to no organized party because he was a Democrat. Until disabused by his readers, William Safire thought that it was Twain who said "It ain't what we don't know that hurts us. It's what we do know that ain't so." After he misspelled "potato" in 1992, Dan Quayle consoled himself by quoting Twain as having said, "You should never trust a man who has only one way to spell a word." No Twain expert could find that one.

"He's easily invoked," said Robert Hirst, General Editor of the University of California's Mark Twain Project, who has worked with Twain's papers for nearly three decades. "People feel they know what kind of perspective he brings toward things."

Some apocryphal comments by Twain have been part of the national conversation for so long that they've achieved "everybody knows Twain said it" status by repetition alone. For example:

TO CEASE SMOKING IS THE EASIEST THING I EVER DID. I OUGHT TO KNOW BECAUSE I'VE DONE IT A THOUSAND TIMES.

In its December 1945 issue, *Reader's Digest* attributed this observation to Twain (giving *Coronet* magazine as the source). It has since become a favorite Twainism. These two sentences have never been found in his works.

WHEN I WAS A BOY OF FOURTEEN, MY FATHER WAS SO IGNORANT I COULD HARDLY STAND TO HAVE THE OLD MAN AROUND. BUT WHEN I GOT TO BE TWENTY-ONE, I WAS ASTONISHED AT HOW MUCH THE OLD MAN HAD LEARNED IN SEVEN YEARS.

Another *Reader's Digest* item, from September 1937. When the Library of Congress queried Twain scholars about its authenticity, none could confirm it. "It's got the right flavor about it," said Robert Hirst, "but I don't know its source." He's still looking.

THE COLDEST WINTER I EVER SPENT WAS A SUMMER IN SAN FRAN-
CISCO.

Even *San Francisco Chronicle* columnist Herb Caen thought Twain said
this. Despite extensive searching no one has ever found such an observation in Twain's works. Its genesis may be an 1879 letter in which Twain
quoted a wag who, when asked if he'd ever *seen* such a cold winter,
replied, "Yes. Last summer." Concluded Twain: "I judge he spent his
summer in Paris."

THE MAN WHO DOES NOT READ GOOD BOOKS HAS NO ADVANTAGE
OVER THE MAN WHO CAN'T READ THEM.

Abby Van Buren once made this observation in her advice column. A
reader said she should have credited the thought to Mark Twain. Abby
apologized, explaining that she genuinely thought the idea was her own.
Perhaps it was. Although this saying is often attributed to Twain, no one
has ever confirmed that he said it.

THE REPORTS OF MY DEATH ARE GREATLY EXAGGERATED.

This could be Twain's single most requoted line. By legend it was the
author's response to a press inquiry about his demise. The actual story
is a bit more complicated.

In 1897 a report reached America that Mark Twain was dying in
London. The *New York Journal* cabled its London correspondent to
find out whether Twain was at death's door. Although he knew the
author to be in good health, the *Journal*'s correspondent sent a reporter
to Twain's house with the cable from New York. Twain sent back this
note: "James Ross Clemens, a cousin of mine, was seriously ill two or
three weeks ago in London but is well now. The report of my illness
grew out of his illness; the report of my death was an exaggeration."

On June 2, 1897, the *Journal* published Twain's response in an
article titled "MARK TWAIN AMUSED." They began one paragraph with
his observation that "The report of my death was an exaggeration."
Over time this comment was much repeated, with "greatly" added to
"exaggerated." Where did the "greatly" come from? Apparently from
Twain himself. In the spring of 1906, the author typed up his recollection of the death rumor episode. In his first draft he recalled telling a

reporter, "Say the report is exaggerated." A few months later Twain retyped his manuscript, then scribbled "greatly" in front of "exaggerated" before mailing it to *The North American Review,* where it was published that fall. According to this memoir, in 1897 Twain had advised the press to "say the report is greatly exaggerated." He hadn't, of course. His original longhand note to the *Journal*'s correspondent has been preserved. But the embellished version is more compelling. It's the one that has lasted, typically said to have been Twain's own cable to the New York press.

THE FINEST CONGRESS MONEY CAN BUY

Library of Congress researchers have never confirmed this popular Twainism. The closest words they found were in a speech Twain wrote but didn't deliver: "I think I can say, and say with pride, that we have some legislatures that bring higher prices than any in the world."

WHENEVER I FEEL AN URGE TO EXERCISE I LIE DOWN UNTIL IT GOES AWAY.

This observation is commonly attributed to Twain. It certainly sounds like the sedentary author. Others who get credit for the witticism include W. C. Fields, Paul Terry, and—most often—former University of Chicago President Robert Maynard Hutchins. According to Hutchins's biographer Harry S. Ashmore, this quip originated with humorist J. P. McEvoy and was one of many that Hutchins had squirreled away to use at appropriate moments.

WAGNER'S MUSIC IS BETTER THAN IT SOUNDS.

Although this observation is commonly put in Twain's mouth, in his autobiography he clearly attributed the line to humorist Bill Nye. Nye himself didn't claim original authorship. According to Twain, "The late Bill Nye once said, '*I have been told* that Wagner's music is better than it sounds.'" (emphasis added)

"We see this all the time," said Robert Hirst about the crediting of other people's words to Twain. "It's like an insurance policy. Attributing something to Mark Twain adds to the joke. When they hear his name, people are disposed to laugh; they're ready to laugh. That's the chief reason he's saddled with so much stuff that isn't his."

This is true of secondhand wit in general. A good line just works better if it's put in the mouth of someone we already think is funny. Calling a knee-slapper "an old Chinese joke" doesn't cut it. However, a name we associate with laughs—Mark Twain, Will Rogers, Dorothy Parker, Woody Allen—starts our smile even before we've heard the joke. As a result, the wits of the hour get far more credit than they're due for funny material. The old line "Even paranoids have real enemies" is sometimes attributed to Woody Allen. When his profile was higher, Henry Kissinger used to get credit for a similar observation. Both Bob Hope and Woody Allen have been credited with saying, "I'm not afraid of dying. I just don't want to be there when it happens." This illustrates how the process can change direction. A prominent wit who gets credit for gags he never uttered may lose luster over time. Material which used to be attributed to this figure then is moved to the mouth of better known figures. Such has been the fate of Wilson Mizner.

Wilson Mizner

For a largely forgotten figure, Wilson Mizner looms large in the annals of misquotation. Well over six feet tall, Mizner was a gambler and literary knockabout with a gift for phrasemaking. Mencken said that Mizner contributed more humorous observations to the national dialogue than any other man of his time. Screenwriter Anita Loos—who modeled the character played by Clark Gable in *San Francisco* after Mizner—predicted accurately that "generations yet to come will be quoting Mizner without ever having heard his name."

More than a half a century after Mizner's death in 1933, many of his hundreds of recorded comments remain fresh. Among them are:

I HATE CARELESS FLATTERY, THE KIND THAT EXHAUSTS YOU IN YOUR EFFORT TO BELIEVE IT.

SLEEP NEVER WORRIED ME, THOUGH; ALL I'VE EVER NEEDED WAS JUST ANOTHER FIVE MINUTES.

THE WORST TEMPERED PEOPLE I'VE EVER MET WERE PEOPLE WHO KNEW THEY WERE WRONG.

A FELLOW WHO'S ALWAYS DECLARING THAT HE'S NO FOOL
USUALLY HAS HIS SUSPICIONS.

I KNOW OF NO SENTENCE THAT CAN INDUCE SUCH IMMEDIATE AND
BRAZEN LYING AS THE ONE WHICH BEGINS: "HAVE YOU READ . . ."

BE URBANE TO EVERYBODY. YOU CAN NEVER TELL IN WHICH POOL
THE NEXT SUCKER WILL BITE.

Mizner had an abiding disdain for "suckers." The gambler figured that those who volunteered to be fleeced in card games deserved whatever they got. His trademark greeting was a hearty **"Hello, Sucker!"** This was adopted by flamboyant speakeasy hostess Texas Guinan (later played by Betty Gable in *Incendiary Blonde*) as her own signature line. The greeting enjoyed a national vogue for a time.

In the early part of this century Mizner popularized and may have coined the phrase **"Never give a sucker an even break."** His good friend W. C. Fields later "ad-libbed" this line during an early performance of the 1923 play *Poppy*. Soon it became *his* signature line, and the title of Fields's last movie. But he was merely the line's publicist. Others attribute this phrase to P. T. Barnum, with no more evidence than that supporting the "sucker born every day" credit. Beginning in 1968, *Bartlett's* attributed "never give a sucker an even break" to vaudeville impresario E. F. Albee. Clifton Fadiman had done the same thing in his 1954 compilation *An American Treasury*. Both probably got the attribution from a 1953 memoir by vaudevilian Joe Laurie, Jr. Laurie despised Albee and claimed that his motto was "Never give a sucker an even break." No one else that I can find ever said this of Albee.

Many have concluded that Wilson Mizner was the line's actual author. More likely it's a saying Mizner picked up in his gambling days in San Francisco and Alaska, then brought to New York in 1905. During his years in Manhattan, Mizner regaled eager listeners with his street humor at tables reserved for him in prominent restaurants. "For nearly two years I saw very little of Wilson except surrounded by a crowd," his brother Addison recalled of their time together in New York. "If they were theatrical people or writers, they would have scraps of paper and a pencil surreptitiously taking down his witticisms to be used later as their own."

Mizner's reputation as a wit was spread largely by this army of Boswells who eagerly repeated his latest mots and reported them in newspaper columns. Though many Miznerisms still circulate, their source is largely forgotten. I recently read a sportswriter's description of a crank phone caller as **"just some mouse studying to be a rat."** Columnist Red Smith said the same thing about Yankees manager Billy Martin. That line was used by Mizner eighty years ago. In a 1983 article on misquotation, a Canadian columnist wrote, **"If you steal from one person it's plagiarism; if you steal from several it's called research."** Mizner made the same observation some seven decades earlier. Many other Miznerisms are still in play, sometimes attributed to him, sometimes to others, or to no one in particular. Among them are:

BE NICE TO PEOPLE ON YOUR WAY UP BECAUSE YOU'LL MEET THEM ON THE WAY DOWN.

Walter Winchell—who loved to report Miznerisms in his newspaper column—sometimes gets credit for this line. So does Jimmy Durante. By now it's a commonplace in show business and sports, usually repeated with no attribution at all. Wilson Mizner said it first.

LIVING IN HOLLYWOOD IS LIKE FLOATING DOWN A SEWER IN A GLASS-BOTTOM BOAT.

New York Mayor Jimmy Walker took this concept from Mizner and made it his own when he said "A reformer is a guy who rides through a sewer in a glass-bottom boat." Others also adapted Mizner's line, to various ends.

LIFE'S A TOUGH PROPOSITION—AND THE FIRST HUNDRED YEARS ARE THE HARDEST.

This observation is attributed both to Mizner and his fellow migrant from San Francisco to New York, cartoonist T. A. "Tad" Dorgan.

Though undeniably original, Mizner also borrowed material from sources known only to him. "Mizner had the sympathy and patience which attracted all sorts of unconventional people," noted biographer Edward Dean Sullivan, "and from such contacts came some of his keenest and most applauded mots." Mizner's friend Jim Tully reached the same conclusion. "He retained and used all things that filled his purpose," Tully wrote of Mizner. "When he read, **'Fame is merely the prolonging of neighborhood gossip,'** he quoted it often, without credit to me. When I mentioned Schopenhauer's observation—**'Dull people are always formal'**—he exclaimed, 'God!' and purloined it." Charged with plagiarism more than once in his brief career as a playwright, Mizner never denied the charge. "Didn't Shakespeare steal, you illiterate peasant—" he told Tully, "and Moliere—and Dante—it's all a stream running nowhere—you dip out the water you need."

In taking this stand, Wilson Mizner was hardly unique. Many of those with a reputation for being clever keep mental archives of well-rehearsed quips—some borrowed—to pull out and repeat "spontaneously" as the occasion demands. Such wit is sometimes taken from earlier epochs. In modern times, **"The only difference between men and boys is the price of their toys"** has been credited to Liberace and Joyce Brothers, among others. A Poor Richard maxim was, "Old boys have their playthings as well as young ones; the difference is only in their price." Poor Richard's **"There's more old drunkards than old doctors"** (echoing Rabelais's "A hundred devils leap into my body, if there are not more old drunkards than old physicians") is another line that won't die, most recently showing up in a Willie Nelson song:

> *But there's more old drunks than there are old doctors*
> *So I guess we'd better have another round*

Such pass-along wit often gets filtered through many mouths before finding its way back home. "From to time to time," reported Steve Allen, "people walk up to you and say, 'Listen, I've got the funniest story to tell you,' and proceed to tell you one of your own jokes." An early editor of the British humor magazine *Punch* found that the magazine's material sometimes circled the globe before ending up back on his desk in new clothing. Humorists tend to be philosophical about this sort of thing. "There's no such thing as a new joke," said Milton Berle. "All jokes are public domain. It's not the gag, it's how you deliver it."

Alexander Woollcott

A bore once monopolized Wilson Mizner's ear at a restaurant. Noticing the pained expression on his listener's face, the bore finally asked if Mizner wanted him to leave. "No," Mizner replied. "But you might move over a little. **I may vomit.**" This mot made the rounds. In time it became a show-stopping line in the mouth of Sheridan Whiteside, the character based on Alexander Woollcott in Moss Hart and George S. Kaufman's play *The Man Who Came to Dinner.* Woollcott was the rotund drama critic for the *New York Times* and other papers after World War I. He later wrote plays himself, and produced best-selling essay collections. Before his death in 1943, Woollcott hosted a popular radio show called *The Town Crier.* Through his various forums, Woollcott propagated much apocrypha and secondhand humor, some of which he attributed to himself. "Most of his anecdotes were already stale when they achieved the dignity of Joe Miller's Joke Book," concluded his biographer Edwin P. Hoyt.

THIS IS THE WAY GOD WOULD HAVE BUILT IT IF HE'D HAD THE MONEY.

Woollcott reportedly said this about Moss Hart's country home in the late 1930s. That observation was also attributed to George S. Kaufman, Wolcott Gibbs, and Frank Case. George Bernard Shaw was supposed to have made the same remark after visiting William Randolph Hearst's opulent San Simeon ranch in 1933. Four years earlier British writer Peter Fleming wrote to his brother in a 1929 letter, "Long Island represents the American's idea of what God would have done with Nature if he'd had the money." That comment was obviously floating about in the twenties and thirties, available for whoever could successfully lay claim to it.

ALL THE THINGS I LIKE TO DO ARE EITHER IMMORAL, ILLEGAL, OR FATTENING.

This line is often attributed to Woollcott, though never with an original source. Biographer Howard Teichmann says the drama critic frequently made such an observation. *Reader's Digest* attributed the line to Woollcott in its December 1933 issue with no citation. W. C. Fields said

"Everything I like is either illegal, immoral, or fattening" in his 1934 movie *Six of a Kind*. Over time it became such a catchphrase that in 1991 CBS newsman Bob Schieffer observed of the Bush administration's effort to dominate interview programs "There is nothing illegal, immoral, or fattening about it" without mentioning Alexander Woollcott or anyone else as a source for that saying.

LET'S GET OUT OF THESE WET CLOTHES AND INTO A DRY MARTINI.

This quip is routinely misattributed to Alexander Woollcott. Woollcott did not coin the line and never claimed he did. *Bartlett's* gave it to him in 1968 (citing *Reader's Digest*), Robert Benchley in 1980. Howard Teichmann said that "ten years of checking" convinced him that Benchley indeed deserved credit for the line. In his 1944 book *Try and Stop Me* Bennett Cerf recounted a whole anecdote about Benchley coming in from a driving rain and delivering this witticism. But according to Benchley's son Nathaniel, "Robert never said, 'Let's get out of these wet clothes and into a dry martini,' although there are people who will swear they were there when he said it. It was a joke in somebody's column, and a press agent picked it up and attributed it to Robert, and it stuck." Based on his own interview with Nathaniel Benchley, Teichmann reached a somewhat different conclusion: "A press agent, working on behalf of Robert Benchley, had come up with the line and, because he wished his weekly salary check to come through, passed it on to a columnist and gave credit to Benchley."

In his 1942 film *The Major and the Minor,* Benchley said to Ginger Rogers, "Why don't you get out of that wet coat and into a dry martini?" This film was written by Charles Brackett and Billy Wilder (who also directed). When *Los Angeles Times* columnist Jack Smith—who calls the wet clothes/martini quip "one of the most durable and rootless lines in the language"—asked Wilder about its origin, the director said he'd always assumed it originated with Benchley himself. But during shooting, Benchley told Wilder that the line originated with his friend Charles Butterworth. Jack Smith considered the case closed until a reader wrote him that a 1937 film called *Every Day's a Holiday* featured the following exchange between Butterworth and Charles Winninger:

WINNINGER (IN WET EVENING CLOTHES): "I'm hot. Soaked all over."

BUTTERWORTH: "You ought to get out of those wet clothes and into a dry martini."

Mae West, who also starred in this film, got screenwriter billing. So conceivably the line is hers. The *Oxford Dictionary of Modern Quotations* includes it under her name. But West was a notorious credit hog who hated to share billing with anyone, no matter how many of her lines they might have written. Conclusion: despite a plathora of candidates, the originator of this quip has yet to be determined.

THERE IS LESS IN THIS THAN MEETS THE EYE.

This line has also been misattributed to Robert Benchley, among others. Its midwife, if not its parent, was actually Alexander Woollcott. In 1922 Woollcott attended a revival of Maurice Maeterlinck's play *Aglavaine and Selysette*. In the next day's *New York Times,* the critic reported that this performance "was best summed up by the beautiful lady in the back row.

" 'There is less in this than meets the eye.' "

The "beautiful young lady in the back row" turned out to be Tallulah Bankhead. At the time Bankhead was an obscure young actress. According to biographer Lee Israel, Bankhead's bon mot was actually a malaprop. The twenty-year-old actress meant to say *"more* than meets the eye" but blew her line. After the remark stormed New York with Tallulah as its source, she knew better than to claim it was anything less than intentional. "I wasn't aware I'd said anything devastating . . ." Bankhead later admitted, "it is only fair to say that most of the wisecracks I have mothered have been accidental quips."

Dorothy Parker

Another figure to whom Bankhead's malaprop has been attributed is Dorothy Parker. Parker was America's premiere wisecracker during the 1920s and 1930s. At that time, saying "Have you heard Dottie Parker's latest?" increased dramatically your odds of being paid attention. The mere mention of her name could elicit a grin of anticipation. As a result, during her heyday Parker rivaled Mark Twain as a flypaper wit. "Everything I've ever said will be credited to Dorothy Parker," moaned her fellow Algonquin Round Tabler George S. Kaufman.

Parker's quips were a columnist's delight. There just weren't enough of them to meet the demand. This is why so many lines were put in her mouth. "I say hardly any of those clever things that are attributed to me," she once insisted. "I wouldn't have time to earn a living if I said all those things."

In one of the most famous stories involving Dorothy Parker, Clare Boothe Luce waved her through a door, saying, "Age before beauty." As Parker glided through the door she was said to have trilled, **"Pearls before swine."** (In another version of this exchange Parker delivered the setup line, Beatrice Lillie the retort.) Luce denied that this encounter ever took place. Parker biographer John Keats concurred. The genesis of *this* legend might have been an Alexander Woollcott short story called "The Pearl," whose heroine explains that she got her name "because I'm cast before swine."

Many of Parker's most famous sayings can be traced back to Woollcott's fawning profile of her in his 1935 best-seller *While Rome Burns*. (She'd written a puff piece about Woollcott for *Vanity Fair*.) Since they were both members of the Algonquin Round Table, it was easy to assume that the drama critic had personally witnessed the episodes he described, or at least had them on good authority. Woollcott's profile included the widely repeated story that when she grew too lonely in her rented office, Parker painted the word MEN on its door. No one ever said they'd actually seen this famous door. How could they? It didn't exist. As Parker herself confirmed, this mystique-building prank took place only in her letter to a friend complaining that unless more visitors came by, she would have to write MEN on her office door.

Some other Parkerisms which were put in play by Woollcott's profile included:

RUNS THE GAMUT OF EMOTIONS FROM A TO B.

Woollcott reported Parker's legendary put-down of Katharine Hepburn's acting in the same year she supposedly made it. His wording was ambiguous. After quoting from a *Life* review in which Parker called *The*

House Beautiful "the play lousy," he added, "more recently she achieved an equal compression in reporting on *The Lake*. Miss Hepburn, it seems, had run the whole gamut from A to B." The reader was free to infer that this assessment could be found in Parker's review of that 1934 play. This is still often reported. There is no such review in *Life* or any other magazine Parker wrote for at the time. Did she make this observation about Hepburn's acting in some other context? Possibly. Hepburn herself reported in her autobiography that Parker said, "Go to the Martin Beck [Theater] and see K.H. run the gamut-t-t of emotion from A to B." According to Hepburn biographer Garry Carey, Parker made such a remark during *The Lake*'s intermission. Carey gave no source. Dorothy Parker's biographers don't discuss the quip. It was Woollcott who made Parker's alleged assessment of Hepburn's acting part of the national conversation.

EXCUSE MY DUST.

Woollcott also popularized the now-common assumption that Parker wanted her tombstone to read, "Excuse my dust." In fact these words appeared as Parker's "epitaph" in a 1925 *Vanity Fair* gag feature. It's not even clear that she wrote them. According to Nora Ephron, Dorothy Parker once said that her gravestone should be inscribed with what later became a bumper sticker classic: "If you can read this, you've come too close."

HOW CAN THEY TELL?

This was supposed to have been Dorothy Parker's reaction to Calvin Coolidge's death in 1933. According to Jim Tully, Wilson Mizner said "How do they know?" when told about the president's death. This was either remarkable serendipity or a case of two wits recycling an old line at an opportune moment.

Will Rogers

Shrewder, smarter, and better read than the rube persona he affected, Will Rogers contributed many enduring quips to the national discourse. Among them are:

AMERICA IS THE ONLY NATION TO GO TO THE POORHOUSE IN AN
AUTOMOBILE.

WE NEVER LOST A WAR AND WE NEVER WON A [PEACE]
CONFERENCE IN OUR LIVES.

INCOME TAX HAS MADE MORE LIARS OUT OF THE AMERICAN
PEOPLE THAN GOLF HAS.

EVERY TIME THEY MAKE A LAW IT'S A JOKE AND EVERY TIME
THEY MAKE A JOKE IT'S A LAW.

I TELL YOU FOLKS, ALL POLITICS IS APPLESAUCE.

Then there's:

BUY LAND. THEY AIN'T MAKIN' ANY MORE OF THE STUFF.

Realtors are fond of quoting this quip from Rogers. No source is ever
given because it's spurious. The humorist looked down on those who
speculated in real estate. He himself owned little land. "There is nothing
that can break a man quicker than land," is an actual quote from
Rogers, "unless it's running a grocery store or dealing in second-hand
cars."

I NEVER MET A MAN I DIDN'T LIKE.

Rogers repeated variations on this theme often. But its original form is
quite a bit different than the version which became his epitaph.

According to his friend Homer Croy, Rogers began composing his
own epitaph in the early 1920s. He tried various possibilities. One was,
"Here lies Will Rogers. Politicians turned honest and he starved to
death." In a more serious vein, Rogers suggested, "He never picked on
a man when he was down." An early version of the epitaph Rogers
finally chose was, "He joked about every prominent man of his time, but
he never met one he disliked."

This slogan first appeared in print after Rogers's 1926 trip to the
Soviet Union. There he had an appointment to meet with Bolshevik
leader Leon Trotsky. Trotsky's star was descending, however, and his

arch-rival Stalin would not let him meet the influential American. Rogers regretted this. As he later told readers of the *Saturday Evening Post,* "I bet you if I had met him and had a chat with him, I would have found him a very interesting and human fellow, for *I have never yet met a man I dident like*" (italics and misspellings in original). This was the first time that Rogers recorded this phrase. He later tried many variations on the theme in his writing and speeches. During some 1930 remarks at a Boston church, Rogers said, "I've got my epitaph all worked out. When I'm tucked away in the old graveyard west of Oologah [Oklahoma], I hope they will cut this epitaph—or whatever you call them signs they put over gravestones—on it, 'Here lies Will Rogers. He joked about every prominent man in his time, but he never met a man he didn't like.' " When the Associated Press reported this remark, it caused a national stir. Rogers's saintly self-epitaph made the popular humorist that much more beloved. According to Croy, the humorist recognized its hyperbole. "In reality there were many men he couldn't abide," wrote Croy. But Rogers knew a good epitaph when he hit on one, and gladly suffered fools as its price.

Groucho Marx

Many of the Marx Brothers' early "ad-libs" were carefully crafted by George S. Kaufman. Groucho Marx called Kaufman the wittiest man he knew. At the same time, he and his brothers embellished Kaufman's lines as they did all others. Groucho in particular was so quick-witted and yet—like most professional entertainers—so willing to acquire material where he found it that it's hard to determine what was his and what wasn't.

I DON'T WANT TO BELONG TO ANY CLUB THAT WOULD HAVE ME AS A MEMBER.

Groucho's best-known line appears in various forms. According to his son Arthur, the version above was part of his letter of resignation from the Friars Club. Groucho's brother Zeppo confirmed this, as did his friend Arthur Sheekman. In his autobiography, Groucho said he wired a group called the Delaney Club, "PLEASE ACCEPT MY RESIGNATION. I DON'T WANT TO BELONG TO ANY CLUB THAT WILL ACCEPT ME AS A

MEMBER." Did this actually happen? Possibly. But, as Nigel Rees asked, "wouldn't it be good to see the original letter?"

TIME WOUNDS ALL HEELS.

A good pun has a thousand parents. Perhaps because it was a line in *The Marx Brothers Go West* (1940), "Time wounds all heels" is sometimes attributed to Groucho. Others to whom it has been credited include Bennett Cerf, Jane Ace (by her husband Goodman), W. C. Fields, and Irving Brecher, screenwriter of *The Marx Brothes Go West*. An early claim to this classic was that of Frank Case. Case, manager of the Algonquin Hotel in its literary heyday, wrote in his 1938 memoir, "What I always say is, 'Time wounds all heels.'" Few remember his name any longer, however, so Case is rarely among those given credit for this durable pun.

I'VE BEEN AROUND SO LONG, I KNEW DORIS DAY BEFORE SHE WAS A VIRGIN.

This is a modular saying, an old Hollywood saw whose subject changes with the context. Groucho sometimes got credit for originating the line. Oscar Levant recycled it in *The Memoirs of an Amnesiac*. I also saw it applied to a presidential aspirant who had converted from an Establishment figure to an insurgent: "I knew Fred Harris before he was a virgin."

Show business quips don't always cross over to the world of politics that way. But within Hollywood the borrowing and reborrowing of good lines is a communal pastime and always has been.

9

Say It Again, Sam

During his half-century as a movie mogul, producer Samuel Goldwyn was renowned for his mangled syntax. When told by an associate that they were having trouble finding Indians as extras, Goldwyn reportedly said, "We can get all the Indians we need at the reservoir." Warned that a script was "too caustic," he allegedly thundered, "To hell with the cost! If it's a good picture we'll make it."

A Polish immigrant (whose original name was Schmuel Gelbfisz), Goldwyn never fully mastered his second tongue. Especially when he was under pressure Goldwyn would tangle his words. Hundreds of malaprops attributed to him included:

IT'S MORE THAN MAGNIFICENT; IT'S MEDIOCRE.

WHAT WE WANT IS A STORY THAT STARTS WITH AN EARTHQUAKE AND WORKS ITS WAY UP TO A CLIMAX.

LET'S HAVE SOME NEW CLICHÉS.

I'LL GIVE YOU A DEFINITE MAYBE.

I DON'T THINK ANYBODY SHOULD WRITE HIS AUTOBIOGRAPHY
UNTIL AFTER HE'S DEAD.

Goldwyn's malaprops became so legendary that the term *Goldwynism* entered the national lexicon in the 1930s. It's persisted to this day. The *Random House Dictionary* defines *Goldwynism* as "a phrase or statement involving a humorous and supposedly unintentional misuse of idiom, as 'Keep a stiff upper chin,' esp. such a statement attributed to Samuel Goldwyn."

Knowing the value of publicity, Goldwyn at first didn't discourage circulation of the many real and spurious malaprops attributed to him. "Look," he told a reporter in 1939, "I should wish to spoil copy? No. If the newspaper boys need copy to write and make people laugh, it is all right with me." His staffers vied to invent Goldwynisms and plant them in the press. Since such talented wisecrackers as Dorothy Parker, George Kaufman, Lillian Hellman, and Eddie Cantor worked for Goldwyn at one time or another, formidable talent was devoted to this pursuit. In the late 1930s Goldwyn's screenwriters even held a contest to see whose concoction would be the first one in print. George Oppenheimer won with "It rolls off my back like a duck."

Visitors to Samuel Goldwyn stayed alert for fresh Goldwynisms. Those who heard one, or thought they did, showed it off like a trophy. Many Goldwyn visitors were not above making up a Goldwynism to report, or even borrowing one from a gag book. When the producer offered Orson Welles a "blank check" during a party conversation, it was said he'd offered Welles a "blanket check." Goldwyn once told publicist Arthur Mayer, "First you have a good story, then a good treatment, and next a first-rate director. After that you hire a competent cast, and even then you have only the nucleus of a good picture." Subsequently, wrote Mayer, "I have seen this story so often in print rewritten by press agents to 'only the mucus of a good picture,' that I now tell it that way myself."

In time it became hard to distinguish an authentic Goldwynism from a counterfeit. In time too the producer of such classic films as *Dodsworth, Wuthering Heights,* and *The Best Years of Our Lives* grew embarrassed about the many bloopers attributed to him. He was especially incensed when the *Reader's Digest* sent him $25 after attributing "blanket check" to him in its "Picturesque Patter of Speech" feature. Toward the end of his career Goldwyn denied that he'd ever uttered a single Goldwynism. "I wish I was smart enough to say some of the things they said I said," he grumbled in 1959. "None of them are true. They're all made up by a bunch of comedians and pinned on me." Goldwyn's loyal wife Frances concurred. After her husband died in 1974, however, Mrs. Goldwyn admitted that as many as half of the malaprops attributed to Sam were authentic. Among them were:

I WAS ON THE BRINK OF AN ABSCESS.

I DON'T CARE IF MY PICTURES DON'T MAKE A DIME, SO LONG AS EVERYONE COMES TO SEE THEM.

I HAD A MONUMENTAL IDEA THIS MORNING, BUT I DIDN'T LIKE IT.

IN THIS BUSINESS IT'S DOG EAT DOG, AND NOBODY'S GOING TO EAT ME.

Other Goldwynisms are more debatable, including many classics.

INCLUDE ME OUT.

Before storming out of a heated discussion about a labor dispute among members of the Motion Picture Producers and Distributors of America, Goldwyn supposedly exclaimed, "Gentlemen, include me out!" Many who were present swore that this was his exit line. According to Goldwyn, his actual words were "Gentlemen, I'm withdrawing from the association." In later years the producer grew philosophical about this classic Goldwynism, going so far as to propose "Include me out" for his own epitaph during a parlor game. Most Goldwynites consider this one authentic. Among other things, his mangling of language was known to happen most often during moments of stress.

A VERBAL CONTRACT ISN'T WORTH THE PAPER IT'S WRITTEN ON.

Screenwriter and Goldwyn-watcher Garson Kanin said of this one, "I would like to think that Goldwyn said [it]. I doubt that he did." The producer himself denied ever saying this. According to movie industry chronicler Norman Zierold, Goldwyn did say of fellow mogul Joe Schenck, "His verbal contract is worth more than the paper it's written on," and reporters gave his words a polish.

I CAN ANSWER YOU IN TWO WORDS: "IM POSSIBLE."

Goldwyn was especially vehement about denying "im possible." His vehemence was justified. According to Goldwyn biographer Alva Johnston, this gag appeared in a 1925 humor magazine. Charlie Chaplin later admitted that he circulated it as a Goldwynism. "It was an old gag from a sketch they used to do in the [music] halls," said Chaplin, "and I thought it would be fun to pin it on Sam."

I READ PART OF IT ALL THE WAY THROUGH.

According to Alva Johnston, a Goldwyn rival once said this to a team of writers. When they howled, the embarrassed producer pleaded, "Boys, I've always been good to you. Don't tell it on me. I'm sensitive. Tell it on Sam."

ANYONE WHO SEES A PSYCHIATRIST OUGHT TO HAVE HIS HEAD EXAMINED.

Lillian Hellman has been credited with coining this Goldwynism. Whether or not she did, it's unlikely that Goldwyn himself ever said it. In 1946 the producer told a reporter that he occasionally went to see a psychiatrist himself. That was two years before this Goldwynism achieved national renown via the ubiquitous *Reader's Digest,* which reported it in December 1948 without giving a source.

WE'LL MAKE HER AN ALBANIAN.

A friend of Arthur Mayer's vouched for one famous story about Goldwyn. The producer was warned that Lillian Hellman's play *The Children's Hour* could not be made into a movie because its main character was a lesbian. "We'll get around that," Goldwyn supposedly replied. "We'll make her an American." This response became a prominent part of the Goldwyn legend, euphonized to "We'll make her an Albanian." Biographer Arthur Marx called this story "An apocryphal Goldwynism if ever there was one." According to Marx, Goldwyn would never have made such a simpleminded observation. In addition, he was too close to Hellman—then under contract to Goldwyn and his frequent lunch partner—to have been so ignorant about her play.

TOO BLOOD AND THIRSTY

Marx also questioned Goldwyn's legendary exchange with James Thurber after the writer complained about the movie based on his story *Walter Mitty*. "I am very sorry that you felt it was too blood and thirsty," Goldwyn was said to have written Thurber. "Not only did I think so," Thurber supposedly wired back, "but I was horror and struck." As Marx pointed out, however, Goldwyn's secretaries would never have let a letter of his go out with so obvious a boner. No such correspondence has been found in the extensive Goldwyn archives. So where did this one originate? Clue: Thurber had no compunctions about peddling spurious quips as authentic.

WHAT WON'T THEY THINK OF NEXT?

In another anecdote, Goldwyn marveled "What won't they think of next?" after being shown a sundial. According to Alva Johnston this old gag had appeared in print (featuring an Italian gardener) long before it was put in Samuel Goldwyn's mouth.

The Hollywood Quip Exchange

In a setting dedicated to the production of fantasy, inventing, misattributing, and pilfering quips can be seen as little more than business as usual. One reason Ronald Reagan was so casual about borrowing other people's words was that this is how it's done where he came of age. In Hollywood, the ravenous hunger of scriptwriters for material, columnists for quips, and egos for inflation created an environment in which any good line quickly becomes public domain. The press has often been an unwitting accomplice to this process. On November 23, 1981, *People* magazine quoted actor Robby Benson as saying, **"There are five stages to an actor's career. First, 'Who's Robby Benson?' Then, 'Get me Robby Benson.' 'Get me a Robby Benson type': That's three. 'Get me a young Robby Benson,' four. And five, 'Who's Robby Benson?' "**

Three and a half years later, on April 29, 1985, *People* ran this item: "Alan Arkin was musing on the various stages in one's acting career. 'First,' he said, 'it's "Who's Alan Arkin?" Then, "Get me Alan Arkin!" Then, "He's too expensive. Get me an Alan Arkin type." Just after that it's, "Get me a *young* Alan Arkin," and then, finally, "Who's Alan Arkin?" ' "

Hollywood is full of such public domain quips with multiple claims to authorship. Among them are:

IF YOU HAVE A MESSAGE, SEND IT BY WESTERN UNION.

This could be the single most repeated cliché in the history of moviemaking. It has been variously attributed not only to Samuel Goldwyn but to Harry Warner, Harry Cohn, Humphrey Bogart, Marlon Brando, George S. Kaufman, Ernest Hemingway, and George Bernard Shaw. Any of them may have said this at one time or another. So might many others involved in moviemaking. Who said it first will probably never be known.

NEVER LET THAT BASTARD BACK IN HERE—UNLESS WE NEED HIM.

This is the classic angry mogul's response to a supplicant who's offended him. At various times it's been put in the mouth of the usual suspects, including Samuel Goldwyn, Harry Warner, and Adolph Zukor. According to Alva Johnston, George M. Cohan first said this during his days as a Broadway producer. Others say it's simply an old vaudeville gag.

I DON'T HAVE ULCERS. I GIVE THEM.

Goldwyn and Cohn were both quoted about giving ulcers rather than having them. RCA founder David Sarnoff said the essence of his managerial style was: "I don't get ulcers. I give them." That line made the rounds of executives, coaches, and sundry bureaucrats. Lyndon Johnson wasn't the only politician to spout this piece of curmudgeonly self-praise. So did Ed Koch when he was mayor of New York. Football coach Vince Lombardi was credited with a somewhat more elegant version: "I don't have ulcers, but I'm a carrier." Basketball coach Bill Fitch later said the same thing. Maybe they all bought the same gift-shop novelty sign: SOME PEOPLE GET ULCERS AND SOME PEOPLE GIVE THEM.

I HAVE A FOOLPROOF DEVICE FOR JUDGING A PICTURE. IF MY FANNY
SQUIRMS, IT'S BAD.

Harry Cohn was most commonly associated with this test of cinematic
appeal. When the *New York Times* reported that *60 Minutes* producer
Don Hewitt assessed a news report's boredom quotient by whether he
"felt an itch in the vicinity of his pants," Hewitt quickly disabused the
paper.

IT ONLY PROVES WHAT THEY ALWAYS SAY—GIVE THE PEOPLE WHAT
THEY WANT TO SEE AND THEY'LL COME OUT FOR IT.

Red Skelton's comment about Harry Cohn's well-attended 1958 funeral
could be his best-remembered line. According to Bert Lahr's son John
Lahr, his father said much the same thing a year earlier about Louis
Mayer's funeral: "If you want a full house, you give the public what it
wants." Samuel Goldwyn and others were credited with saying about
Mayer, "The reason so many people showed up at his funeral was
because they wanted to make sure he was dead." Later the same thing
would be said about Cohn.

I'VE BEEN RICH AND I'VE BEEN POOR. RICH IS BETTER.

This line is generally credited to singer Sophie Tucker. Others think
comedian Joe E. Lewis said it first. Since Tucker and Lewis often
performed together, they had many an opportunity to borrow each
other's material.

FROM BIRTH TO AGE EIGHTEEN, A GIRL NEEDS GOOD PARENTS.
FROM EIGHTEEN TO THIRTY-FIVE, SHE NEEDS GOOD LOOKS. FROM
THIRTY-FIVE TO FIFTY-FIVE, SHE NEEDS A GOOD PERSONALITY. FROM
FIFTY-FIVE ON, SHE NEEDS GOOD CASH.

Sophie Tucker's other well-known saying has also been attributed to
novelist Kathleen Norris, who was her contemporary. According to
Bartlett's, Tucker said this in 1953, when she was sixty-nine and Norris
was seventy-three.

LIFE BEGINS AT FORTY.

Tucker is also sometimes credited with "Life begins at forty," because she sang that song so often. This song was based on a book with the same title.

JUST KNOW YOUR LINES AND DON'T BUMP INTO THE FURNITURE.

This famous acting advice is attributed to Noel Coward in Britain, Spencer Tracy in America. Nigel Rees, who said he's also seen this admonition attributed to Alfred Lunt, gives the nod to his countryman. But wasn't it Coward who wrote, "The only thing that really saddens me over my demise is that I shall not be here to read the nonsense that will be written about me. . . . There will be lists of apocryphal jokes I never made and gleeful quotations of words I never said. *What* a pity I shan't be here to enjoy them!"?

You'd think that the inventing, rewriting, and borrowing of show business lines would stop at the film canister wall, where a celluloid record exists to settle bets. That's not the case. Movie lines are as easy to misremember as any other—perhaps more so, since they're repeated so often.

Movie Misquotes

MISREMEMBERED LINES

As my four-year-old and I watched *The Wizard of Oz,* I said, "this is where Dorothy says, **'We're not in Kansas anymore.'** " My son knew better. "No, Dad," he responded, "it's 'Toto, I have a feeling we're not in Kansas anymore.' " He was right.

WHAT WE'VE GOT HERE IS A FAILURE TO COMMUNICATE.

Our memories understandably add an "a" to Strother Martin's classic line from *Cool Hand Luke.* He actually said, "What we've got here is failure to communicate."

ME TARZAN, YOU JANE.

Johnny Weissmuller himself got it wrong when he said in a 1932 interview, "I didn't have to act in *Tarzan, the Ape Man*—just said, 'Me

Tarzan, you Jane.'" He didn't. In a decision on copyrights handed down by the Court of Appeals for the Second Circuit (Hartford, Connecticut), an excerpt from the screenplay of that 1932 movie reported the exact words used when Tarzan met Jane after chasing away an ape that was bothering her:

JANE: Thank you for protecting (*point to herself*) me.

TARZAN: (*tapping her on the chest*) Me.

JANE: No. (*pointing to herself*) I'm only me for me.

TARZAN: (*tapping her*) Me!

JANE: No. (*pointing to him*) To *you* I'm *you*.

TARZAN: (*tapping himself on the chest*) You?

JANE: No. (*pause*) I'm Jane Parker. Understand? Jane.

TARZAN: (*tapping her*) Jane.

TOGETHER: (*Tarzan taps her*) Jane.

TARZAN: (*tapping her*) Jane.

JANE: (*nodding*) Yes, Jane.

JANE: (*pointing to him*) You? (*Tarzan does not respond; she points to herself*) Jane.

TARZAN: (*tapping her*) Jane.

JANE: (*pointing to him*) And you? You?

TARZAN: (*tapping himself*) Tarzan. Tarzan.

JANE: (*slowly*) Tarzan.

TARZAN: (*alternately tapping her and himself, harder and harder each time*) Jane. Tarzan. Jane. Tarzan. Jane. Tarzan. Jane. Tarzan. Jane. Tarzan. Jane. . . .

JANE: (*exasperated*) Oh, please stop. Let me go. I can't bear this. (*realizing he can't understand*) Oh, what's the use?

BORROWED LINES

• In *Blaze*, Paul Newman played former Louisiana governor Earl Long. At one point Long says, **"The poor people of Louisiana have only three friends: Jesus Christ, Sears and Roebuck, and Earl Long."**

Atlanta Journal-Constitution columnist Lewis Grizzard said he grew up hearing this line attributed to Georgia governor Gene Talmadge, and using his name.

• The late boxing trainer Cus D'Amato often talked about fear being a boxer's friend (because it made him cautious and alert). This observation appeared in Sylvester Stallone's *Rocky V,* along with several others taken from a 1985 CBS-TV interview with D'Amato. D'Amato's thoughts were put in the mouth of Rocky's trainer, played by Burgess Meredith.

• In *All That Jazz,* the Bob Fosse character played by Roy Scheider said, **"To be on the wire is life. The rest is waiting."** Several years before that 1982 movie, this line was attributed to wire-walker Karl Wallenda. Nearly half a century before Scheider read his line, race-car driver Rudolf Caracciola was quoted as saying, "To race is to live. All the rest is simply waiting."

• According to the aging movie star played by Peter O'Toole in *My Favorite Year* **"Dying is easy. Comedy is hard."** Some think that line originated with Edmund Kean. Others attribute it to English actor Edmund Gwenn. In response to the comment "It must be very hard," Gwenn was quoted as having said on his deathbed in 1959, "It is. But not as hard as farce."

• In *The Best Man* (1964), Henry Fonda lip-synced the words of Alamo hero Sam Houston when he said about Cliff Robertson, **"He has every characteristic of a dog except loyalty."**

• In 1981's *The Four Seasons,* Carol Burnett said repeatedly, **"Are we having fun yet?"** That line subsequently became T-shirt common. Long before *The Four Seasons* appeared, "Are we having fun yet?" was the signature line of Bill Griffith's cartoon character Zippy the Pinhead.

SIGNATURE LINES

Many lines clearly associated with particular actors are apocryphal. It's one more case of our remembering what we want to have heard, not what was actually said.

Greta Garbo

I WANT TO BE ALONE.

Greta Garbo did say this, to John Barrymore, in the movie *Grand Hotel*. In time the sentiment was attributed to the reclusive actress herself. Garbo didn't like this. She once told a friend, "I never said 'I want to be alone.' I only said, 'I want to be *let* alone!' There is all the difference." A subsequent book of movie lines cooperated, reporting that Garbo said, "I vant to be left alone," in *Grand Hotel*.

Charles Boyer

COME WITH ME TO THE CASBAH.

Charles Boyer's signature line was never said by him in the movie *Algiers,* or any other. Boyer thought it was invented by his press agent. The line was a staple of Boyer impersonators, who probably didn't care whether he said it or not.

Mae West

WHY DON'T YOU COME UP AND SEE ME SOMETIME?

What Mae West actually told Cary Grant in *She Done Him Wrong* was, "Why don't you come up sometime and see me?" This provocative suggestion caught the public's fancy in its euphonized form. West herself used the new version in her next movie, *I'm No Angel*.

W. C. Fields

W. C. Fields was an unusually strong magnet for spurious signature lines such as "No man who hates dogs and children can be all bad" and "Never give a sucker an even break." One reason Fields so often gets credit for the latter is that it was the title of his 1941 movie. But those words do not appear in the film itself, and Fields fought against using them as its title, preferring "The Great Man." After losing this fight, he moaned, "What does it matter; they can't get that on a marquee. It will probably boil down to *Fields—Sucker*."

After "dogs and children," and "never give a sucker," Fields's most famous line was:

ON THE WHOLE, I'D RATHER BE IN PHILADELPHIA.

There's a widespread assumption that these words appears on W. C. Fields's tombstone. What actually is written on the vault holding his ashes is, "W. C. Fields, 1880–1946." The more popular version originated as part of the same 1925 *Vanity Fair* feature that reported Dorothy Parker's epitaph as "Eat my dust." Fields's exit line was given as, "I would rather be living in Philadelphia." Whether this spoof epitaph was his own invention wasn't clear. (Ghostwriters produced magazine pieces which appeared under Fields's byline.) After he died, "I'd rather be in Philadelphia" became Fields's epitaph in the public mind, usually beginning, "On the whole . . ." Bennett Cerf reported this version in 1944, and *Bartlett's* followed suit in its next four editions.

YOU CAN'T CHEAT AN HONEST MAN.

This was a common credo among the con men Fields so often portrayed. It became the title of a 1939 Fields movie, but was no more original to him than titles such as *The Old Army Game* or *So's Your Old Man.*

IT'S NOT A FIT NIGHT OUT FOR MAN OR BEAST.

This movie title was a Fields line in a revue during the late 1920s. Fields himself later wrote in a letter, "I do not claim to be the originator of this line as it was probably used long before I was born in some old melodrama."

W. C. Fields was an inspired comedian but not always an original one. Like so many other entertainers, he had few qualms about borrowing material which suited his purposes. As writer David Robinson observed of Fields's performances, "He largely improvised his own dialogue, except when it was written by gagmen he admired, like Dickens or Lewis Carroll."

Cary Grant

JUDY! JUDY! JUDY!

Without this line to recite, Cary Grant impersonators would have been lost. Grant once had some sound men listen through all of his movies for the line. They couldn't find it. Where did he think it originated? "I vaguely recall," said Grant, "that at a party someone introduced Judy Garland by saying, 'Judy, Judy, Judy,' and it caught on, attributed to me."

OLD CARY GRANT FINE. HOW YOU?

In Hollywood, Cary Grant was famous for intercepting a telegram sent to his studio inquiring, "HOW OLD CARY GRANT?" He responded, "OLD CARY GRANT FINE. HOW YOU?" Great story. Grant agreed. "That story has been attributed to various people over the years," he once observed. "I wish I could say it was true, but it's not."

James Cagney

YOU DIRTY RAT!

Before receiving the American Film Institute's Life Achievement Award in 1975, James Cagney had someone check all of his films to see if he'd ever said, "You dirty rat!" He hadn't. "I never said, 'Mmmmm, you dirty rat,' " Cagney told the audience, "but I thank all of you who have given me credit for it." Where did this line come from? In *Blonde Crazy,* Cagney did call someone "a dirty, double-crossing rat." Cagney mimics may have bumper-stickered this line into the more popular version.

ALL RIGHT, YOU GUYS!

"Most of my imitators also say, 'All right, you guys!' which I don't remember ever saying," Cagney wrote in his autobiography. He thought this line sounded more like the Bowery Boys, and that his impersonators might have gotten it from them.

At the American Film Institute tribute, producer Paul Keyes teased the honoree by saying that what Cagney actually said in his movies was "Judy! Judy! Judy!"

"Mind if I use that?" said Cagney.

"You were going to anyway," responded Keyes.

Cagney subsequently issued this advisory to Frank Gorshin, a lead-ing impersonator of him: "Oh Frankie, I never said 'MMMMmmm, you dirty rat!' What I actually said was 'Judy, Judy, Judy.' "

Humphrey Bogart

DROP THE GUN, LOUIE.

Humphrey Bogart denied ever saying this line in any of his many roles as a heavy. In *Casablanca* he did say, "Not so fast, Louis."

TENNIS, ANYONE?

Supposedly this was Bogart's only line in his first Broadway play. Some claim to have heard him say "Tennis, anyone?" but usually years after the fact, and with no evidence other than their memory. During a 1951 interview, Bogart told William Safire that to clear the stage of excess characters in some of his early plays, he would walk on in tennis gear, racket in hand, and say something like "It's forty-love out there. Anyone care to come out and watch?" Bogart added, "The lines I had were corny enough, but I swear to you, never once did I have to say, '*Tennis, anyone?*' " Bogart did refer to his early parts as " 'Tennis, anyone?' roles." *The Oxford Dictionary of Quotations,* thinks this phrase might have its roots in a line from Shaw's 1914 play *Misalliance:* "Anyone for a game of tennis?"

PLAY IT AGAIN, SAM.

The most famous of all misquoted movie lines appears neither in the script nor the film of *Casablanca.* The closest words are, "Play it, Sam. Play 'As Time Goes By.' " These words are uttered by Ilsa (Ingrid Bergman), not Rick (Humphrey Bogart). Later Rick does say, "If she can stand it I can. Play it!" After years of hearing his words misquoted, the cowriter of *Casablanca*'s script—Howard Koch—speculated that " 'again' simply underlined the average person's nostalgic memory of the scene (so familiar on posters and on the covers of film anthologies) in which Bogart sits drinking and brooding while Dooley Wilson sings, 'As Time Goes By.' " In *The Spoilers,* a 1956 movie, Anne Baxter did say, "Play it again, Sam." This line later became the title of a Woody Allen play and movie. Describing how he imitated Bogart as a teenager, Woody Allen wrote, "I was walking like Bogart, talking like Bogart, curling my lip and saying, . . . 'Play it again, Sam.' (I know he never actually said 'Play it again, Sam,' but I said it enough for both of us.)"

The Vast Wasteland

As with movie stars, signature lines are routinely put in the mouths of television personalities, or come to them secondhand.

DID YOU EVER WONDER WHY . . . ?

For the twentieth anniversary program of *60 Minutes,* Andy Rooney reviewed all of his taped segments. None included the introduction made famous by impersonator Joe Piscopo on *Saturday Night Live.* As with Cagney, Grant, Boyer, et al., concocted words proved more suggestive of the character impersonated than any he'd actually said.

BEAM ME UP, SCOTTY.

According to Trekkers, William Shatner did say "Scotty, beam me up," once, in Star Trek's fourth episode. What he more commonly said was "Beam us up, Mr. Scott," or "Enterprise, beam us up." In time our ears euphonized his actual command to the livelier version, one better suited to the T-shirts and bumper stickers on which it commonly appears.

I LAUGHED ALL THE WAY TO THE BANK.

In 1954, on the heels of his success on television, Liberace capped a triumphal thirty-day tour with the first piano concert held at Madison Square Garden since Paderewski played there two decades earlier. His performance was a sellout. New York's music reviewers were underwhelmed by the winks, grins, and candelabra of this Gorgeous George of the keyboard. In response Liberace quipped, "I cried all the way to the bank." This cheeky retort caught the public's fancy. In time it became a cliché. But a funny thing happened to Liberace's riposte on its way to the quote collections. His original statement, about *crying* all the way to the bank, had a bit of irony and bite. But Americans aren't supposed to cry, even in jest. As the years went by, Liberace's quip gradually evolved into "I *laughed* all the way to the bank." By now this is the accepted version. Even the *Morris Dictionary of Word and Phrase Origins* (1988) reports that Liberace told critics he was "laughing all the way to the bank." Today it's rare to see the original version in print. My collection of printed variations of Liberace's retort over the years breaks down this way:

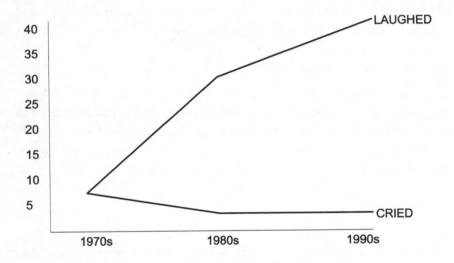

One article about chicken maven Frank Perdue said he "cackled" all the way to the bank, and another, about a busy tavern owner, said she "bubbled" all the way.

Watching television at times can feel like seeing a video collection of warmed-over, misattributed quotations. In the CBS series *WIOU* a news producer played by Mariette Harley said, "Television news is like sausage. People who love it shouldn't see it being made," without mentioning Bismarck. A video-taped Hans Christian Anderson fable, which did not list Mark Twain in its credits, featured a Chinese emperor who observes, "The rumors of my death have been greatly exaggerated."

Television has an inexhaustible hunger for bumper-stickered

phrases. Since it is so dependent on sound bites, and because sports are such a TV staple, athletes who use brief, quotable lines are the media's crown jewel. But few of them do. Sports figures sometimes need help from the press to punch up their words. Fortunately, that hasn't proved to be a problem.

10

Say It Ain't So!

On July 5, 1946, the Brooklyn Dodgers led the National League. Their arch-rivals, the New York Giants, were in seventh place—next to last. As his team was about to play the Giants, Dodgers manager Leo Durocher held court for a group of sportswriters. Although the Giants had beaten his team the day before, Durocher ridiculed their pathetic record and dinky home runs. Red Barber, Brooklyn's radio announcer, asked Durocher why he didn't admit that the Giants' home runs were as good as anyone's. "Why don't you be a nice guy for a change?" needled Barber.

Durocher leaped to his feet. "A nice guy?" he shouted. "A nice guy! I been around in baseball for a long time and I've known a lot of nice guys. But I never saw a nice guy who was any good when you needed him. Go up to one of those nice guys some time when you need a hundred to get you out of a jam and he'll always give you that, 'Sorry, pal. I'd like to help you but things are not going so good at the ranch.' That's what they'll give you, those nice guys. I'll take the guys who ain't nice. The guys who would put you in a cement mixer if they felt like it.

142

But you get in a jam and you don't have to go to them. They'll come looking for you and say, 'How much do you need?' "

Winking to his colleagues, a reporter asked Durocher if he was a nice guy. "No," said the Dodgers' manager. "Nobody ever called me that."

Durocher pointed at the Giants' dugout, saying, "Nice guys! Look over there. Do you know a nicer guy than [Giants' manager] Mel Ott? Or any of the other Giants? Why they're the nicest guys in the world! And where are they? In seventh place!

"The nice guys over there are in seventh place. Well let them come and get me."

He waved contemptuously toward the other dugout. "The nice guys are all over there. In seventh place."

That's it, folks. That's the genesis of **"Nice guys finish last,"** as reported by Frank Graham of New York's *Journal-American*. Graham, whose accuracy was respected by Durocher and most others, devoted his entire column to the Dodger manager's views on nice guys. "LEO DOESN'T LIKE NICE GUYS," it was titled. No other reporter present even mentioned Durocher's tirade in his coverage the next day. When Graham's original column was reprinted in *Baseball Digest* that fall, Durocher's references to nice guys finishing in "seventh place" had been changed to "last place" and "in the second division." Before long Leo's credo was bumper-stickered into "Nice guys finish last."

Somebody needed to say it. Enough of us were feeling that way about the gloomy prospects of decent folks. No one was better qualified than the irascible Durocher to put this feeling into words. For years Durocher protested to no avail that he hadn't said "Nice guys finish last." But his actual words—"The nice guys over there are in seventh place"—didn't have much snap. Journalists routinely ignored his protests. Eventually Durocher stopped trying to correct the record. The four words which made him famous far beyond the ballpark made their way into *Bartlett's*. Durocher's 1975 autobiography was called *Nice Guys Finish Last*. In that book he recalled the 1946 conversation with Frank Graham and his colleagues as concluding with him saying of the Giants, "Take a look at them. All nice guys. They'll finish last. Nice guys. Finish last." By the late 1970s Durocher had taken to saying that yes, he'd said nice guys finish last, but not in the sense it's usually taken. No quotation collector ever looked it up. As a result, a wide range of contexts are given for Durocher's famous comment. One English collection reported that Durocher said nice guys finish last in July 1952, about a player of his own named "Mellott." When Durocher died in 1991, nearly every obituary reported that he'd said "Nice guys finish last." Lucky for him. If we remembered what Leo Durocher actually said—that the nice guys over there are in seventh place—for how long would we be likely to be remember his name?

There's a reason that we cling so tenaciously to spurious sayings from the world of sports. Far beyond that world, the rest of us depend on figures such as Durocher to say things we want said but would be embarrassed to say ourselves. As child-adults, sports figures are allowed to point out that the emperor is buck naked. The rest of us can then quote them, our claim to maturity intact. Quoting someone like Yogi Berra gives public speakers an opportunity to show they're in touch with the common folks but not on their level. Spicing their discourse with a line from Casey Stengel allows intellectuals to display some range at little risk to their image. In his day, Muhammad Ali was always good for a clever, down-to-earth remark about this issue or that. He fed the rest of us a lot of lines. Sports quotes are just very useful all around. As a result, such comments are more than usually subject to the axiom that what needs saying will be said, and by the person we want to have said it.

In 1920, "Shoeless Joe" Jackson was one of eight Chicago White Sox players accused of deliberately losing the 1919 World Series at the behest of gamblers. It was as if Mother Teresa had been caught selling phony splinters from the true cross. The baseball players' sin cast a pall over America's secular religion. Not just baseball but the American sense of self was on trial. Someone needed to tell these ball players how hurt we felt, how let down, and plead with them to deny the charges. That someone appeared in a widely reprinted article by sportswriter Hugh Fullerton. This is how Fullerton reported the scene at the courthouse where Shoeless Joe had just testified before a grand jury:

> After an hour, a man, guarded like a felon by other men, emerged from the door. He did not swagger. He slunk along between the guardians, and the kids, with wide eyes and tightening throats watched, and one, bolder than the others, pressed forward and said:

"It ain't so, Joe, is it?"

"Yes, kid, I'm afraid it is."

And the world of faith crashed around the heads of the kids. Their idol lay in dust, their faith destroyed. Nothing was true, nothing was honest; there was no Santa Claus.

Then, and not until then, did Jackson, hurrying away to escape the sight of the faces of the kids, understand the enormity of the thing he had done.

Fullerton's prose poetry caught the public's fancy. His boy's plaintive question became the Black Sox scandal's focusing phrase. Somewhere along the way his words were given a polish, euphonized from the pedestrian "It ain't so, Joe, is it?" to the terser, more poetic, **"Say it ain't so, Joe."** It took some historical rewriting to produce this version, however. A 1940 history of the Associated Press placed its reporter at Jackson's side as he made his way through a mob of boys. "One tiny youngster timidly stepped up to the outfielder and tugged at his sleeve," wrote the history's author. " 'Say it ain't so, Joe,' " he pleaded. Joe Jackson looked down. 'Yes, kid, I'm afraid it is.' The crowd of little fans parted silently to make a path. 'Well I'd never thought it,' gulped the youngster. 'I'd never thought it.' " That history took a bit of liberty with this report from the *Chicago Herald* of September 29, 1920:

> As Jackson stepped out of the building, one little urchin in the crowd grabbed him by his coat sleeve.
>
> "It ain't true, is it Joe?"
>
> "Yes, kid, I'm afraid it is," Jackson replied.
>
> "Well, I'd never have thought it," the boy exclaimed.

Other newspapers reported similar scenes. None used the phrase "Say it ain't so, Joe." Jackson himself always denied that this or anything like it was ever said to him. "I guess the biggest joke of all," he commented in later years, "was that story that got out about 'Say it ain't so, Joe.' It was supposed to have happened . . . when I came out of the court room. There weren't any words passed between anybody except me and a deputy sheriff. . . . He asked me for a ride and we got in the car together and left. There was a big crowd hanging around in front of the building, but nobody else said anything to me."

Another legendary sports saying of doubtful authenticity is **"Win**

one for the Gipper." This is a distillation of an emotional locker room speech coach Knute Rockne gave Notre Dame football players as they were about to play Army in 1928. Rockne invoked the name of a former player, George Gipp, whose deathbed request eight years earlier supposedly had been to use his memory to motivate the Fighting Irish for a big game. " 'Rock,' " the coach said Gipp told him, " 'some day when things look real tough for Notre Dame, ask the boys to go out there and win one for me.' Well, I've never used Gipp's request until now. This is the time." A New York *Daily News* writer later reported Rockne's locker room speech in a feature story headed, "GIPP'S GHOST BEAT ARMY/ IRISH HERO'S DEATHBED REQUEST INSPIRED NOTRE DAME." Two years later Rockne himself embellished the legend when he wrote in a magazine that the dying Gipp told him, " 'Some time, Rock when the team's up against it, when things are wrong and the breaks are beating the boys—tell them to go in there with all they've got and win just one for the Gipper." In 1940, an adaptation of these words—"Someday, when things are tough, maybe you can ask the boys to go in there and win just one for the Gipper"—provided the dramatic climax of a movie featuring Ronald Reagan as George Gipp. That movie, and Reagan's lifelong fixation with his role, ensured that the pithy, if probably apocryphal "Win one for the Gipper" would become a permanent part of America's athletic-political lore.

When it comes to sports homilies, Knute Rockne is an all-American flypaper figure. The legendary football coach is given credit for all manner of things he never said, or even believed. A Philadelphia lawyer once complained that "there's no Knute Rockne of the courtroom who says it's not whether you win or lose, it's how you play the game." The credo of sports troubador Grantland Rice couldn't have been farther from that of Notre Dame's hard-bitten coach. "When the going gets tough, the tough get going," is sometimes attributed to Rockne. But biographer Jerry Brondfield concluded that he was no more its author than were John Mitchell or Joseph Kennedy, who also get credit for the line. This is just one more slogan of unknown paternity which has been posted in locker rooms for decades.

On the other hand, Brondfield thought that Notre Dame's coach may have originated a line for which he rarely gets credit. That line is, "You show me a good and gracious loser and I'll show you a loser." Brondfield was told that Rockne said this in the 1920s, to a colleague who complimented a fellow coach for being "such a good and gracious loser." In its terser form, **"Show me a good loser and I'll show you a loser"** became a bedrock American adage. Richard Nixon said he was told this in the 1930s by his college football coach, Wallace "Chief" Newman. "There is no way I can adequately describe Chief Newman's influence on me," Nixon later wrote. Jimmy Carter was also fond of this slogan. So are countless American men. "Show me a good loser" is commonly attributed to Leo Durocher, for no better reason than "it sounds like him."

The world of sports is filled with such orphan quotations searching for a home. Others include:

The Sweet Science

THE BIGGER THEY ARE, THE HARDER THEY FALL.

This boxing maxim is sometimes attributed to John L. Sullivan, occasionally to James Corbett, but most often to Bob "Ruby Robert" Fitzsimmons. Fitzsimmons popularized the slogan in 1900 when—after knocking out a much larger opponent—he said, "You know the old saying, 'The bigger they are, the further they have to fall.'" In 1926 Albert Payson Terhune reported seeing a version of this saying on an old English sporting print. Among various related proverbs recorded in seventeenth century England was "The higher standing the lower fall."

WE WAS ROBBED!

This is one of two comments by Joe Jacobs to make *Bartlett's*. Jacobs was a colorful, rambunctious fight manager beloved by sportswriters for his Runyonesque syntax. According to *Bartlett's,* after heavyweight champion Max Schmeling lost a 1932 title fight to Jack Sharkey, "Jacobs, Schmeling's manager, shouted this protest against the decision." In an oral history recorded some forty years after that fight, referee Gunboat Smith said these were Jacobs's words. Most quote collections and boxing histories concur. The *New York Times*'s 1940 obituary of Jacobs recalled him saying, "We wuz robbed." But a survey of the major New York newspapers turned up these reports of his manager's words the day after Schmeling lost the decision:

"JOE JACOBS . . . SAID HIS CHAMPION HAD BEEN ROBBED." *Daily Mirror*

". . . JOE JACOBS, SAID THEY WERE ROBBED." *Daily Mirror*

"I WAS ROBBED OF THE DECISION." *Times*

"HE WAS ROBBED." *Evening Post*

"WE'VE BEEN ROBBED!" *American* (reported by Damon Runyon)

"IT WAS A BARE-FACED ROBBERY." *American*

"HE WAS JOBBED." *American* (reporting a postfight radio interview with Jacobs)

It's conceivable that the New York reporters all gave Jacobs a hand with his diction. Or perhaps the version that's gone down in history is the one we wanted to hear, and heard.

I SHOULD OF STOOD IN BED.

"No quotation book that calls itself a quotation book can look you in the eyes these days unless it includes, 'I should of stood in bed,' " noted sportswriter John Lardner in 1951. This is still true. Jacobs's second most familiar quotation has achieved the status of a classic, despite some confusion about when and why he said it. *Bartlett's* first reported that the fight manager made this comment to New York sportswriters after returning from the 1934 World Series in Detroit, where he'd bet on Chicago, who lost. In 1934 Detroit played St. Louis in the World Series. In its next edition *Bartlett's* changed the date to 1935. I found no such remark by Joe Jacobs reported by any New York newspaper in the days following the 1935 World Series between Detroit and Chicago. According to the *Morris Dictionary of Words and Phrases*, Jacobs said he should of stood in bed after one of his fighters fought before a poor house. Professor Matthew Bruccoli of the University of South Carolina said Jacobs made this observation when one of his fighters got beat. *Los Angeles Times* columnist Jim Murray thought the line began with boxing manager Joe Gould. When Murray's colleague Jack Smith mentioned that attribution in his column, a reader wrote to say that he'd seen "I should of stood in bed" attributed to Joe E. Wall, manager of a Brooklyn baseball team, in a New York city tabloid in 1931 or 1932.

According to John Lardner they're all wrong. "As it happens," he reported of Jacobs's immortal words, "the great man coined them two feet from your correspondent's ear. It was the only time I ever heard a famous quotation in the making." Lardner explained that Joe Jacobs sat right behind him while watching his first live baseball game on the frigid opening day of the 1935 World Series. When a companion asked what he thought of the game, Jacobs replied, "I should of stood in bed."

WE'LL WIN, BECAUSE GOD'S ON OUR SIDE.

This thought is as old as the Crusades, as modern as Saddam Hussein. It is what Joe Louis is often credited with saying soon after the attack on Pearl Harbor. His actual words—to a Madison Square Garden rally—were a bit more modest: "We're gonna do our part, and we will win, because we are on God's side." During the Civil War, when a delegation of southerners told Lincoln that "God is on our side," the President responded, "It is more important to know that we are on God's side."

I AM THE GREATEST.

Muhammad Ali never claimed to have coined his own signature line. Late in his career the boxer told a reporter that he didn't even believe it. Ali explained that he got the idea from wrestler Gorgeous George, whose boasting filled seats. "I saw an opportunity to do the same thing," Ali explained. "So I started the 'I am The Greatest' thing. I began with the poetry and predicting rounds. And it worked. They started coming in with their ten and twenty dollar bills to see the braggin' nigger." Biographer Thomas Hauser pointed out that Ali was bragging long before he saw Gorgeous George wrestle, however. Wilfred Sheed, another Ali biographer, thought his famous boast may have originated with the boxer's father.

FLOAT LIKE A BUTTERFLY, STING LIKE A BEE.

There is general agreement that Ali's crony Drew "Bundini" Brown was the source of his famous credo.

America's Pastime

DON'T LOOK BACK. SOMETHING MIGHT BE GAINING ON YOU.

Satchel Paige's classic maxim (part of a longer list) is routinely mis-quoted. "Someone might be gaining on you" is the most common version. Then there's the more paranoid "They might be gaining on you." All-Star outfielder Barry Bonds once said, "Like they say: 'Don't look back, somebody might be in front of you.' " According to Cleveland Cavalier coach Lenny Wilkens, "I think Satchel Paige said, 'If you look back, someone will step on you.' "

YOU COULD LOOK IT UP.

Casey Stengel was famous for saying this repeatedly during his heyday as a manager, from the 1940s through the 1960s. "You Could Look it Up," was the title of a James Thurber short story which ran in the *Saturday Evening Post* in 1941. That story, about a baseball manager named Squawks Magrew, included lines like "This was thirty, thirty-one year ago; you could look it up" and "Well, sir, it'll all be there in the papers of thirty, thirty-one year ago, and you could look it up."

Malaprops sometimes get passed back and forth between Casey Stengel and Yogi Berra. Berraisms which have been attributed to Stengel include "The game isn't over until it's over," and "It's déjà vu all over again." These are only two of a long list of popular Berra sayings dating back nearly half a century.

During "Yogi Berra Night" in his hometown of St. Louis in 1947, the Yankee catcher said, **"I'd like to thank everyone who made this night necessary."** That was an early Berraism. Many to come earned him a reputation as Sam Goldwyn in spikes. Like Goldwyn, he was given a hand by publicists and reporters who put simpleminded remarks in the mouth of the All-Star catcher (an eighth-grade dropout). "Most of the stories attributed to Yogi are the products of the fertile minds of witty correspondents traveling with him," concluded sportswriter Jimmy Powers.

Early in his career Berra was quoted as responding to a manager who suggested he think before hitting the ball, **"Think! How the hell are you gonna think and hit at the same time?"** This seemed to be a classic Berraism—insight wrapped up in a deceptively simpleminded observation. But according to writer Ed Fitzgerald that line was put in Yogi's mouth by a sportswriter.

As with Twain, Goldwyn, and Parker, the demand for Berra remarks far exceeds the supply. This is why counterfeit sayings from the master are as common as freshly made "antiquities" in Middle Eastern flea markets. He himself once observed, "I really didn't say everything I said." Discovering what Yogi did or didn't say is no easy task. Among other things, Berra is a helpful, but not definitive expert on his own commentary. His wife Carmen is no more definitive. Joe Garagiola, Berra's best friend since childhood, is a bit more helpful. The former Cardinal catcher—who popularized many Berraisms as a banquet speaker and television personality—says he can distinguish real from spurious Berraisms because "the real ones . . . make sense. They're not clever or witty, not plays on words—just his unique way of looking at things."

From George Bush on, citing Yogi Berra has long been a national pastime. "It has become a way to invoke the authority of the Common Man," observed Jack Rosenthal of the *New York Times*. Spouting Berraisms is a way to express simple truths with little risk of looking like a simpleton. Heck, you're just quotin' ole Yog'. This can be risky, however. As Rosenthal pointed out, when British press magnate Robert Maxwell came to New York to buy the *Daily News,* he went the extra mile to show he was hep to American ways. "As Yogi Bear once said," noted Maxwell, "a thing is not done until it is done."

IT AIN'T OVER TILL IT'S OVER.

This is *the* classic Berraism. It's probably authentic. Yogi said that when he was managing the Mets in 1973. No one else has ever claimed authorship of this line. Berra himself said he said it, though he insisted his actual words were "It *isn't* over until it's over."

YOU CAN OBSERVE A LOT BY WATCHING.

Another classic. Yogi said this in an October 24, 1963 press conference after being named manager of the Yankees. Explaining how he'd prepared himself for the job during his previous year as a coach, Berra told reporters, "You can observe a lot by watchin'." (In his autobiography Yogi mistakenly thought his actual words were "You can see a lot just by observing.") This Berraism is continually requoted because—like "It' ain't over till it's over"—the words contain wisdom disguised as a tautology.

These two are the most authentic Berraisms. The authenticity quotient of the rest ranges from dubious to spurious.

IT'S DÉJÀ VU ALL OVER AGAIN.

In recent years this saying has climbed the charts of Yogi Berra's hit parade. This charming observation has become such a catchphrase that it's often used without even mentioning Berra. That's probably just as well. Yogi denies that he ever said it. It's unlikely that he did. Like the many spurious Goldwynisms, this is the kind of thing Berra "should" have said, but probably didn't. Among other things, *déjà vu* is not a term he would be likely to use in any context.

A WRONG MISTAKE

Berra was thrilled to hear himself quoted this way by George Bush during a 1988 campaign debate, even though he denied ever saying these words. In *The Wit and Wisdom of Yogi Berra,* sportswriter Phil Pepe said that when he was asked how the powerful Yankees could have lost the 1960 World Series to the less awesome Pirates, Berra explained, "We made too many wrong mistakes." Pepe gave no source. The author admitted that trying to distinguish real from spurious Berraisms was not something he cared to get into.

BASEBALL IS NINETY PERCENT MENTAL. THE OTHER HALF IS PHYSICAL.

Another one that "sounds like Yogi." The earliest date I've seen it assigned to him is 1979. A collection of sports quotes published that year but written earlier credited Phillies manager Danny Ozark with "Half of this game is ninety percent mental." In 1977 Milwaukee Brewer outfielder Jim Wohlford was quoted as saying that "ninety percent of this game is half mental." But quoting Danny Ozark or Jim Wohlford to this effect would add exactly zero to the retelling. So this line has joined the Berra lore. Along the way numbernesia has kicked in. Berra said he's seen the comment requoted a number of ways, including "Baseball is 50 percent mental and the other ninety percent is physical."

ALWAYS GO TO OTHER PEOPLE'S FUNERALS; OTHERWISE THEY WON'T GO TO YOURS.

Berra denied ever saying this, and with good reason. Clarence Day's 1935 book *Life with Father* included the line "If you don't go to other men's funerals, they won't come to yours."

NOBODY EVER GOES THERE ANYMORE; IT'S TOO CROWDED.

Yogi said he did say this one—about Ruggeri's restaurant in St. Louis. Carmen Berra thought her husband said it about a New York restaurant. According to Phil Pepe it was Charlie's in Minneapolis. In addition to those candidates, Joe Garagiola said he'd heard this Berraism applied to restaurants in Boston, Kansas City, and Sarasota, Florida. In the 1940s Dorothy Parker was supposed to have said the same thing about Chasen's in Los Angeles. If so, she might have borrowed the remark from a 1943 *New Yorker* story by John McNulty. In this story, McNulty wrote of a couple of characters: "They were talking about a certain hangout and Johnny said, 'Nobody goes there any more. It's too crowded.' "

Some of the words put in Yogi's mouth are simply absurd. A number of people, including General Norman Schwarzkopf, thought Yogi said, **"The future ain't what it used to be."** This is an old saw, more reliably attributed to science fiction author Arthur Clarke. When his wife told him that she'd gone to see *Dr. Zhivago* a second time, Yogi was famous for responding, **"Dr. Zhivago, again? What's the matter with you now?"** Quote maven Paul Dickson thought this probably was an old joke with Berra's name dropped in.

When the House Budget Committee Chairman observed, "Like Yogi Berra said, **'When you reach the crossroads, take it,'** " a *New York Times* reporter asked Yogi about that one. "You mean the roads crossing thing?" Berra replied. "Yeah, I probably did say it one time. I say a lot of things I don't remember."

A Collision Sport

FOOTBALL ISN'T A CONTACT SPORT, IT'S A COLLISION SPORT. DANC-
ING IS A CONTACT SPORT.

Vince Lombardi typically gets credit for this line. If he did say it,
Lombardi may have got the line from Michigan State's football coach
Duffy Daugherty, to whom it's also credited. In 1986, Chicago Bears
coach Mike Ditka chimed in with "I don't call football a contact sport.
I call it a collision sport."

WINNING ISN'T EVERYTHING, IT'S THE ONLY THING.

This is among the most hallowed of American sports creeds, rivaled
only by "Nice guys finish last." It is routinely attributed to Vince
Lombardi. By the time I grew interested in misquotes, Green Bay's
renowned coach was no longer alive. I'd heard that his signature line
had appeared in a 1953 movie called *Trouble Along the Way*. When this
movie was released, Vince Lombardi was an obscure assistant coach at
West Point. While in Los Angeles on other business I went to Warner
Brothers studios and reviewed the dialogue transcript for *Trouble Along
the Way*. Sure enough, on Page 4 of Reel 5-A, the daughter of a football
coach played by John Wayne says of him, "Listen, like Steve says,
'Winning isn't everything, it's the only thing!' " In a telephone conversation, Melville Shavelson, the movie's producer-screenwriter, told me
that this line came from UCLA football coach Red Sanders. UCLA's
athletic department referred me to a 1955 *Sports Illustrated* profile of
Sanders. This profile quoted Sanders as having said, " 'Sure, winning
isn't everything. It's the only thing."

Before going to Los Angeles, Sanders coached at Vanderbilt from
1940 to 1948. Both Vanderbilt's 1946–1948 sports information director
and a sports columnist for the Nashville *Banner* have confirmed that
Sanders used this saying at the time. No one knows whether it was
original to him. Sanders was a quotable, well-read man. "Winning isn't
everything" may have been his own coinage. Or it could just be one of
those locker room bromides whose author will never be known. In later
years the line was credited not only to Vince Lombardi but to Washington Redskin coach Joe Kuharich, University of Maryland coach Jim
Tatum, and Chicago White Sox owner Bill Veeck.

A 1962 profile of Lombardi in *Life* magazine attributed this saying to Green Bay's coach. Six years later, Jerry Kramer's best-selling memoir *Instant Replay* gave added exposure to Lombardi's putative slogan. In some interviews the coach said he'd used those words and regretted it. On other occasions he denied saying them at all. In the late 1960s a former player of Lombardi's asked his old coach about the quote so routinely associated with him. Lombardi said he'd been misquoted but knew that trying to correct the record would be futile. Later he did try, protesting that his real philosophy was, "Winning isn't everything, the *will* to win is the only thing." In a 1962 *Esquire* profile, Green Bay's coach had been quoted as saying, "Winning isn't everything, but wanting to win is!" In a book on football published after his 1970 death, Lombardi wrote, "I have been quoted as saying, 'Winning is the only thing.' That's a little out of context. What I said is that 'Winning is not everything—but making the effort to win is." Certainly this version reflected Lombardi's philosophy better than the one so often ascribed to him. Lombardi was too shrewd a coach and psychologist to emphasize winning per se. That's for the Donald Trumps, George Steinbrenners, and Billy Martins. But on the eve of our debacle in Vietnam *someone* had to say that winning was the only thing. Lombardi was the most prominent candidate. He got the job.

Sports quotes, like any others, must suit their times. When "Winning isn't everything" first appeared in print under Red Sanders's name, we weren't so receptive to that message. Nor was Sanders famous enough to make his comment familiar. We not only needed a better known name to associate with that creed, but an appropriate moment for it to become one of our most familiar quotations. A similar fate befell "Nice guys finish last." Although Leo Durocher's original comments about nice guys were made in 1946, it took years for the bumper stickered version to catch on. Well into the 1950s profiles were written about Durocher which didn't even mention his famous misquotation. As late as the early 1960s, writer Nelson Algren compared Durocher favorably with Camus because of the insight of his classic comment: "Nice guys finish second." This was not the only time Algren got it wrong.

11

The Literary Lift

"Immature poets imitate; mature poets steal."

T. S. ELIOT

"A good composer does not imitate; he steals."

IGOR STRAVINSKY

Nelson Algren is the source of one of our most popular pieces of folk wisdom: **"Never play cards with a man called Doc. Never eat at a place called Mom's. Never sleep with a woman whose troubles are worse than your own"** (the wording varies). In his 1956 novel *A Walk on the Wild Side,* Algren attributed these rules to a prison convict. During a subsequent interview, Algren said he'd gotten them from an old black woman. When lecturing, the novelist sometimes offered this advice as his own. Today it is routinely credited to Algren himself. In her 1990 biography of Algren, Bettina Drew did not include this bit of folk wisdom because she didn't think it sounded like him. Drew thought Algren may have gotten the "rules" from an old friend named Dave Peltz. Peltz, who met Algren in the 1930s when both worked on the WPA Writer's Project, now owns a construction business in Gary, Indiana. During an interview he recalled cooking up the rules and including them in a letter to Algren without saying they were his. Why not? "Because he wouldn't have paid as much attention," explained Peltz. "He always felt that people on the outside, people in the

156

underground, were wiser than those of us who were in the mainstream, who belonged to the middle class. So I attributed this quote to a black lady who was the madam of a neighborhood whorehouse."

How did he come up with the rules? According to Peltz, "Never play cards with a man named Doc" is an old gambler's expression. "Never eat at a place called Mom's" reflected the fact that there were so many restaurants called "Mom's" in those days, few of which were any good. " 'Never go to bed with somebody whose troubles are worse than your own' was purely mine," he added, "because I knew he [Algren] had a problem of getting involved with people who were in worse trouble than he was. And he would suffer for it."

What reaction did Peltz get from Algren to his rules?

"I got no reaction from him, except that he began to use them in all of his lectures."

How does he feel when seeing his rules quoted so often as Algren's?

"I'm amused."

If Peltz is right, Nelson Algren was taking part in a great tradition: the literary lift. When it comes to borrowing material wherever they find it, writers are right up there with politicians, coaches, and standup comedians. Tending to be more creative, they're more likely to put a fresh spin on words they've appropriated. By the same token, they're less likely to admit the loan. "I am not very scrupulous, I own," admitted Byron, "when I have a good idea, how I came into possession of it." As a result, some of the better known elements of our literary heritage are not exactly what we thought them to be.

Consider this celebrated exchange:

F. SCOTT FITZGERALD: **The rich are not like you and me.**

ERNEST HEMINGWAY: **Yes, they have more money.**

That dialogue never took place, at least not between Fitzgerald and Hemingway. Yet there's a reason for the widespread assumption that it did. In 1926 Fitzgerald published a short story called "The Rich Boy." The third paragraph of his story included these lines: "Let me tell you about the very rich. They are different from you and me. They possess and enjoy early, and it does something to them, makes them soft where we are hard, and cynical where we are trusting, in a way that, unless you were born rich, it is very difficult to understand." Ten years later, Hemingway published an early version of "The Snows of Kilamanjaro" in *Esquire*. His story included this passage: "He remembered poor Scott Fitzgerald and his romantic awe of them [the rich] and how he had started a story once that began, 'The very rich are different from you and me.' And how someone had said to Scott, Yes, they have more money."

Though Hemingway didn't say so, the reader was free to infer that this rejoinder was his. *The Crack-Up*—Fitzgerald's published miscellany—included this jotting from his notebook: "They have more money. (Ernest's wisecrack.)" *Crack-Up* editor Edmund Wilson added a footnote for context: "Fitzgerald had said, 'The rich are different from us.' Hemingway had replied, 'Yes, they have more money.' " No wonder we assume that this exchange actually took place. Edmund Wilson said it did. He was wrong. Here's what really happened: Several years before writing "Snows of Kilamanjaro," Hemingway had lunch with his editor, Maxwell Perkins, and critic Mary Colum. Perkins later wrote a relative that during this lunch Hemingway commented, "I am getting to know the rich." Colum responded, "The only difference between the rich and other people is that the rich have more money." When Hemingway's subsequent story suggested that Scott Fitzgerald, not himself, was the object of this topper, Perkins wrote Fitzgerald, "I was present when that reference was made to the rich, and the retort given, and you were many miles away."

In response to Fitzgerald's protest, Hemingway changed Fitzgerald's name to "Julian" in the book *Snows of Kilamanjaro*. Correcting the record proved easier than revising the popular misapprehension, however. Some forty years after Hemingway's little conceit, writer Larry L. King spoke for many when he observed, "To this day, I read or hear of that 'exchange' between Hemingway and Fitzgerald as if it actually happened."

Hemingway had already been involved in another literary lift: **"You are a lost generation."** Gertrude Stein is famous for pinning this label on Hemingway and his peers. In an unpublished forward to *The Sun Also Rises*, the novelist said Stein got that term—*une génération perdue*—from the owner of a Paris auto repair shop who used it to describe those World War I veterans whom he couldn't train as mechanics. (Hemingway later recounted a different version of this story in *A Move-*

able Feast.) Stein herself said she'd picked up the term *"génération perdue"* in 1924, from the proprietor of a hotel in Belley. "He said that every man becomes civilized between the ages of eighteen and twenty-five," wrote Stein. "If he does not go through a civlizing experience at that time in his life he will not be a civilized man. And the men who went to war at eighteen missed the period of civilizing, and they could never be civilized. They were a lost generation." In either case Stein was merely the reporter and Hemingway the publicist of this now-familiar phrase.

Literary lifting has a long tradition, even among writers of stature. Incorporating existing sayings into one's work is the most common form. In an 1822 novel called *The Fortunes of Nigel,* for example, Sir Walter Scott wrote, "The waterman declared that he would **rather have her room than her company.**" This observation drew on a sort of aphoristic revolving fund:

FOR SUCH A SCOFFING PRELATE, HIS ROOM HAD BEEN BETTER THAN HIS COMPANY.
> Richard Stanyhurst, *Description of Ireland,* 1577

I HAD RATHER HAVE YOUR ROOM AS YOUR COMPANY.
> *The Marriage of Wit and Wisdom,* 1579

I HAD AS LIEF HAVE THEIR ROOM AS THEIR COMPANY.
> Robert Greene, *Farewell to Folly,* 1591

BETTER HIS ROOM THAN [HIS] COMPANY.
> Philemon Holland, translator, *Plutarch's Morals,* 1603

SHE WOULD RATHER HAVE HIS ROOM THAN HIS COMPANY.
> Samuel Hieron, *Works,* ii, 1617

PREFERRING HIS ROOM, AND DECLINING HIS COMPANY.
> Thomas Fuller, *A Wounded Conscience,* 1646

Forty-three years after Scott drew on this literary treasure trove, Dickens did too when he wrote in *Our Mutual Friend,* "Let me have your room instead of your company."

In such cases authors have adapted material that is virtually public domain. In other cases this is less clear.

• After she met Byron, but before she became his mistress, Lady Caroline Lamb wrote of him in her journal: **"Mad, bad and dangerous to know."** More than a century later Evelyn Waugh used these very words to describe his associates at Oxford in the 1920s. Mordecai Richler repeated the phrase twice in nearly identical passages separated by over a hundred pages in his 1980 novel *Joshua Then and Now.* (*Time*'s reviewer chided Richler for borrowing from Waugh.)

• In *Huckleberry Finn,* Mark Twain used the phrase **"you pays your money and takes your choice."** It's understandable to assume that this American-sounding phrase began with Twain. In fact, nearly four decades before *Huckleberry Finn* was published, *Punch* ran a cartoon called "The Ministerial Crisis" in which a customer is told by a showman, "Which ever you please, my little dear. You pays your money, and you takes your choice."

• Readers old enough to know that the term **"mean streets"** didn't originate as the title of a Martin Scorsese film generally attribute this phrase to Raymond Chandler. Chandler's most celebrated single sentence was, **"Down these mean streets a man must go who is not himself mean, who is neither tarnished nor afraid."** This appeared in his 1944 essay "The Simple Art of Murder." The hook phrase in that sentence dates back at least to 1894 when Arthur Morrison published a book about London's East End called *Tales of Mean Streets.*

• In George Orwell's 1939 novel *Coming Up for Air,* one character observed that **"there's a thin man inside every fat man."** Six years later, in *The Unquiet Grave,* Cyril Connolly wrote, "Imprisoned in every fat man a thin one is wildly signalling to be let out." Today Connolly's livelier version is better remembered than Orwell's earlier one.

• When *People* quoted jet-setter Hélène Rochas as saying "After thirty, you get the face you deserve," it noted that this paraphrased an observation by George Orwell. On April 17, 1949, the last words written in Orwell's manuscript notebook were, **"At fifty, everyone has the face he deserves."** But Orwell was hardly the only one to whom this thought had occurred. According to Clifton Fadiman, when Lincoln was taken to task for turning down an older job applicant whose face put him off, the President told a cabinet member, "Every man over forty is responsible for his face." Others think Lincoln said this about those over thirty. Arthur Schlesinger, Jr., said House Speaker Sam Rayburn told him this anecdote about Lincoln, except the cutoff was age fifty. *The Viking Book of Aphorisms* attributed "A man of fifty is responsible for his face" to Lincoln's secretary of war, Edwin Stanton. A collection of Mae West quotes included, "A man has more character in his face at forty than at twenty—he has suffered longer." In 1956 Coco Chanel was quoted as saying, "Nature gives you the face you have at twenty, it is up to you to merit the face you have at fifty." This was several years after Orwell's journal entry, of course, as was Albert Camus's 1960 line in *The Fall*, "Alas, after a certain age every man is responsible for his face." In his novel *The American Ambassador,* Ward Just wrote of a character, "if at forty everyone has the face he's earned . . ."

As usual with such a quote, numbers vary in the retelling. For ready reference:

	FACE AT OR AFTER			
	30	40	50	UNSPECIFIED
Orwell			X	
Lincoln I		X		
Lincoln II	X			
Lincoln III			X	
Stanton			X	
West		X		
Chanel			X	
Camus				X
Just		X		
Rochas	X			

Oscar Wilde

As an unabashed borrower and involuntary lender of good lines, Oscar Wilde was a leading literary cross-pollinator. When David Frost was asked by *Playboy*'s interviewer to discuss the subject of the queen, he responded, "The queen is not a subject," not acknowledging Wilde as the source of this mot. In *An Ideal Husband* Wilde wrote "Life is never fair," perhaps inspiring John F. Kennedy's similar observation—"Life is unfair"—nearly a century later. The term "beautiful people," (as in the Beatles' "How does it feel to be one of the beautiful people?") was one Wilde used often, as he did in an 1879 letter to Harold Boulton: "I could have introduced you to some very beautiful people."

Even as he was loaning out his lines, Wilde was notorious for acquiring material wherever he found it. James McNeill Whistler rarely missed an opportunity to make this point. "What has Oscar in common with Art," Whistler once asked, "except that he dines at our tables and picks from our platters the plums for the pudding that he peddles in the provinces?" On another occasion, after Whistler got off a good line, the painter reported that Wilde told him, "I wish I'd said that." "You will, Oscar, you will," Whistler said he responded. Wilde, Whistler concluded, "has the courage of the opinions of others." His one-time friend responded by using this phrase in his play *The Decay of Lying*.

Some examples of give and take in Wilde's work include:

GOOD AMERICANS, WHEN THEY DIE, GO TO PARIS.

Wilde was so taken with this line that he used it twice: in his 1890 novel *The Picture of Dorian Gray,* and three years later in the play *A Woman of No Importance.* This thought had already appeared four decades earlier, in Oliver Wendell Holmes's 1853 *Autocrat of the Breakfast Table.* There it was attributed to "one of the wittiest of men" (now known to be his friend Thomas Gold Appleton). Wilde might have gotten it from that source, or during his 1882 visit to America where Holmes was one of his hosts.

GIVE ME THE LUXURIES, AND ANYONE CAN HAVE THE NECESSARIES.

Wilde was said to have used this line in conversation. In *The Autocrat of the Breakfast Table,* Holmes quoted "my friend, the Historian"

(John Lothrop Motley) as saying, "Give us the luxuries of life and we will dispense with the necessities." Holmes himself sometimes gets credit for this line, as does Frank Lloyd Wright.

PLEASE DO NOT SHOOT THE PIANIST. HE IS DOING HIS BEST.

Though he didn't claim them, these words are sometimes put in Wilde's mouth. They are also attributed to Mark Twain. In fact, as Wilde reported in "Impressions of America," this admonition was on a sign he saw in a Leadville, Colorado saloon.

I CAN RESIST EVERYTHING EXCEPT TEMPTATION.

That observation gained its broadest audience as a line in Wilde's play *Lady Windermere's Fan*. It has also been attributed to Mark Twain, Mae West, and W. C. Fields. Whether or not the words were original to Wilde, he was their primary disseminator.

EXPERIENCE . . . IS MERELY THE NAME MEN GIVE TO THEIR MISTAKES.

This line appears in both *The Picture of Dorian Gray* and *Lady Windermere's Fan*. According to Leo Rosten, credit for these words also has been given to Shaw, G. K. Chesterton, Sydney Smith, Samuel Butler, and Voltaire. Rosten himself thought this was an old Jewish folk saying. In a 1915 speech, surgeon J. Chalmers Da Costa said, "What we call experience is often a dreadful list of ghastly mistakes."

NOWADAYS PEOPLE KNOW THE PRICE OF EVERYTHING AND THE VALUE OF NOTHING.

This version appeared in *The Picture of Dorian Gray*. In *Lady Windermere's Fan*, a cynic is defined as "a man who knows the price of everything and the value of nothing." Several years later Elbert Hubbard took credit for "Too many people nowadays know the price of everything and the value of nothing."

IN THIS WORLD THERE ARE ONLY TWO TRAGEDIES. ONE IS NOT GETTING WHAT ONE WANTS, AND THE OTHER IS GETTING IT.

Among his many divisions of life into two, this line from *Lady Winder-mere's Fan* is Wilde's best known. In *Man and Superman* Shaw later wrote, "There are two tragedies in life. One is to lose your heart's desire. The other is to gain it." Elbert Hubbard then chimed in with "On man's journey through life he is confronted by two tragedies: One when he wants a thing he can not get; and the other when he gets a thing and finds he does not want it." In recent years Irving Kristol has promulgated Kristol's Law: "Being frustrated is disagreeable, but the real disasters in life begin when you get what you want." This version had another antecedent in Thomas Huxley's 1876 observation that "a man's worst difficulties begin when he is able to do as he likes." A corollary was subsequently offered by Logan Pearsall Smith: "There are two things to aim at in life; first to get what you want; and, after that, to enjoy it." Wilde had already noted in *An Ideal Husband:* "When the gods wish to punish us they answer our prayers."

WE HAVE REALLY EVERYTHING IN COMMON WITH AMERICA NOWA-DAYS, EXCEPT, OF COURSE, LANGUAGE

This was Wilde's articulation of a fairly widespread sentiment, in *The Canterville Ghost.* Similar thoughts have been attributed to Churchill, Shaw, and others.

George Bernard Shaw

Like Wilde, George Bernard Shaw was not shy about incorporating other people's words into his work. *Man and Superman,* for example, includes the line, "Very nice sort of place, Oxford, I should think, for people that like that sort of place." This brought to mind an earlier assessment of a book of poetry attributed to Abraham Lincoln: "For people who like that sort of thing, that is about the sort of thing they would like." A line from Jefferson Davis's 1861 inaugural as president of the Confederacy—"All we want is to be left alone"—was echoed in Shaw's 1904 play, *John Bull's Other Island:* "All we ask now is to be let alone." When such parallels were called to his attention, Shaw responded, "If I find in a book anything I can make use of, I take it gratefully. My plays are full of pillage of this kind."

At the same time, Shaw was so quotable that he got credit for far more quotations than were his due. He was among those credited with Horace Walpole's line, **"The world is a comedy to those that think, a tragedy to those that feel."** Though well known for his withering view of Americans ("I have defined the hundred percent American as a ninety-nine percent idiot"), Shaw strenuously denied saying "Oh, all Americans are blind, deaf, and dumb anyway," after being introduced to Helen Keller. "I tell you," Shaw said during the flap over this incident, "I have been misquoted everywhere, and the inaccuracies are chasing me round the world."

Disputed Shawisms include:

YOUTH IS A WONDERFUL THING. WHAT A CRIME TO WASTE IT ON CHILDREN.

Somebody said this, and it sounds like Shaw, so he usually gets credit for the quip. The earliest known attribution of this observation to Shaw was in a 1940 book called *10,000 Jokes, Toasts, & Stories.* According to this book Shaw bemoaned youth being wasted on children during a dinner conversation. *Reader's Digest* ran the line with no source in 1940. It has since become a standard part of the Irish playwright's lore. Shaw expert Dr. Stanley Weintraub thought this might be one of many observations which originated elsewhere, perhaps with Wilde, and ended up on Shaw's doorstep.

ENGLAND AND AMERICA ARE TWO COUNTRIES SEPARATED BY THE SAME LANGUAGE.

This is another Shawism which *Reader's Digest* ran without a source, in 1942. It subsequently showed up in quote collections, attributed to Shaw. The Library of Congress could not find this observation in any of Shaw's published work. Its genesis may be Wilde's earlier line, "We have really everything in common with America nowadays, except, of course, language."

BUT SUPPOSE THE CHILD INHERITED YOUR BRAINS AND MY BEAUTY?

Shaw's celebrated response to a beautiful woman who proposed that they produce a child with her looks and his intellect is generally said to have been made to dancer Isadora Duncan. Biographer Hesketh Pearson (who knew Shaw personally) reported that the exchange involved a Swiss woman who wrote him, "You have the greatest brain in the world, and I have the most beautiful body; so we ought to produce the most perfect child." According to Pearson, who gave no source, Shaw responded, "What if the child inherits my body and your brains?"

WHO ARE WE TWO AGAINST SO MANY?

Bennett Cerf said that this was Shaw's response to a heckler when he took the stage after a preview showing of the film of *Pygmalion*. "My friend," Cerf reported Shaw saying, "I quite agree with you, but what are we two against so many?" In Alexander Woollcott's version, the playwright's curtain speech after one of his plays opened was interrupted by a heckler who shouted, "Shut up, Shaw. Your play is rotten!" "You and I know that," Woollcott said Shaw replied, "but who are we among so many?" According to Hesketh Pearson the play was *Arms and the Man,* and Shaw responded to the "Boo!" of a boy in the audience with "I quite agree with you, my friend, but what can we two do against a whole houseful of the opposite opinion?" Who knows if any such exchange ever took place, and if so, where?

THE TROUBLE, MR. GOLDWYN, IS THAT YOU ARE ONLY INTERESTED IN ART AND I AM ONLY INTERESTED IN MONEY.

This was Shaw's legendary response to Samuel Goldwyn's interest in filming the playwright's work as the works of art they were meant to be. Shaw himself passed along a clipping describing the exchange to Bennett Cerf, who tagged it "apocryphal." This widely circulated story seems to have been one of many which originated with Goldwyn publicist Howard Dietz.

Shaw was a major flypaper figure. Even the hoary "Messages are for Western Union" has been put in his mouth. He also was a generous source of loans. The Kennedys set up a special account for *Back to*

Methuselah's "You see things; and you say 'Why?' But I dream things that never were; and I say, 'Why not?' " Malcolm Fraser, who was Australia's prime minister from 1975 to 1983, drew on the same play for his motto, "Life wasn't meant to be easy." (In *Back to Methuselah,* a Shaw character said, "Life was not meant to be easy, my child; but take courage: it can be delightful.") The playwright's oft-quoted "All professions are conspiracies against the laity" has been attributed to others, including economist Kenneth Boulding. Another Shawism which floats about in different forms and many mouths is "He who can, does. He who cannot, teaches."

Borrowed Titles

In 1937, Thomas Wolfe met Lincoln Steffens's widow, Ella Winter, at a dinner party. Wolfe told her about the strain of a recent visit to his hometown of Asheville, North Carolina. "But don't you know you can't go home again?" asked Winter. This question put Wolfe's own feelings into words. He eagerly asked Winter's permission to use it as a book title. She consented. Her offhand observation now lives on as the classic title of Wolfe's novel *You Can't Go Home Again.*

Borrowing book titles from other sources—the Bible, lines of poetry, sayings—has a long and honorable history. Nonetheless, it's interesting to see how often the authors of books with borrowed titles themselves get credit for those titles. For example:

• *Stranger in a Strange Land* will always be associated with Robert Heinlein's 1961 novel by that title. Its genesis is Exodus 2:22, "I have been a stranger in a strange land." Long before that, in 406 B.C., Sophocles used the term "stranger in a strange country." Around 270 B.C., "Stranger in a strange land" was among Theocritus's *Inscriptions.*

• Ernest Hemingway's *For Whom the Bell Tolls* originated, of course, in John Donne's "never send to know for whom the bell tolls; it tolls for thee."

• *Gone with the Wind* drew on Ernest Dowson's poem *Non Sum Qualis Eram Bonae Sub Regno Cynarae:* "I have forgot much, Cynara! gone with the wind . . ."

Such cases are fairly well known, and involved no implication by the author that their title was original. In other cases this isn't so clear. Tom

Wolfe's 1979 book *The Right Stuff* made those words an American catchphrase. Over a century before that, the term "right-colored stuff" was English slang for money. More to the point, the term "right sort of stuff" had been used to describe manly virtues for at least that long. Even more to the point, a 1908 novel by Ian Hay was called *The Right Stuff*.

The Best and the Brightest was not only the title of David Halberstam's examination of our descent into Vietnam, but became one of the most repeated catchphrases of modern times. Halberstam thought it was original to him. However, Episcopalians had long been singing a hymn called "The Brightest and the Best" when his book appeared in 1972. This hymn was written by Anglican Bishop Reginald Heber in 1819. In the mid-nineteenth century, Charles Dickens referred to a family in *Little Dorritt* as "the best and the brightest." Half a century later, Rudyard Kipling wrote in a 1903 poem: "So the best and the brightest leave us."

In 1947, columnist Walter Lippmann published a book called *The Cold War.* Many subsequently credited Lippmann with coining this term. However, financier Bernard Baruch had already used the phrase in a speech he gave earlier that year. Baruch did not coin it himself. Pulitzer Prize-winning editor and writer Herbert Bayard Swope included this phrase in a 1946 speech he drafted for Baruch. The financier thought "cold war" too strong a term for U.S.-Soviet relations at the time, but changed his mind the next year. When its paternity came into question in 1949, Baruch wrote Swope a letter confirming his original authorship. Lippmann thought he'd heard a French version, *"la guerre froide,"* in the 1930s. The term actually has an even longer history. According to Australian historian Joseph Siracusa, German Social Democrat Eduard Bernstein used the German words *"ein kalter Krieg"* in a 1893 newspaper article. Bernstein's translated words were: "This continued arming, compelling the others to keep up with Germany, is itself a kind of warfare. I do not know whether this expression has been used previously, but one could say it is a cold war." Political scientist Adda B. Bozeman has pointed out that in the thirteenth century, a Spanish writer named Don Juan Manuel used the Spanish term *"guerra fria"* to describe the tense coexistence of Christians and Moslems in his country.

Conservative economist Milton Friedman is more associated than anyone else with the saying **"There's no such thing as a free lunch."**

This is largely because he published a book by that title in 1975. But Friedman never claimed to have originated this saying. He had no idea who did. In 1991 the editor of *The Oxford Dictionary of Modern Quotations* happily announced that the mystery was solved: Robert Heinlein used the phrase "There ain't no such thing as a free lunch" in his 1966 novel *The Moon Is a Harsh Mistress*. This phrase was so central to that work of science fiction that it was abbreviated as "tanstaafl." But Robert Heinlein was far from the first person to conclude that free lunches had hidden costs. Burton Crane had already warned that there was no free lunch in his 1959 book *The Sophisticated Investor*. Ten years earlier, newspaper columnist Walter Morrow told readers the same thing. Undoubtedly this saying was circulating long before that. The observation that there's no free lunch is so obvious that it's hard to imagine it wasn't made soon after the first plate of hard-boiled eggs was set out for paying drinkers in a New Orleans saloon in 1838. Lexicographer Stuart Berg Flexner said the phrase "free lunch" became common in the 1840s as the institution itself worked its way to both coasts. In 1854, a San Francisco publication reported that "the excitement during the week on the subject of the 'free lunches' has been of the most intense character." In 1882, the *Chicago Times* observed that Oscar Wilde was following a "free-lunch route" across America. Thirteen years later, an essay in *The Philistine* proposed a "Free Lunch League."

According to economist Robert Hessen, the observation that free lunches aren't really free could be at least a century old. Conservative economists have relied on this observation for decades to get their point across. Because his book is so associated with the adage, Milton Friedman still gets credit for it, even among academic colleagues. This goes to show that despite its emphasis on scholarship, academia is no less likely than any other part of society to cherish its own misquotations.

12

Misquote U.

The classic definition of higher education is **"Mark Hopkins on one end of a log and a student on the other."** This definition is generally attributed to James Garfield. Garfield, the last President born in a log cabin, attended Williams College in the mid-1850s when Mark Hopkins was its president. He and Hopkins developed a close relationship. Years later, at an 1871 gathering of Williams alumni, Garfield (then an Ohio congressman) argued passionately against an ambitious building program for the college. Although no one recorded his remarks, in later years a number of those present recalled different versions of the future President's defense of humanistic education. This 1871 meeting is generally assumed to be the setting where Garfield observed that an ideal college consisted of Mark Hopkins, a student, and a log.

Nearly seven decades after the Williams alumni meeting, a quote detective named Carroll Wilson set out to investigate James Garfield's most quotable quote. Wilson's diligent sleuthing determined that (a) Garfield's words only became a common-place long after they were uttered; (b) it was the hook word *log* which captured our imagination and made this quote so memorable; but that (c) this word was grafted on to Garfield's purported remarks only after he'd died and couldn't correct the record.

Witnesses to Garfield's 1871 plea for teacher-based education varied widely in their memory of his actual words. Nobody recalled hearing about any log. According to one contemporary account, the Ohio congressman said "he would rather have Dr. Hopkins in a brick shanty than them all [physical appointments]." Another reported Garfield's words as, "Give me Mark, with a piece of birch-bark to write upon, and I'll defy all the colleges in the country." Yet a third recalled him saying that "other colleges might parade their varied departments, their long roll of professors, their piles of stately buildings, as evidences of superior educational advantages, but one year with grand old Mark Hopkins is worth them all."

These were the only contemporary reports Wilson could find. None had attracted much attention. After Garfield was assassinated in 1881, however, many reminiscences about the martyred President harked back to his impassioned plea to the Williams alumni ten years earlier. In the process Garfield's words took on a new luster. One eulogist now recalled that he'd said, "Give me a log cabin in the center of the state of Ohio, with one room in it and a bench with Mark Hopkins on one end of it and me on the other, and that would be a college good enough for me." An 1882 book about Garfield's views on education quoted his words as, "Give me a log hut, with only a simple bench, Mark Hopkins at one end and I at the other, and you may have all the buildings, apparatus and libraries without him." A subsequent speechmaker recalled that Garfield had said "he would rather be taught in a college where Mark Hopkins was teacher, though the buildings had nothing but pine slabs to cover them, than in the best endowed university of the country, under ordinary teaching." Another Williams alumnus thought Garfield's words were: "A pine bench with Mark Hopkins at one end of it and me at the other, is a good enough college for me!"

That was close to what Carroll Wilson finally concluded Garfield had actually said in 1871: "A log cabin (in the woods), with a pine bench in it with Mark Hopkins at one end and me at the other, is a good enough college for me." This was a perfectly good observation. But, concluded Wilson, "as a 'familiar quotation' . . . no success at all. The idea is all right, but the expression is too complicated." Before Garfield's comment could become a quote-book commonplace it needed a Boswell to help out with syntax and publicity.

This Boswell appeared in the form of John Ingalls. Though widely forgotten today, at the end of the nineteenth century Ingalls was one of America's best known orators. A former Senator from Kansas, he was a senior at Williams when Garfield was a freshman. The two had struck up a friendship. They remained friends until Garfield's death. After losing his race for the Senate in 1891, Ingalls spent the last decade of his life crisscrossing the country giving lectures. His ability as an orator was said to rival that of William Jennings Bryan. Ingalls's specialty was coining pithy, memorable phrases. One eulogizer called him "the greatest phrase-maker of his time." A collection of his lectures was published in 1902. One lecture was titled, "Garfield: the Man of the People." In it, Ingalls said of the late President, "He always felt and manifested a peculiar interest in his alma mater and in President Hopkins, whom he regarded as the greatest and wisest instructor of the century. 'A pine log,' he said, 'with the student at one end and Doctor Hopkins at the other, would be a liberal education.' "

Though not there to enjoy it, Garfield had his log at last. We can't prove that Ingalls supplied it. But, as Carroll Wilson pointed out, this form of Garfield's now-familiar quotation was unknown in 1891 when John Ingalls took to the lecture circuit. By the time he died in 1900, after becoming one our most famous platform personalities, it had become one of our most familiar quotations. Since Ingalls was a friend of Garfield's and a Williams man to boot, there was no doubt in Carroll Wilson's mind that he'd found the source of Garfield's quote at last.

Colleges and universities are as likely to harbor misquotes as any other segment of society. Each department, every discipline, has hallowed phrases which were never said, have been drastically altered, or have been misattributed for years.

Psychology

SOMETIMES A CIGAR IS JUST A CIGAR.

This line is beloved by showboat psychology professors who imitate Groucho Marx while telling students that Freud said that sometimes a cigar is just a cigar. These are words we desperately want Freud to have said (smokers especially). But no one has any evidence that he did. Peter Gay's 1988 biography of Freud—which discusses his love of cigars at length—mentions no such comment. Nor does Elisabeth Young-Bruehl's 1988 biography of his daughter Anna, to whom psychiatry's patron saint is supposed to have made the remark. Where did it originate? Psychology professor Alan Elms of the University of California at Davis has spent years trying to find out. "I've tried quite a variety of avenues," reported Elms, "talked to a number of Freud scholars. None panned out." Elms speculated that this comment may have begun with a comedian who was spoofing the psychiatrist, and eventually ended up in Freud's mouth.

LOVE AND WORK

These two words—about life's proper goals—are among Freud's most quoted. This could be because they're the perfect rationale for a post-modern Protestant ethic. Evidence that Freud said them is hazy at best. His alleged observation was publicized by Erik Erikson's 1963 book *Childhood and Society.* After referring to "Freud's shortest saying," Erikson wrote: "Freud was once asked what he thought a normal person should be able to do well. The questioner probably expected a complicated answer. But Freud, in the curt way of his old days, is reported to have said: '*Lieben und arbeiten*' (to love and to work)."

Erikson was scrupulous enough to say that Freud was "reported to have said" this. But he gave no source. In his 1960 collection *The Great Quotes,* George Seldes included this excerpt from Theodor Reik's 1957 book *Love and Lust:* "Work and love—these are the basics. Without them there is neurosis." Many subsequent quote collections attributed these words to Reik. The closest passage I could find in Reik's book is: "There are only two roads that lead to something like human happiness. They are marked by the words: love and achievement." This was also the best that the Library of Congress could come up with. Freud was not mentioned as the source of this observation by Reik.

Even if Freud (or Reik) did conclude that love and work were life's aim, this thought was hardly original. In an 1856 letter, Tolstoy wrote, "One can live magnificently in this world, if one knows how to work and how to love."

Natural Sciences

BUT STILL IT DOES MOVE.

Galileo's suggestion that the earth moved around the sun, not vice versa, was considered heretical by reactionary clerics. To make this point they threatened to torture the astronomer until he recanted. In 1633 Galileo did recant, admitting to his inquisitors that earth was the stationary center of the universe. He is famous for then whispering, *"Eppur si muove."* ("But still it does move.") This intellectual equivalent of a child's crossed fingers has long been an important symbol to scientists that despots might abuse their bodies but could never claim their minds. Galileo's disclaimer first appeared in print more than a century after his 1642 death. "The moment he was set at liberty," reported an Italian history book in 1757, "he looked up to the sky and down to the ground, and, stamping with his foot, in a contemplative mood, said, *Eppur si muove;* that is, *still it moves,* meaning the earth." As a comment murmured before his inquisitors, this remark gained widest circulation in a French book published in 1761. It was then repeated so often that it became a routine part of Galileo's lore. No serious student of the astronomer's life thinks he was reckless enough to actually whisper *"Eppur si muove,"* or anything like it with thumb screws and body racks hovering in the background.

IF I HAVE SEEN FARTHER, IT IS BY STANDING ON THE SHOULDERS OF GIANTS.

Isaac Newton is generally credited with coining this aphorism in 1675. Nearly three centuries later, sociologist Robert Merton devoted an entire book to questioning this attribution. Merton discovered that in various forms, the saying about dwarves seeing farther from the shoulders of giants had been around for centuries before Newton repeated it in a letter to Robert Hooke. The portrayal of dwarfs on shoulders was common in medieval religious art, including some stained-glass windows of the cathedral at Chartres. Early in the twelfth century (ca. 1126), Bernard of Chartres was quoted as saying that "in comparison with the ancients, we stand like dwarfs on the shoulders of giants." This was the earliest record of the saying that Merton found. Variations on this theme appeared frequently after that, in a wide range of cultures. (It was central to the debate about whether moderns knew more than ancients, or were merely dwarfs astride these giants' shoulders.) Robert Burton gave the phrase a boost in 1624 when he repeated it in *Anatomy of Melancholy,* citing his contemporary, Didacus Stella. In 1891, John Bartlett misattributed Burton's version of this saying to the Roman poet *Lucan* (A.D. 39–65), rather than *Luke,* whom Didacus Stella gave as his source. This error continued through *Bartlett's* fifteenth edition in 1980, fifteen years after Merton's book was published. Merton called their mistake "an unfruitful error concocted out of a lazy citation."

For all of that, to this day the saying about dwarfs seeing farther astride giants is routinely misattributed to Isaac Newton. How did Newton get credit for a phrase which was at least five centuries old when he repeated it? Merton has concluded that this is just one more case of our putting an already familiar quotation in the most famous plausible mouth. In Merton's words, the aphorism "became Newton's own, not because he deliberately made it so but because admirers of Newton made it so."

SURVIVAL OF THE FITTEST

These words usually come to mind in conjunction with the name Charles Darwin. In fact it was Herbert Spencer who condensed Darwin's theory of evolution into this pithy phrase. Spencer did so in his book *Principles of Biology.* Darwin endorsed and even admired this restatement of his theory, writing in *The Origin of Species,* "The expression often used by Mr. Herbert Spencer of the Survival of the Fittest is more accurate, and is sometimes equally convenient."

THERE IS NO HITCHING POST IN THE UNIVERSE.

Albert Einstein once noted in a letter to George Seldes, "Many things which go under my name are badly translated from the German or are invented by other people." The physicist said this to explain his suggested deletion from Seldes's quotation collection of, among other things, his famous observation that "there is no hitching post in the universe." This was said to have been Einstein's response to a reporter's request for a one-line definition of his theory of relativity. Einstein didn't delete "God does not play dice," the bumper-stickered version of his 1926 observation: "I, at any rate, am convinced that *He* is not playing at dice."

IF ONLY I HAD KNOWN, I SHOULD HAVE BECOME A WATCHMAKER.

Since his death in 1955, Albert Einstein has often been quoted as saying words to this effect. ("Plumber" is sometimes substituted for "watchmaker.") Whatever the wording, the implication is that Einstein regretted a career which led him to help invent the atomic bomb. He said no such thing. The genesis of this remark is in a 1954 letter in which Einstein used similar words to make a very different point. Einstein's letter, in response to a series of articles in *The Reporter* on the status of scientists in America, included these lines: "If I would be a young man again and had to decide how to make my living, I would not try to become a scientist or scholar or teacher. I would rather choose to be a plumber or a peddler in the hope to find that modest degree of independence still available under present circumstances."

Political Science

VOTE EARLY AND VOTE OFTEN.

This credo of crooked politicians gets passed around. Boston Mayor James Michael Curley was said to have been guided by such a principle in the early part of this century. Some reference books quote Representative William Porcher Miles as reporting in an 1858 speech that the slogan was "openly displayed on the election banners in one of our northern cities." Others say it originated with Martin Van Buren's son John, a prominent New York lawyer in the mid-nineteenth century. Later that century Josh Billings wrote, " 'Vote early and vote often,' is the politishun's golden rule. Du unto others az yu would be dun by." Trying to pin this catchphrase on anyone in particular is probably a futile exercise.

NOBODY EVER WENT BROKE UNDERESTIMATING THE INTELLIGENCE
OF THE AMERICAN PUBLIC.

Beloved by elitists of all political hues, H. L. Mencken's most familiar
quotation takes various forms. "Taste" and "idiocy" are sometimes
substituted for "intelligence," depending on what point the quoter is
trying to make. The reason Mencken's citers have such wide latitude on
this quotation is that it does not appear in his published works. *Bartlett's* calls the remark "attributed." According to George Seldes,
Mencken's actual words—made in reference to the success of *Reader's
Digest*—were, "There's no underestimating the intelligence of the
American public." Mencken's associate Charles Angoff wrote Seldes
that he'd heard Mencken make such an observation many times. But the
closest Mencken comment on the record did not even mention Americans. In a 1926 column he wrote, "No one in this world, so far as I
know—and I have searched the records for years, and employed agents
to help me—has ever lost money underestimating the intelligence of the
great masses of the plain people."

IF FASCISM COMES TO AMERICA IT WILL BE ON A PROGRAM OF
AMERICANISM.

This observation is attributed to Huey Long, the Louisiana populist
active on the national scene in the 1930s. Writer Robert Cantwell reported that Long said this during a conversation with him. His comment
was widely repeated, and to this day is Long's best-remembered quotation. Cantwell later told historian Arthur Schlesinger, Jr., that these
weren't Long's actual words. He didn't say what Long's actual words
were.

Fine Arts

LESS IS MORE.

Although it is generally attributed to architect Ludwig Mies van der
Rohe, this phrase appeared long before his birth in Robert Browning's
1855 poem "Andrea del Sarto":

> *Well, less is more, Lucrezia; I am judged.*

A German mentor of Mies was said to have used "less is more" as his own motto. But the words suit Mies so well that we've left them in his mouth. "He knew he was associated with that phrase," said biographer Franz Schulze, who interviewed many of Mies's associates, "but I've never heard anyone acknowledge that they heard him say 'less is more,' or 'God is in the details.' "

GOD IS IN THE DETAILS.

According to Schulze, Mies's other famous maxim may have originated in a line by Flaubert: *"Le bon Dieu est dans le détail"* ("The good God is in the details"). Since the architect—a stonemason's son—was so obsessed with his buildings' components, this phrase suited him to a T-square. "It's quite possible that he said it to someone," speculated Schulze, "or it's quite possible that a journalist attributed this to him because it sounded like something he might have said." Another Mies biographer, David Spaeth, thought Michaelangelo might have written something about details being Godlike. But even if Mies didn't originate this saying, said Spaeth, "It's so appropriate to him that if he didn't say it, he should have."

WHEN I HEAR THE WORD CULTURE, I REACH FOR MY GUN.

This line is commonly attributed to Hitler's henchman Hermann Göring. It actually originated in *Schlageter,* a 1933 play by Nazi poet Hanns Johst. Two translations of the line in question are, "Whenever I hear the word culture . . . I release the safety-catch of my Browning [pistol]" and "When I hear the word culture, I uncock my revolver's safety catch."

Creative Writing

TYPING RATHER THAN WRITING

In 1991 I heard a literature professor dismiss romance novelists as hacks engaged in "typing rather than writing." That sounded like a smart rap of their unoriginal knuckles. Truman Capote said the same thing about Jack Kerouac in the late 1950s.

EASY WRITING MAKES HARD READING.

This observation has been attributed to Ernest Hemingway. It has many antecedents. Among them are:

WHAT IS WRITTEN WITHOUT EFFORT IS IN GENERAL READ
WITHOUT PLEASURE.

> Samuel Johnson, 1776

YOU WRITE WITH EASE TO SHOW YOUR BREEDING.
BUT EASY WRITING'S CURST HARD READING.

> Richard Sheridan, 1816

READ OVER YOUR COMPOSITIONS, AND WHEREVER YOU MEET WITH
A PASSAGE WHICH YOU THINK IS PARTICULARLY FINE, STRIKE IT OUT.

This admonition is routinely ascribed to Samuel Johnson. But what Johnson clearly said to Boswell (about a wordy historian named William Robertson) was, "I would say to Robertson what an old tutor of a college said to one of his pupils: 'Read over your compositions, and wherever you meet with a passage which you think is particularly fine, strike it out.' " In *Pudd'nhead Wilson,* Twain echoed this tutor's advice when he wrote, "As to the adjective: when in doubt, strike it out."

WRITING IS EASY. YOU JUST SIT DOWN AT THE TYPEWRITER, OPEN UP
A VEIN, AND BLEED IT OUT DROP BY DROP.

Sportswriter Red Smith was frequently quoted to this effect. (Other versions include "There's nothing to writing. All you do is sit down at a typewriter and open a vein"; "Writing is easy. I just open a vein and bleed"; and "Writing a column is easy. You just sit down at your typewriter until little drops of blood appear on your forehead.") Red Smith was a fine, exacting writer. No doubt he made such an observation. But Smith may not have been the first to do so. Gene Fowler, who died in 1960, is supposed to have said, "Writing is easy: all you do is sit staring at a blank sheet of paper until the drops of blood form on your forehead." Thomas Wolfe has been quoted as saying: "Writing is easy. Just put a sheet of paper in the typewriter and start bleeding." Whoever said it first, the comment has a distinguished ancestor in Sydney Smith's observation in the late 1830s that a colleague wrote "drop by drop."

Economics

BAD MONEY DRIVES OUT GOOD.

"Gresham's Law" was not authored by sixteenth century English financier Sir Thomas Gresham. It originated with Scottish economist Henry Dunning MacLeod in 1857. "MacLeod was endowed with a marvelous ability for reading into a text what is not there," noted Raymond de Roover in a monograph on Gresham. "Nowhere does Gresham state either explicitly or implicitly that bad money drives out the good." Copernicus and others had already noted that when too much base money was in circulation, good coins tended to be hoarded, sent abroad, or melted down. Generalizing from this specific point to the broader observation that bad money drives out good was MacLeod's doing, not Gresham's. Gresham's only contribution to that "law" was the prestige of his name, posthumously loaned.

IF YOU HAVE TO ASK HOW MUCH THEY COST, YOU CAN'T AFFORD THEM.

This is what J. Pierpont Morgan allegedly said when asked the price of yachts. Reports of Morgan's famous comment tend to be of the "someone said he said it" variety. Similar observations have been attributed to other wealthy men. Billionaire J. Paul Getty was credited with various versions of a corollary: "If you know how much you are worth, you are not worth much." One of the silver-hoarding Hunts of Texas was also quoted as saying, "People who know how much they're worth usually aren't worth that much."

UNDER CAPITALISM MAN EXPLOITS MAN. UNDER COMMUNISM IT IS JUST THE REVERSE.

Just after his fall from power, former Soviet leader Mikhail Gorbachev was credited with making this observation. By then it had been around for at least a couple of decades. Some quote collections attribute the comment to "Anonymous." Economist John Kenneth Galbraith has also been cited as its source.

Marxist Studies

KARL MARX

RELIGION . . . IS THE OPIUM OF THE PEOPLE.

Although generally attributed to Marx—from the introduction to his *Critique of the Hegelian Philosophy of Right* (1844)—this thought was not original to him. According to historian Gertrude Himmelfarb such an observation was common among young Hegelians before Marx put it in print. Marx was the first to publish this phrase, however, and he usually gets author's credit.

WORKERS OF THE WORLD, UNITE! YOU HAVE NOTHING TO LOSE BUT YOUR CHAINS.

This famous call to revolution is a rewrite of what Marx and Engels wrote in *The Communist Manifesto:* "The proletarians have nothing to lose but their chains. They have a world to win. Working men of all countries, unite!"

VLADIMIR ILYICH LENIN

Hair-raising comments by the likes of Lenin were long a staple of anti-Communist propaganda. The fact that most were spurious and known to be spurious didn't stop their propagation. To note just a few:

THE CAPITALISTS ARE SO HUNGRY FOR PROFITS THAT THEY WILL SELL US THE ROPE WITH WHICH TO HANG THEM.

Shortly after Lenin's 1924 death, writer I. U. Annenkov copied some fragmentary notes by the Bolshevik leader which he found in a Moscow archive. Among them was, "They [capitalists] will furnish credits which will serve us for the support of the Communist Party in their countries and, by supplying us materials and technical equipment which we lack, will restore our military industry necessary for our future attacks against our suppliers. To put it in other words, they will work on the preparation of their own suicide." The more dramatic version with its hook words *rope* and *hanging* lasted longer. No proof has been found that Lenin said any such thing, and many have tried hard to find it. In his autobiography Barry Goldwater wrote of Stalin, "He also said something to this effect: 'When it comes time to hang the capitalists, they will sell us the rope.' "

THE BEST WAY TO DESTROY THE CAPITALIST SYSTEM IS TO DEBAUCH THE CURRENCY.

In a 1920 book, John Maynard Keynes wrote that Lenin "is said to have declared that the best way to destroy the Capitalist System is to debauch the currency." Ever since Keynes wrote that, Lenin's alleged remark has been put directly in his mouth by debunkers. Researchers at the Library of Congress have never been able to find this sentence in Lenin's writing.

PROMISES ARE LIKE PIE CRUST, MADE TO BE BROKEN.

Ronald Reagan was especially fond of citing this Leninism, which he thought he'd read somewhere. In a 1905 article for the magazine *Proletarii,* Lenin did write, "Promises are like pie crust, leaven to be broken," calling this "an English proverb." The point Lenin was trying to make was not that he believed this proverb, but that his Bolshevik rivals did. The "proverb" actually came from the pen of Jonathan Swift and appeared in his *Polite Conversation.* The fact that this had long been clear didn't prevent anti-Communists from quoting Swift's words as proof of Lenin's cynicism. After the *U.S. News & World Report* so quoted the Bolshevik leader in 1958, a spokeswoman for the magazine admitted in a letter to author Morris Kominsky that they knew Lenin was quoting Swift. But the magazine never publicly acknowledged its misattribution. Kominsky's efforts to correct the record among others who attributed Swift's words to Lenin—including Secretary of State John Foster Dulles—were no more successful.

THE UNITED STATES . . . WILL FALL INTO OUR HANDS LIKE A RIPE FRUIT.

Ronald Reagan was also fond of putting these words in Lenin's mouth. When Kominksy asked the Library of Congress about their authenticity, he got this response: "According to Mr. Pistrak of the United States Information Agency, an expert on Communist statements, it is extremely improbable that Lenin ever made the statement you quote. The Library of Congress, Mr. Pistrak, and others have searched fruitlessly for verification of this quotation. In addition, according to Mr. Pistrak, since Lenin was almost wholly uninterested in the United States (his interest lay in the hope of a Communist revolution in Europe), it is unlikely he would have made such a statement."

USEFUL IDIOTS OF THE WEST

Of Lenin's supposed depiction of non-Communist dupes, a Library of Congress staffer reported in 1987, "We get queries on *useful idiots of the West* all the time. We have not been able to identify this phrase among [Lenin's] published works."

Theology

- In I Timothy 6:10 "the love of money," not money itself, is called **"the root of all evil."**
- **"Pride goeth before** destruction," not **"a fall,"** is what we actually find in Proverbs 16:18.
- **"The lion shall lie down with the lamb,"** in Isaiah 11:6, is "The wolf also shall dwell with the lamb, and the leopard shall lie down with the kid; and the calf and the young lion and the fatling together; and a little child shall lead them.
- "Can the **leopard change his spots?"** is an abridgement of the original "Can the Ethiopian change his skin, or the leopard his spots?" from Jeremiah 13:23.
- **"Let us eat, drink and be merry, for tomorrow we die"** is a composite of these Biblical passages: "Let us eat and drink; for tomorrow we shall die," from Isaiah 22:13, and "take thine ease, eat, drink, and be merry," from Luke 12:19, and "A man hath no better thing under the sun, than to eat, and to drink, and to be merry," Ecclesiastes 8:15.

GOD HELPS THOSE WHO HELP THEMSELVES.

According to a survey published in 1991, fifty-six percent of Americans polled thought that the proverb "God helps those who helps themselves" comes from the Bible. It doesn't. Over five centuries before the birth of Christ, Aesop wrote, "The gods help them that help themselves." A monotheistic version was recorded by James Howell in 1659: "God helps him, who helps himself." In *Discourses on Government* (1698), Algernon Sidney wrote, "God helps those who help themselves." Poor Richard picked up the beat half a century later when he observed, "God helps them that help themselves."

CLEANLINESS IS NEXT TO GODLINESS.

This conviction is often assumed to be biblical. In fact it wended our way circuitously, via John Wesley. In a sermon published in 1791, the founder of Methodism advised that " 'Cleanliness is indeed, next to godliness.' " Since the phrase is in quotation marks, it's easy to assume that Wesley was quoting the Bible. He wasn't. The inspiration for this Protestant cornerstone came from the Talmud: "The doctrines of religion are resolved into carefulness; carefulness into vigorousness; vigorousness into guiltlessness; guiltlessness into abstemiousness; abstemiousness into cleanliness; cleanliness into godliness."

GOD, GIVE US THE SERENITY TO ACCEPT WHAT CANNOT BE CHANGED; GIVE US THE COURAGE TO CHANGE WHAT SHOULD BE CHANGED; GIVE US THE WISDOM TO DISTINGUISH ONE FROM THE OTHER.

In various forms "The Serenity Prayer" is most commonly associated with Alcoholics Anonymous. AA credits theologian Reinhold Niebuhr as the prayer's author. The theologian is said to have composed this prayer in 1934. When questions were raised about its originality, he responded, "It may have been spooking around for years, even centuries, but I don't think so. I honestly do believe that I wrote it myself." In a comment made soon before his 1971 death, Niebuhr seemed less certain: "Subconscious or even unconscious traces, of course, always play their part in all forms of art—in music as well as literature—and J. S. Bach, T. S. Eliot, Shakespeare (and Jesus, for that matter) often echoed material from the past." According to Mowbray of London, the publishing arm of the Anglican church, variations on the serenity prayer have been in common use for centuries.

GO PLACIDLY AMID THE NOISE AND THE HASTE, AND REMEMBER WHAT PEACE THERE MAY BE IN SILENCE. . . . (etc., etc.)

The admonition known as "Desiderata" became quite popular in the 1960s after it was supposedly discovered during reconstruction of Old St. Paul's Church, Baltimore. This advice was said to date from St. Paul's founding in 1692. It subsequently appeared on posters, in essays, and on greeting cards. Before his 1965 death, Adlai Stevenson was planning to use the exhortation on his Christmas cards, explaining that it was an ancient poem. In fact, "Desiderata" was written by Terre Haute lawyer Max Ehrmann in 1927. His widow renewed Ehrmann's copyright in 1954. Two years later, the rector of St. Paul's included the poem in some mimeographed material for his congregation. Someone then reprinted it, saying that "Desiderata" had been discovered at St. Paul's with the 1692 date on it. This myth fueled its enormous popularity (to say nothing of saving poster makers lots of royalty fees). In 1973 a federal court ruled that anyone reprinting "Desiderata" owed royalties to the current owner of its copyright.

Gender Studies

BURN YOUR BRA.

"Burn your bra" is often thought to have been a feminist slogan. It was anything but. This presumed rallying cry of the sixties grew out of a 1968 protest against the Miss America pageant. Demonstrators were invited to discard symbols of restriction, such as brassieres. None were burned. Some may have gone up in smoke on other occasions, especially when television cameras were present. But these would have been isolated incidents. In an era of widespread draft card and flag burning, however, it wasn't hard to imagine that blazing bras were lighting up the sky. That image remains an exciting one, however inaccurate.

SISTERHOOD IS POWERFUL.

This slogan is attributed to *Ms.* editor Robin Morgan in many quote collections. It was the title of a 1970 collection of feminist writing she edited. Morgan was forced to scuttle her original title—*The Hand That Cradles the Rock*—after discovering that S. J. Perelman had already used this as the title of a story. In her book's introduction, Morgan wrote that she now preferred *Sisterhood is Powerful,* but said nothing about its origins. The slogan was also the title of a March 15, 1970 magazine article by Susan Brownmiller. Brownmiller said she got it off a button. According to a history of feminism, "sisterhood is powerful" first appeared in a January 1968 pamphlet written by radical feminist Kathie Amatniek.

THE ONLY MAN IN MY CABINET

When Golda Meir was a member of David Ben-Gurion's cabinet during the 1950s and 1960s, Israel's Prime Minister reportedly called her "the only man in my cabinet." Some said Ben-Gurion's words were earthier, that he'd really said Meir was the only member of his cabinet with balls. Meir tried to debunk both versions. She found it ironic that Ben-Gurion's alleged remark should be considered a compliment. Meir wondered how a man would feel about being described as the only, or best, woman in a cabinet. The comment actually had a long pedigree. Late last century, Salvation Army founder William Booth reportedly said, "My best men are women." In 1959, Samuel Goldwyn called his wife "the best man I have." British politician Barbara Castle later referred to the Tories' Margaret Thatcher as "the best man among them."

CALL ME MADAM.

When Frances Perkins was appointed Secretary of Labor by Franklin Roosevelt in 1933—the first woman to join any President's cabinet—journalists were puzzled about how to address her. She suggested "Miss Perkins." When a reporter pointed out that they called male cabinet members "Mr. Secretary," she deferred to the Speaker of the

House. The Speaker suggested "Madam Secretary." Some press accounts reported that this suggestion came from Perkins herself. It quickly evolved into "Call me madam." In 1950 this became the title of Irving Berlin's successful Broadway musical. Eleanor Roosevelt herself perpetuated the misquote when she wrote in a 1954 book (coauthored with Lorena Hickock), "Some fool reporter wanted to know what to call [Perkins]. . . . 'Call me Madam,' she replied."

Sexuality

CLOSE YOUR EYES AND THINK OF ENGLAND.

This advice on how to endure sexual intercourse sounds so Victorian that it is often attributed to Queen Victoria herself. The suggestion's originator was more likely to have been a Lady Alice Hillingdon. In 1912, Lady Hillingdon reportedly wrote in her journal, "I am happy now that Charles [her husband] calls on my bedchamber less frequently than of old. As it is, I now endure but two calls a week, and when I hear his steps outside my door I lie down on my bed, close my eyes, open my legs and think of England."

LOVE IS TWO MINUTES . . . OF SQUISHING NOISES.

In the early 1980s, punk rocker Johnny Rotten was famous in certain circles for this depiction of lovemaking. Depending on the memory of the quoter (and perhaps his staying power), the length of love's duration varied widely. One quote collection thought love's squishing noises lasted for two minutes and fifty-two seconds. According to Nigel Rees, a graffiti writer in London said, "Love is three minutes of squelching noises." In the magazine *Private Eye,* Auberon Waugh stuck to the squelching version, but reduced its length to "two and a half minutes."

THAT WAS THE MOST FUN I'VE HAD WITHOUT LAUGHING.

Woody Allen said this about sex with Diane Keaton in *Annie Hall.* It has been requoted often since that movie appeared in 1977, and even became the title of a 1990 quotation book. Thirty-five years before

Allen's movie premiered, in the more inhibited World War II era, H. L. Mencken's book of quotations included: "Love is the most fun you can have without laughing." This was attributed to "Author Unidentified," typically a euphemism for Mencken himself.

These, then, are the best of history's false phrases, spurious sayings, and familiar misquotations. Obviously, there is no shortage of supply. Nor is there likely to be one. Our thirst for pertinent remarks that can be attributed to someone we've heard of is unquenchable. The unanswered question in all of this is, so what? In the broad scope of things, does it matter that we misquote so routinely?

13

Could You Look It Up?

Midway through Jimmy Carter's presidency, a newspaper column by Georgia state Senator Julian Bond reported this striking observation written by H. L. Mencken half a century earlier:

On those dark moments when I fear the Republic has trotted before these weary eyes every carnival act in its repertoire, I cheer myself with the thought that someday we will have a President from the deserts of the Deep South . . . The President's brother, a prime specimen of Boobus Collumnus Rubericus, will . . . gather his loutish companions on the porch of the White House to swill beer from the bottle and snigger over whispered barnyard jokes about the darkies. The President's cousin, LaVerne, will travel the Halleluyah circuit as one of Mrs. [Aimee Semple] McPherson's soldiers in Christ, praying for the conversion of some Northern Sodom's most satanic pornographer as she waves his works—well thumbed—for all the yokels to gasp at . . . The President's daughter will record these events with her box camera . . . The incumbent himself, cleaned of his bumpkin ways

by some of Grady's New South Hucksters, will have charm compara-
ble to that of the leading undertaker of Dothan, Alabama.

When *Los Angeles Times* reporter Jeff Prugh asked about his source
for this bit of Menckeniana, Bond replied that he'd copied it from a
publication he could no longer recall. A check with various Mencken
experts—including one who spent more than a week poring over his
writings (from the late 1920s especially)—produced no results. Alistair
Cooke pointed out to Prugh that the word *pornographer* was not common in the twenties. Bond then found his source: a column in a Cleveland newspaper which included the passage in question, saying it came
from an essay in *The Nation* by Calvin Trillin. Trillin told Prugh that
the resuscitated piece of Menckeniana had been "making the rounds of
Washington egghead circles lately." Pressed for his source, Trillin
would only say that it had come to him typewritten on a letter-sized
sheet. Revealing who had given him this sheet would be "endangering
my source," said Trillin. There the trail ended. Bond concluded that
he'd been an unwitting participant in a hoax. His parting thought was,
"Of course I was never taken in, I tell myself now, but if Mencken didn't
write it, he should have."

An implicit question throughout this book has been: Do we really
want to know when we misquote? It's not always clear that we do. I'm
reminded of this every time I happen upon a pithy remark that perfectly
illustrates some point I want to make, then must decide how much effort
it's worth to verify the remark. Any consumer of quotations routinely
faces this dilemma. At the Mark Twain Project, Robert Hirst is regularly asked whether a quote is Twain's, by those who aren't sure they
want to know. "People are looking for confirmation of their line,"
explained Hirst. "They have a mixed interest in finding the answer. If
it's 'yes,' they're delighted. If it's 'no,' they may say it's 'attributed'
anyway."

Ambivalence about verifying quotations is common among politicians, entertainers, wits, journalists, authors, academics, public speakers, and anyone else who trades in other people's words. This is understandable. Attempting to confirm the accuracy of a pertinent comment
is risky. Should a great quotation prove to be apocryphal, or misattributed, we may have to stop using it. In many cases, we prefer blissful

ignorance. Even quotations known to be apocryphal—Hitler on disorderly youth, George Smathers on Claude Pepper, the many made-up Leninisms—live on long after they've been debunked. Even though Alva Johnston pointed out in 1937 that Sam Goldwyn's alleged reaction to sundials—"What won't they think of next?"—was an old gag, this popular Goldwynism continues to be repeated as authentic. As early as 1944, H. Allen Smith noted in a book that Leo Rosten, not W. C. Fields, put the "dogs and children" line into play. Many others subsequently confirmed this fact in print. We continue to credit those words to Fields anyway. They just *sound* so much like him.

A good misquote never dies. We don't necessarily want it to. "There is a fine old crusted tradition of misquoting not lightly to be broken," wrote Bernard Darwin in his introduction to *The Oxford Dictionary of Quotations,* "and it might seem almost pedantry to deck these ancient friends in their true but unfamiliar colors."

Does it matter? Who cares who said something first, as long as it gets said? Isn't an improvement on vintage quotation preferable to the original itself?

As we've seen, misquotes often do improve on real ones. Dan Buck, Pat Schroeder's assistant, once jotted in his notebook a comment he recalled Ted Williams making about his casual attire: "When you bat .400, you don't have to wear a necktie." Some time later Buck discovered that Williams's actual words were, "You don't have to wear a necktie if you can hit." I like Buck's version better.

In such cases, the misquoter does us a favor and perhaps deserves at least as much credit as the quoted. Consider how the same point was made by two historians separated by nearly a century:

Bear-baiting was esteemed heathenish and unchristian; the sport of it, not the inhumanity gave offense.	The Puritan hated bear-baiting, not because it gave pain to the bear, but because it gave pleasure to the spectators.
David Hume *The History of* *Great Britain,* 1754	T. B. Macaulay *History of* *England,* 1848

Macaulay undoubtedly borrowed this idea from Hume. But he expressed it so much better that his is by far the more familiar version. It should be.

To open Chapter 11, I cited T. S. Eliot's often-quoted (and misquoted) observation that "Immature poets imitate. Mature poets steal." This glib-sounding remark was part of a longer, more thoughtful discussion of literary debts. As Eliot pointed out, it is not the taking of a loan from someone else's work that should concern us, but the manner in which this transaction is negotiated. "One of the surest of tests is the way in which a poet borrows," he wrote. "Bad poets deface what they take, and good poets make it into something better, or at least something different. The good poet welds his theft into a whole of feeling which is unique, utterly different from that from which it was torn; the bad poet throws it into something which has no cohesion."

If borrowed material does improve on the original, and if art is served in the process, aside from the thrill of the chase why should we concern ourselves at all with misquotation?

Consider this: In a facetious 1962 *Esquire* feature on tips for college students, Robert Benton and Gloria Steinem attributed "Immature artists imitate. Mature artists steal" to literary critic Lionel Trilling. Since then, T. S. Eliot's comment has been credited to Trilling in at least five reputable quote collections (including *The Oxford Dictionary of Modern Quotations*). The joke was not only on Trilling but on anyone else who took this attribution seriously. One reason for concerning ourselves with misquotation is to avoid accepting counterfeit currency as if it were legitimate.

Gag or no gag, original authors deserve credit for their own words. This is especially true when pilfered material is not improved but vandalized, or when lip-synced comments are passed off as original. Without the vigilance of a William Safire, Nigel Rees, or Justin Kaplan, the Elbert Hubbards of this world will always try to pose as its Ralph Waldo Emersons. For the sake of an accurate record, if nothing else, it's important to collect the best information available about who actually said what. Librarians are continually asked to find the correct wording and attribution of vaguely remembered quotations. Many prove to be apocryphal. According to Charles Anderson of the Evanston (Illinois) Public Library, "the Spurious Quote question probably plagues reference librarians more than any other type." Isn't it better for them to have accurate information with which to answer such questions?

The tools available for verifying familiar phrases, sayings, and quotations are far less dependable than they ought to be. Quotation collections routinely combine garbled words and mistaken attributions with authentic material. Many do so without citing sources. But even cited sources are no guarantee of accuracy. Anyone who tries to trace quotations back to their origins is struck by how elusive such citations can be. Dates are often wrong, as are contexts, sources, volume numbers, and page numbers. Such confusion is so common—even in reliable works of reference—that after a time it isn't even surprising. Miscitation almost feels like the norm.

In one striking case, a number of books report that "I disapprove of what you say, but will defend to the death your right to say it," is based on a sentence in Voltaire's February 6, 1770 letter to a M. le Riche. Voltaire did write a letter to François Louis Henri Leriche on February 6, 1770. This letter does include a familiar quotation. But that quotation is: **"God always favors the heaviest battalions."** Voltaire's letter includes nothing like, "I detest what you write," etc. (Two familiar quotations in one short letter would be remarkable.) He wrote to nobody else that day. How did this mistake occur? The guilty party seems to be one Norbert Guterman, a translator and essayist. Guterman's 1963 book of French quotations mistakenly reported that Voltaire's February 6, 1770 letter to Leriche included this sentence: "I detest what you write, but I would give my life to make it possible for you to continue to write." It didn't. Guterman died in 1984, so we may never know where this sentence actually came from.

This is the Achilles heel of quotation collections: An initial error in one will be repeated so often by others that over time it gains authority through repetition alone. The need to untangle such webs of inaccuracy makes misquotation correction a worthwhile enterprise.

In the process one can sometimes expose misquotations which distort the historical record and malign individuals. For example, in a 1963 biography of Barry Goldwater, Stephen Shadegg reported that John Kennedy said at his inauguration: **"Ask not what your government can do for you, ask what you can do for your government."** This subtle but significant rewording of "ask not what your *country* can do" altered the position of a Democratic President to better suit a conservative bias. Shadegg's misquotation of Kennedy didn't catch on, but other such misquotations have: Robert Walpole's "Every man has his price," Herbert Hoover's "Prosperity is just around the corner," and Charles Colson's "I'd walk over my own grandmother to get Richard Nixon elected."

In some cases misquotes don't just discredit individuals but entire professions. When he was chief justice of the Supreme Court, Warren Burger noted in a libel decision, "Consideration of these issues inevitably recalls the aphorism of journalism attributed to the late Roy Howard that **'too much checking on the facts has ruined many a good news story.'** " Staff members of Indiana University's Roy Howard Memorial Center could find no evidence that the late editor-in-chief of the Scripps-Howard newspaper chain ever made such a comment. They let Burger know. In Burger's revised opinion, this saying was cited as an unattributed aphorism. The public deserved better fact checking from its chief justice.

Checking facts doesn't just prove that many presumed quotes are actually misquotes. Sometimes sayings thought to be spurious prove to be authentic. For example:

- Some quote mavens have concluded that Lincoln's comment **"The Lord prefers common-looking people. That is the reason he makes so many of them"** is apocryphal. Such collectors usually suggest that this observation originated without evidence in a 1928 book on U.S. Presidents. Twenty years earlier, however, in 1908, that comment appeared in John Hay's published diary. Hay, Lincoln's private secretary, wrote on December 23, 1863: "The President to-night has a dream:—He was in a party of plain people, and, as it became known who he was, they began to comment on his appearance. One of them said:—'He is a very common-looking man.' The President replied:—'The Lord prefers common-looking people. That is the reason he makes so many of them.' " While not conclusive, Hay's diary entry suggests that this is a genuine Lincoln saying, not a spurious one.

- For years it was taken for granted that Mark Twain said, **"Everybody talks about the weather but nobody does anything about it."** This became one of his most repeated lines. But a new generation of quote sleuths traced the remark to an 1897 editorial in the *Hartford Courant*. That editorial was unsigned, its contents unattributed. The

Courant's staff at the time included Charles Dudley Warner, Twain's friend and collaborator. In recent years Warner has been given credit for this observation about the weather. According to misinformation collector Tom Burnam, Twain himself attributed the remark to Warner. *Courant* editor Charles Hopkins Clark did too. But a closer reading of the editorial in question reveals that its actual wording was: *"A well known American writer* said once that, while everybody talked about the weather, nobody seemed to do anything about it (emphasis added)." In a 1923 memoir, journalist Robert Underwood Johnson—who knew Twain—wrote, "Nor have I ever seen in print Mark's saying about the weather, 'We all grumble about the weather, but' (dramatic pause) '—but—but nothing is *done* about it.' " Conclusion: Until better evidence comes along, let's give this one back to Twain.

• **"Nuts!"** General Anthony McAuliffe's 1944 response to a German request for surrender during the Battle of the Bulge is often assumed to be a misquote. It certainly sounds like one. As military oaths go, the exclamation is a little limp. It's certainly less profane than one might imagine. Although some contend that this was not McAuliffe's original message, no one has proven otherwise. David Maxey, a former editor at *Look* magazine, told me that during an extended interview with General McAuliffe, the former military commander never wavered in his contention that this was exactly what he said. Since McAuliffe never swore during their "long, liquid lunch," Maxey concluded that he was probably telling the truth. "He was not a salty fella," said Maxey. "It sounds accurate."

The need to give credit where due makes quote verification more than mere nitpicking. In *The Art of Time,* Jean-Louis Servan-Schreiber cited this excerpt from a book by French intellectual Jacques Attali: **"In the modern industrial age the key machine is not the steam engine, but the timepiece."** In 1934—ten years before Attali was born—Lewis Mumford wrote, "The Clock, not the steam-engine, is the key-machine of the modern industrial age." As this example suggests, ethical questions are raised by some forms of misquotation. Plagiarism, an extreme form, is theft. Anyone who deliberately puts his own name to someone eles's writing has stolen that person's property. Worse, the plagiarist has subjected the plagiarized to involuntary servitude, pressed him into service as an unpaid, unacknowledged ghostwriter. He has also deceived the public into thinking he's done work, had thoughts, and written words that weren't his. This is wrong.

But how about everyday borrowing? When she hears a good line, one friend of mine tells her husband, "I wish I'd said that. And I will!" My friend speaks for many. Lip-syncing other people's quips as if we'd made them up ourselves is a national pastime. Is it wrong to borrow a phrase here and a sentence there? I guess so. But it's a meager sort of sin, and pretty universal. Misquotation is the parking ticket of intellectual crimes. Those who make their living by trading in words tend to be philosophical about the give and take of public discourse. Just as they steal, so are they stolen from. Many see themselves as part of a revolving fund to which they both deposit and withdraw. "The most original writers borrowed from one another," Voltaire reportedly said. "The instruction we find in books is like fire. We fetch it from our neighbor's, kindle it at home, communicate it to others, and it becomes the property of all."

Some forms of misquotation exist on a hazier ethical plane than others. When noted figures are credited with quips they didn't coin, we can hardly call them to task for not taking the initiative to point this out. Some do anyway. When *People* quoted Garry Trudeau as saying that he was trying to perfect a life-style that didn't require his presence, the cartoonist wrote them to point out that this line originated with comedian George Carlin.

Those who get credit for their own remarks but with garbled wording resign themselves to the thought that being misquoted is better than not being quoted at all. Only comments worth repeating are worth misrepeating. In a sense the ultimate flattery is to be quoted so often that your words are routinely mangled. "An author should be delighted, not annoyed, when he hears himself persistently misquoted," wrote Hesketh Pearson. "He could receive no higher compliment. It proves that the world has frequent and urgent need of his thoughts and will rather change the manner in which he expresses them than do without the things expressed."

Unlike the casual misquotation which is unavoidable in conversation, however, an indifference to their audience is implied by writers and lecturers who disseminate verbal apocrypha that could easily have been looked up.

In 1992, Lester Thurow, the Dean of MIT's Sloan School of Management and a Harvard Ph.D., spoke to the National Press Club. "Remember the economic advice of Benjamin Franklin in *Poor Richard's Almanac, 1755?*" Thurow asked his listeners. " 'Build a better mousetrap and the world will beat a path to your door.' " *Time*'s drama critic had earlier attributed the lines **"Play up! Play up! and play the game!"** to their obvious author. "Only one man could have written those bully lines," he wrote, "Rudyard Kipling." Any number of readers—who'd had these lines drilled into them in school—wrote *Time* to point out that Sir Henry Newbolt actually composed those bully lines. A writer in *TV Guide* later reported, "A critic once wrote of a one-legged tap dancer: **'The miracle is not that he does it well, but that he does it at all.'** " If this was so, that critic borrowed liberally from Samuel Johnson's classic observation about clergywomen: "Sir, a woman's preaching is like a dog's walking on his hinder legs. It's not done well; but you are surprised to find it done at all." *TV Guide*'s writer could have looked it up. So could the Middle East expert who suggested in a *New York Times* essay that Johnson's observation had something to do with a dog playing a fiddle.

Such gaffes reduce the credibility of a writer or speaker. Nonetheless, those who do make an effort to attribute material—however botched the wording and inaccurate the attribution—at least have taken a shot. Others merely requisition dimly remembered quotations. As Clifton Fadiman has pointed out, "We prefer to believe that the absence of inverted commas guarantees the originality of a thought, whereas it may be merely that the utterer has forgotten its source."

In some cases, "forgotten" is a charitable way to describe a lip-syncer's claim to unattributed remarks. When former Yankee pitcher Jim Bouton said of Howard Cosell, "He's the guy who changed his name, wears a toupee and then tells it like it is," he neglected to credit that line to columnist Jimmy Cannon. And when Richard Burton called Elizabeth Taylor **"a secret wrapped in an enigma inside a mystery,"** he didn't mention that Churchill had already called Russia "a riddle wrapped in a mystery inside an enigma."

To make sure that credit is given where due, and because of our need for a reliable historical record, it's important to keep track of who said what as best we can. Jay Leno makes a point of jotting down quotations on index cards so they can be verified before he uses them in his *Tonight Show* monologue. This is admirable. But Leno has a staff for that sort of thing. The rest of us don't. Therefore, unavoidably, we misquote. Everyone does. Given a choice between using the best version we can remember of a good quotation during conversation or skipping it altogether, we'd be silly not to use the quote. Conversation would be far poorer if no one dared to misquote. Short of carrying *Bartlett's* around like a Walkman, misquotation is unavoidable. (As we've seen, even having *Bartlett's* at hand is no guarantee of accuracy.) We have always misquoted and always will.

This is not due to faulty memory alone. Misquotations meet our need to have certain observations made at certain times: to clarify an unclear episode, verbalize a widespread feeling, or stir a populace. In an article on misquotation, book dealer Morris Rosenblum observed that "invariably, the inventors of memorable statements have been inspired by a dramatic feeling that an epic situation demands an epic phrase." In other words, it takes two to misquote: one to peddle a spurious saying, another to buy it. Apocrypha can't be sold as authentic material without an eager customer.

Does it matter? In the broad scheme of things, not really. Compared to alleviating problems such as hunger, pollution, and the continued slaughter of innocents, putting accurate words in the right mouth is and should be a modest priority. Exposing plagiarism and correcting misrepresentation is somewhat more important. And for the sake of our collective memory, it does matter that we verify historically important sayings and quotations. A people with an accurate historical memory are that much closer to genuine self-understanding. Accepting apocryphal comments as if they were accurate implies that misinformation is as good as real information. Doing so limits our ability to assess who we are and where we've come from. Finding out who actually said what is a step toward actual self-awareness. By examining false phrases, spurious sayings, and familiar misquotations, we can gain understanding of ourselves individually and as a people. What makes us respond to apocryphal words at a given point in time? Why do we want noted figures to have said something they didn't say? Who do we want to have said what? These are revealing questions. Examing not only *how* we misquote but *why* tells us something about ourselves that we can't learn any other way.

Bibliography

The following books were especially helpful to me in preparing my own.

Bailey, Thomas. 1976. *Voices of America: The Nation's Story in Slogans, Sayings, and Songs.* New York: The Free Press.

Baker, Daniel B. 1992. *Power Quotes.* Detroit: Visible Ink Press.

Barnes & Noble Book of Quotations. 1987. (Robert I. Fitzhenry, ed.) New York: Barnes & Noble.

Bartlett, John. 1891. *Familiar Quotations.* 9th ed. Boston: Little, Brown.

———. 1914. *Familiar Quotations.* 10th ed. (Nathan Haskell Dole, ed.) Boston: Little, Brown.

———. 1937. *Familiar Quotations.* 11th ed. (Christopher Morley, ed.) Boston: Little Brown.

———. 1948. *Familiar Quotations.* 12th ed. (Christopher Morley, ed.) Boston: Little, Brown.

———. 1955. *Familiar Quotations.* 13th ed. Boston: Little, Brown.

———. 1968. *Familiar Quotations*. 14th ed. (Emily Morison Beck, ed.) Boston: Little, Brown.

———. 1980. *Familiar Quotations*. 15th ed. (Emily Morison Beck, ed.) Boston: Little, Brown.

Bent, Samuel Arthur. [1887] 1968. *Familiar Short Sayings of Great Men: With Historical and Explanatory Notes*. [Boston: Houghton Mifflin] Detroit: Gale Research.

Benham, Sir William Gurney, [1907] 1949. *Benham's Book of Quotations, Proverbs, and Household Words*. New York: Putnam's.

Berger, Josef. 1963. *Who Said It?* New York: Collier Books.

Boller, Paul F. 1967. *Quotemanship.* Dallas: Southern Methodist University Press.

Boller, Paul F., & Ronald L. Davis. 1987. *Hollywood Anecdotes*. New York: Morrow.

Boller, Paul F., & John George. 1989. *They Never Said It: A Book of Fake Quotes, Misquotes and Misleading Attributions*. New York: Oxford University Press.

Bombaugh, Charles C. 1905. *Facts and Fancies for the Curious*. Philadelphia: Lippincott.

Burnam, Tom. 1975. *The Dictionary of Misinformation*. New York: Thomas Y. Crowell.

———. [1980] 1981. *More Misinformation*. [New York: Lippincott & Crowell] New York: Ballantine.

Cerf, Bennett. 1944. *Try and Stop Me: A Collection of Anecdotes and Stories, Mostly Humorous*. New York: Simon & Schuster.

Colombo, John Robert. 1979. *Popcorn Paradise: The Wit and Wisdom of Hollywood*. New York: Holt, Rinehart and Winston.

Concise Oxford Dictionary of Proverbs. 1982. Oxford: Oxford University Press.

Copeland, Lewis, & Faye Copeland. [1939, 1940] 1965. *10,000 Jokes, Toasts and Stories*. Garden City, NY: Doubleday.

Dickson, Paul. 1978. *The Official Rules*. New York: Delta.

———. 1980. *The Official Explanations*. New York: Delacorte.

———. 1991. *Baseball's Greatest Quotations*. New York: HarperCollins.

Evans, Bergen. [1968] 1978. *Dictionary of Quotations*. [New York: Delacorte] New York: Avenel.

Fadiman, Clifton. 1955. *An American Treasury, 1455–1955*. New York: Harper and Brothers.

Fennell, John P. 1989. *"You Ain't Heard Nothin' Yet!": 501 Famous Lines From Great (and Not-So-Great) Movies*. New York: Citadel Press.

Flexner, Stuart Berg. 1982. *Listening to America*. New York: Simon & Schuster.

Frost, Elizabeth. 1988. *The Bully Pulpit: Quotations from America's Presidents*. New York: Facts on File.

Gee, Renie. 1989. *Who Said That?* (Graham Donaldson and Maris Ross, eds.) London: David & Charles.

Green, Jonathon. 1988. *Says Who?* London: Longman.

Harnsberger, Caroline Thomas. 1964. *Treasury of Presidential Quotations*. Chicago: Follett.

The Harper Book of American Quotations. 1988. (Gorton Carruth and Eugene Ehrlich, eds.) New York: Harper & Row.

Harris, Leon A. 1964. *The Fine Art of Political Wit*. New York: Dutton.

Haun, Harry. 1980. *The Movie Quote Book*. New York: Lippincott and Crowell.

Hendrickson, Robert. 1981. *The Literary Life and Other Curiosities*. New York: Viking.

Herbert, George. 1640. *Outlandish Proverbs*. London.

Hoyt, Jehiel Keeler. 1922. *Hoyt's New Cyclopedia of Practical Quotations*. (Kate Louise Roberts, ed.) New York: Funk and Wagnalls.

King, W. Francis H. 1958. *Classical and Foreign Quotations: A Polyglot Dictionary of Historical and Literary Quotations, Proverbs and Popular Sayings*. New York: Frederick Ungar.

Latham, Edward. [1904] 1970. *Famous Sayings and Their Authors*. [London: Swan Sonnenschein] Detroit: Gale.

Levant, Oscar. 1965. *The Memoirs of an Amnesiac*. New York: Putnam's.

Lewis, Alec. 1980. *The Quotable Quotations Book*. New York: Thomas Y. Crowell.

The Macmillan Dictionary of Quotations. [1987] 1989. New York: Macmillan.

Magill, Frank N. 1965. *Quotations in Context.* New York: Harper & Row.

Mathews, Mitford M. 1951. *A Dictionary of Americanisms on Historical Principles.* Chicago: University of Chicago Press.

Mencken, H. L. 1942. *A New Dictionary of Quotations on Historical Principles from Ancient and Modern Sources.* New York: Knopf.

Miller, William. 1977. *Fishbait: The Memoirs of the Congressional Doorkeeper.* Englewood Cliffs, NJ: Prentice-Hall.

Morris, William, & Mary Morris. 1988. *Morris Dictionary of Word and Phrase Origins.* New York: Harper & Row.

The Morrow Book of Quotations in American History. 1984. (Joseph P. Conlin, ed.). New York: Morrow.

Newcomb, Robert H. 1957. "The Sources of Benjamin Franklin's Sayings of Poor Richard." Ph.D. diss., University of Maryland.

The Oxford Dictionary of English Proverbs. 3d ed. 1970. Oxford: Clarendon Press.

The Oxford Dictionary of Quotations. 2d ed. [1941] 1955. London: Oxford University Press.

The Oxford Dictionary of Quotations. [1979] 1980. New York: Oxford University Press.

The Oxford Dictionary of Modern Quotations. 1991. (Tony Augarde, ed.) Oxford, England: Oxford University Press.

Partridge, Eric. 1977. *A Dictionary of Catch Phrases.* New York: Stein and Day.

Partridge, Eric, & Paul Beale. 1986. *A Dictionary of Catch Phrases.* New York: Stein and Day.

Pearson, Hesketh. [1934] 1973. *Common Misquotations.* [London: Hamish Hamilton] London: Folcroft.

Pepper, Frank S. 1987. *The Wit and Wisdom of the 20th Century.* New York: Peter Bedrick Books.

Peter, Laurence. [1977] 1979. *Peter's Quotations.* [New York: Morrow] New York: Bantam.

Platt, Suzy. 1989. *Respectfully Quoted: A Dictionary of Quotations Requested from the Congressional Research Service.* Washington, D.C.: Library of Congress.

The Reader's Digest Treasury of Modern Quotations. 1975. New York: Reader's Digest Press.

Rees, Nigel. 1979. *"Quote . . . Unquote."* New York: St. Martin's Press.

——. 1981. *Love, Death and the Universe.* New York: Macmillan.

——. 1984. *Sayings of the Century.* London: Allen & Unwin.

——. 1989. *Why Do We Quote . . . ?* London: Blandford Press.

——. 1991. *The Phrase That Launched 1,000 Ships.* New York: Dell.

Ringo, Miriam. 1980. *Nobody Said it Better: 2700 Wise and Witty Quotations about Famous People.* Chicago: Rand McNally.

Rowes, Barbara. 1979. *The Book of Quotes.* New York: Dutton.

Safire, William. 1978. *Safire's Political Dictionary.* New York: Random House.

——. [1980] 1981. *William Safire on Language.* [New York: Times Books] New York: Avon.

——. 1982. *What's the Good Word?* New York: Times Books.

——. 1984. *I Stand Corrected.* New York: Times Books.

——. 1986. *Take My Word For It.* New York: Times Books.

——. [1988] 1989. *You Could Look It Up.* [New York: Times Books] New York: Holt.

——. 1990. *Language Maven Strikes Again.* New York: Doubleday.

——. 1991. *Coming to Terms.* New York: Doubleday.

Samuel, Viscount. 1947. *A Book of Quotations.* London: Cresset Press.

Seldes, George. [1960] 1967. *The Great Quotations.* [New York: Lyle Stuart] New York: Pocket Books.

Seldes, George. 1985. *The Great Thoughts.* New York: Ballantine.

Shenkman, Richard, & Kurt Reiger. [1980] 1982. *One-Night Stands with American History: Odd, Amusing and Little-Known Incidents.* [New York: Morrow] New York: Quill.

Shenkman, Richard. [1988] 1989. *Legends, Lies and Cherished Myths of American History.* [New York: Morrow] New York: Perennial.

——. 1991. *I Love Paul Revere, Whether He Rode or Not.* New York: HarperCollins.

Shipps, Anthony W., 1990. *The Quote Sleuth: A Manual for the Tracer of Lost Quotations.* Urbana, IL: University of Illinois Press.

Simpson, James B. 1957. *Best Quotes of '54, '55, '56.* New York: Crowell.

———. 1964. *Contemporary Quotations.* New York: Crowell.

———. 1988. *Simpson's Contemporary Quotations.* Boston: Houghton Mifflin.

Spinrad, Leonard, & Thelma Spinrad. 1975. *Treasury of Great American Sayings.* West Nyack, NY: Parker.

Stephens, Meic. 1990. *A Dictionary of Literary Quotations.* London: Routledge.

Stevenson, Burton. 1964. *The Home Book of Quotations, Classical and Modern.* 10th ed. New York: Dodd, Mead.

———. 1948. *The Macmillan Book of Proverbs, Maxims, and Famous Phrases.* New York: Macmillan.

Stimpson, George. 1946. *A Book About a Thousand Things.* New York: Harper & Brothers.

———. 1948. *Information Roundup.* New York: Harper & Brothers.

Sugar, Bert Randolph. 1979. *The Book of Sports Quotes.* New York: Quick Fox.

Tripp, Rhoda Thomas. [1970] 1987. *The International Thesaurus of Quotations.* [New York: Harper & Row] New York: Perennial.

Tuleja, Tad. 1982. *Fabulous Fallacies.* New York: Harmony Books.

Udall, Morris, with Bob Neuman & Randy Udall. 1988. *Too Funny to be President.* New York: Holt.

Wagner, Walter. 1975. *You Must Remember This.* New York: Putnam's.

Walsh, William S. 1892. *Handy-Book of Literary Curiosities.* Philadelphia: Lippincott.

Who Said What When. [1988] 1991. New York: Hippocrene Books.

Wilson, Carroll A. 1935. *First Appearance in Print of Some Four Hundred Familiar Quotations.* Middletown, CT: Wesleyan University.

Woods, Henry F. [1945] 1950. *American Sayings: Famous Phrases, Slogans and Aphorisms* [New York: Duell, Sloan and Pearce] New York: Perma Giants.

Notes

These notes indicate my sources of information and suggest leads for anyone interested in pursuing further the origins of specific quotations. I've tried in all cases to give the most obvious reference to text material for which sources are cited: the first few words of quotations, the names of key parties, or other identifying information.

In general, I've cited only the most pertinent sources (avoiding, for example, citing repeated illustrations of the same misquotation). Original sources of quotations are referred to only if they were actually examined. Otherwise, such citations are referred to along with the secondary source in which they've been reported. "Letter" refers to a letter to the author. "Interview" refers to an interview with a source by the author, in person or by telephone.

Sources listed in the bibliography are referred to by last name of author (or first name of title for publications without an author), and date of publication for authors with more than one entry. Publications cited frequently are referred to in the source notes by the following abbreviations:

> Bartlett's—Bartlett's *Familiar Quotations,* fifteenth edition (1980) except where indicated.
>
> CODP—*The Concise Oxford Dictionary of Proverbs* (1982).
>
> Harper—*The Harper Book of American Quotations* (1988).

Home Book—*The Home Book of Quotations, Classical and Modern*, tenth edition (1964).

Hoyt's—*Hoyt's New Cyclopedia of Practical Quotations* (1922).

Macmillan—*The Macmillan Dictionary of Quotations* (New York: Macmillan, 1987, 1989).

MPMFP—*The Macmillan Book of Proverbs, Maxims, and Famous Phrases* (1948).

Morrow—*The Morrow Book of Quotations in American History* (1984).

ODEP—*The Oxford Dictionary of English Proverbs*, third edition (1970).

Oxford—*The Oxford Dictionary of Quotations*, third edition (1979, 1980) except where indicated.

Oxford Modern—*The Oxford Dictionary of Modern Quotations* (1991).

Reader's Digest Treasury—*The Reader's Digest Treasury of Modern Quotations* (1975).

Newspapers cited frequently are referred to by the following abbreviations:

BG—*Boston Globe*

CT—*Chicago Tribune*

DDN—*Dayton Daily News*

NYDN—*New York Daily News*

NYT—*New York Times*

PDN—*Philadelphia Daily News*

PI—*Philadelphia Inquirer*

USAT—*USA Today*

WSJ—*Wall Street Journal*

WP—*Washington Post*

CHAPTER 1: WHY MISQUOTES DRIVE OUT REAL QUOTES

1. Bierce: *The Devil's Dictionary,* New York: Dover, 1958, 106.

Donatus: Bent, iv.

Rosten: *Saturday Review,* June 12, 1976, 12; Leo Rosten, *The Power of Positive Nonsense* (New York: McGraw-Hill, 1977), 113–7; Safire 1989, 142; Morris, 21; Los Angeles *Evening Herald and Express,* February 17, 1939; *Time,* February 27, 1939, 30; H. Allen Smith, *Lost in the Horse Latitudes* (Garden City, NY: Doubleday, Doran, 1944), 191–2.

2. Worth: *Harper's Monthly,* November, 1937, 663; Will Fowler letter to LAT *Calendar,* March 30, 1986.

Darnton: Meyer Berger, The Story of *The New York Times, 1851–1951* (New York: Simon & Schuster, 1951), 460–2.

Biden-Simpson: Senate Judiciary Hearings on the Confirmation of Clarence Thomas, October 13, 1991.

3. Congreve, *The Mourning Bride,* 1697, III:1; I:1.

Addison, *Cato,* 1713, IV:1.

"Don't look a gift horse," MPMFP, 1182; CODP, 91.

"There is safety," CODP, 196.

"Necessity," Magill, 679–80.

"If the shoe fits," CODP, 31; King, 92.

"You can't have," (Heywood, 1546) MPMFP, 274; CODP, 109; Stimpson 1946, 163.

"gild," William Shakespeare, *King John,* 1596–7, IV:2.

4. "Discretion," Henry IV, Part I, 1597, V:4.

"There's method," Hamlet, 1600, II:2.

"Alas!" Ibid., V:1.

Warhol: catalog to exhibit of Andy Warhol photographs, Moderna Museet, Stockholm, February–March 1968; Bob Colacello, *Holy Terror: Andy Warhol Close Up* (New York: HarperCollins, 1990), 1; NYT, July 7, 1987.

Dozens of variations: "Now that": Robert Taylor, BG, October 1, 1977; "You know": Roger Simon, *Wild Turkey,* 1974 (New York: Warner, 1986), 134; "What did": Christine Kraft, Channel 39 (Philadelphia, PA), August 15, 1983; "Andy Warhol's": George Vecsey, NYT, August 15, 1982; "In the future": Jack

Hicks, *TV Guide,* August 2, 1980, 18; "In art": wall display, Swarthmore-Rutledge K–8 School, Swarthmore, PA, September 20, 1989; "Everybody is": *Dayton Journal Herald,* August 31, 1977.

5. Truman: "If you can't," *Time,* April 28, 1952, 19; *Public Papers,* 1952, 1085–1086; *Mr. Citizen* (New York: Bernard Geis Associates, 1960), 229.

"I don't care," John J. O'Grady, *Creative Computing,* July 1980, 64.

"It's a recession," (London) *Observer,* April 13, 1958, in *Oxford Modern,* 218.

Pascal: Blaise Pascal *Pensees, The Provincial Letters,* provincial letter 16, 571 (1941), in Platt, 389; King, 151.

6. Koppel: ABC-TV, December 26, 1991.

Hemingway: Dorothy Parker, *The New Yorker,* November 30, 1929, 31.

Barnum: Pelton, interview, December 17, 19, 1991; Robert Edmund Sherwood, *Here We Are Again: Recollections of an Old Circus Clown* (Indianapolis: Bobbs-Merrill, 1926), 192–3; Stimpson 1946, 2–3; A. H. Saxon, *P. T. Barnum: The Legend and the Man* (New York: Columbia University Press, 1989), 334–7.

7. "Elementary": Oxford Modern, 69; Partridge 1977, 56; "The Crooked Man," in Sir Arthur Conan Doyle, *The Memoirs of Sherlock Holmes* (London: John Murray, 1893, 1974), 147; review of *The Return of Sherlock Holmes,* NYT, October 19, 1929; Rees 1984, 92–3; Rees 1991, 53.

Ali: Thomas Hauser, *Muhammad Ali: His Life and Times* (New York: Simon & Schuster, 1991); interview, December 7, 1991.

8. Wilson: Platt, 71; NYT, January 23, 1953; Bartlett's, 817; Fadiman, 194; Harper, 116.

9. Oxford, 233; Macmillan, 153; *Bully Pulpit,* Frost, 36.

Platt: interview, December 5, 1990.

Safire 1978, xii–xiii; Rees 1989, 2.

9–10. "You can never be": Duchess of Windsor: *Esquire,* August, 1973, 93; Ralph G. Martin, *The Woman He Loved* (New York: Simon & Schuster, 1973, 1974), 505; NYT, May 4, 1980; *People,* December 27, 1983–January 3, 1984, 55. Paley: *Philadelphia Magazine,* October, 1978, 6; *People,* May 31, 1982, 58; Harvey A. Levenstein, *Revolution at the Table* (New York: Oxford, 1988), 205. Capote: Lewis, vii, 23; Clarke, interview, December 10, 1990.

10. Platt: xiii–xiv.

Weinberg: *San Francisco Chronicle,* November 15, 1964; interview, December 5, 1990; Gleason, *San Francisco Chronicle,* November 18, 1964; *Washington Post,* March 23, 1970; *Bill of Rights Journal,* Winter 1988, 15. Rubin, *Growing (Up) at 37* (New York: M. Evans, 1976), 7.

CHAPTER 2: THE RULES OF MISQUOTATION

13. Sherman: *Harper's Weekly,* June 24, 1871; William Tecumseh Sherman, *Memoirs of Gen. W. T. Sherman, Written by Himself* (New York: Charles L. Webster, 1891), 466; Lloyd Lewis, *Sherman: Fighting Prophet* (New York: Harcourt, Brace and Company, 1932), 631.

14. Pogo: Kelly, Mrs. Walt and Bill Crouch, Jr., ed., *The Best of Pogo* (New York: Simon & Schuster, 1982), 156, 224; Platt, 102.

Ford: CT, May 25, 1916; Allan Nevins and Frank Ernest Hill, *Ford: Expansion and Challenge* (New York: Scribner's, 1957), 129–42; Walter Karp, "Henry Ford's Village," in *A Sense of History* (New York: American Heritage, 1985), 659–62.

15. De Gaulle: Ernest Mignon, *Les Mots du General* (Paris: Librairie Artheme Fayard, 1962), 57; *Newsweek,* October 1, 1962, 34; Oxford, 173; Lewis, x. Over 400 French cheeses, CT, December 1, 1991.

Longworth: *Newsweek,* February 11, 1974, 52; Ringo, 219; NYDN, February 14, 1933; Fleeson, Joseph P. Lash, *Eleanor and Franklin* (New York: Norton, 1971; Signet, 1973), 802; NYT, February 21, 1980. Longworth denial, Lash, 802. Lowell: *A Fable for Critics* (Freeport, NY: Books for Libraries Press, 1890, 1972), 78.

15–16. Armstrong: NYT, July 21, 1969, July 31, 1969; WP (Reuters), July 20, 1989; Clark DeLeon, PI, July 19, 1989, July 26, 1989. William Poundstone, *Big Secrets* (New York: Quill/Morrow, 1983), 183–4.

16. Stein: "Sacred Emily," in William Harmon, ed., *The Oxford Book of American Light Verse* (New York: Oxford University Press, 1979), 293; Rees 1979, 40; Rees 1984, 90; Rees 1991, 28; Green, 725; Janet Hobhouse, *Everybody Who Was Anybody: A Biography of Gertrude Stein* (New York: Putnam's 1975, 1976), 73, 139, 175, 185, 205.

Sutton: Willie Sutton with Edward Linn, *Where the Money Was* (New York: Viking, 1976), 120.

Lansky: Robert Lacey, *Little Man: Meyer Lansky and the Gangster Life* (Boston: Little, Brown, 1991), 284–5, 315, 423. NYT, January 16, 1983.

17. Stengel: Robert Creamer, *Stengel: His Life and Times* (New York: Simon & Schuster, 1984), 299. Jarvis: Norman Lear letter to *Newsweek,* November 6, 1978, 8–9.

17–18. Kissinger: Fallaci, *The New Republic,* December 16, 1972, 21; Mike Wallace letter to *Playboy,* December 1982, 16; *Esquire,* June 1975, 104; Henry Kissinger, *The White House Years* (Boston: Little, Brown, 1979), 1410.

18. Seattle: Susan Jeffers, *Brother Eagle, Sister Sky: A Message from Chief Seattle* (New York: Dial, 1991); Joseph Campbell, with Bill Moyers, *The Power of Myth* (New York: Doubleday, 1988) 34–5; National Public Radio, *Weekend Edition,* June 8, 1991; *Newsweek,* May 4, 1992, 68.

19. Hitler: Beatty, *Saturday Review,* May 17, 1969, 10, December 20, 1969, 12; *Esquire,* November 1970, 44; Platt, 33–4; William O. Douglas, *Points of Rebellion* (New York: Vintage Books, 1969, 1970), 58; *Parade,* April 26, 1970; Boller and George, 45–6.

20. Socrates: *Forbes,* April 15, 1966, 5, 85.

Zack: Paul Tsongas, *Heading Home* (New York: Knopf, 1984), 160.

21. Greeley: Henry Luther Stoddard, *Horace Greeley: Printer, Editor, Crusader* (New York: Putnam's, 1946), 93; William Harlan Hale, *Horace Greeley: Voice of the People* (New York: Harper & Brothers, 1950), 195–6; Glyndon G. Van Deusen, *Horace Greeley: Nineteenth-Century Crusader* (Philadelphia: University of Pennsylvania, 1953), 173; Jules Archer, *Fighting Journalist: Horace Greeley* (New York: Julian Messner, 1966), 109; Erik Lunde, *Horace Greeley* (Boston: G. K. Hall, 1981), 19, 29, 87, 102; Lunde letter, March 11, 1992; Suzanne Schulze, *Horace Greeley: A Bio-Bibliography* (Westport, CT: Greenwood Press, 1992). Greeley-Soule: Charles Roll, *Colonel Dick Thompson* (Indianapolis: Indiana Historical Collection, 1948), 135–6; Walsh, 1083–4.

22. "If men could get": *Ms.,* March, 1973, 89; Gloria Steinem, *Outrageous Acts and Everyday Rebellions* (New York: Holt, Rinehart and Winston, 1983), 8.

"the little man": Safire 1978, 401–2; Safire, *NYT Book Review,* December 24, 1978; Safire, NYT, March 22, 1980.

"weaned on a pickle": Alice Roosevelt Longworth, *Crowded Hours* (New York: Charles Scribner's, 1933; Arno Press, 1980), 337.

23. "a vast wasteland": NYT, May 10, 1961; NYT, May 4, 1986; John Bartlow Martin, *It Seems Like Only Yesterday* (New York: Morrow, 1986), 203.

"chewing gum": Simpson 1957, 233; Simpson 1964, 400; Simpson 1988, 377.

Wright: Fadiman, 838; Sullivan: *Lippincott's,* March 1896, in Bartlett's, 681; NYT, April 9, 1959 in Reader's Digest Treasury; Oliver Wendell Holmes, *The Autocrat of the Breakfast Table* (New York: A. L. Burt, 1858, 1900), 121.

24. Anderson: *RQ,* Spring 1987, 291.

Wicker: NYT, January 1, 1982; NYT, July 27, 1963; *Public Papers,* John F. Kennedy, July 26, 1963, 603; NYT, July 27, 1963; Platt, 239; Herman Kahn, *On Thermonuclear War* (Princeton: Princeton University Press, 1961) 20, 40.

Colson: WSJ, October 15, 1971; Charles W. Colson, *Born Again* (Old Tappan, NJ: Fleming H. Revell, 1976), 57. Colson letter, March 17, 1992.

Tweed: Albert Bigelow Paine, *Thomas Nast: His Period and His Pictures* (New York: Chelsea House, 1980), 164, 197; Leo Hershkowitz, *Tweed's New York: Another Look* (Garden City, NY: Anchor Press/Doubleday, 1978), xviii.

25. F.P.A.: Robert MacKenzie, *TV Guide,* March 11, 1978, 36; Levant, 163; Robert E. Drennan, ed., *The Algonquin Wits* (New York: Citadel Press, 1968), 36. Bevin: Macmillan, 433; Oxford Modern, 33; Rees 1984, 233; Sir Roderick Barclay, *Ernest Bevin and the Foreign Office 1932–1969* (London: Sir Roderick Barclay, 1975), 78.

Holmes: Jack Smith, *Chicago Sun-Times,* February 14, 1977; Anthony and Sally Sampson, ed., *The Oxford Book of Ages* (Oxford: Oxford, 1985, 1988), 174; Fadiman, 783. Clemenceau: Macmillan, 400. von Wrangel: Smith, *Chicago Sun-Times,* February 14, 1977.

25–26. "If people don't want to come": Berra: Phil Pepe, *The Wit and Wisdom of Yogi Berra* (New York: St. Martin's, 1988), 151. Hurok: *Time,* October 1, 1979, 83. "I don't care": Goldwyn: Ezra Goodman, *Bogey: The Good–Bad Guy* (New York: Lyle Stuart, 1965), 112. Cohan: John McCabe, *George M. Cohan: The Man Who Owned Broadway* (Garden City: Doubleday, 1973), 196; Fadiman, 833. Barnum: Garson Kanin, *Hollywood* (New York: Viking, 1974), 296. Truman: John J. O'Grady, *Creative Computing,* July 1980, 64. Curley: Vic Gold, *P.R. as in President* (Garden City: Doubleday, 1977), in Dickinson 1978, 34. Sullivan: Ringo, 159; Safire 1978, 574; Rees 1984, 60; Rees 1991, 11.

26. Longworth: Platt, 376; Miller, 103–4; Carol Feisenthal, *Alice Roosevelt Longworth* (New York: G. P. Putnam's, 1988), 161. Connelly: James R. Gaines, *Wit's End* (New York: Harcourt, Brace, Jovanovich, 1977), 30; Howard Teichmann, *Smart Aleck: The Wit, World and Life of Alexander Woollcott* (New York: Morrow, 1976), 112; Malcolm Goldstein, *George S. Kaufman* (Oxford: Oxford, 1979), 67.

Weiss: Sugar, 116. Duchess: Rees 1989, 229; Partridge 1977, 103. Duke-Ewing: D. L. Stewart, DDN, October 1, 1991; Macmillan, 208.

26–27. Gorbachev aide: BG, August 22, 1991; Acheson: Macmillan, 3; Talleyrand, et al.: King, 388; Home Book, 337; Baker, 75.

27. "Living well": Calvin Tomkins, *Living Well is the Best Revenge* (New York: Viking, 1962), 126; Herbert: Herbert, #524; Lyly: ODEP, 476.

Courter: Gay Courter, *Flowers in the Blood* (New York: Dutton, 1990), 553; interview, December 7, 1991; Walter Bagehot, *Literary Studies, Volume One* (New York: Dutton, 1879, 1911, 1951), 152.

Barnard: *Printer's Ink,* December 8, 1921, 96; March 10, 1927, 114; Bartlett's 12th, 1213; Rees 1991, 27; Macmillan, 409.

CHAPTER 3: POOR RICHARD'S PLAGIARISM

30. Canetti: Macmillan, 500.

Franklin: Esmond Wright, *Franklin of Philadelphia* (Cambridge: Belknap/Harvard, 1986), 53–5; Carl Van Doren, *Benjamin Franklin* (New York: Viking, 1938), 110–3, 266–8; Carl Van Doren, in *Meet Dr. Franklin* (Philadelphia: The Franklin Institute, 1943), 232–4. Theodore Hornberger, *Benjamin Franklin* (Minneapolis: University of Minnesota Press, 1962), 11–2, 23–6; Stuart A. Gallacher, "Franklin's *Way to Wealth;* a Florilegium of Proverbs and Wise Sayings," *Journal of English and Germanic Philology,* 48: 229–51, April 1949; Charles W. Meister, "Franklin as a Proverb Stylist," *American Literature,* 24: 157–66, May, 1952; Robert H. Newcomb, "The Sources of Benjamin Franklin's Sayings of Poor Richard," Ph.D. diss., University of Maryland, 1957.

"An ounce of prevention": Meister, 164.

"There are no gains": MPMFP, 924; Newcomb, 292.

"A word to the wise": MPMFP, 261; CODP, 250; King, 66; Meister, 161.

31. Newcomb: interview, December 26, 1991; Newcomb, 12, 50, 81, 228, 240, 367.

"Success has ruined": Newcomb, 138, 351.

"A man in a passion": Newcomb, 77, 313.

"For want of a nail": Newcomb, 361; Herbert, *Outlandish Proverbs* #499.

"Love your neighbor": Newcomb, 327; Herbert, #141.

"Marry your sons": Newcomb, 88, 348; Herbert, #149.

"Nothing dries": Newcomb, 328; Herbert, #659.

32. "At 20 years": Newcomb, 110.

"Don't throw stones": Newcomb, 351; Herbert, #196; Howell: Newcomb, 351.

Newcomb: Newcomb, 16, 143, 158, 240; interview.

Fuller: Newcomb, 100.

32–33. "We do not inherit": *RQ*, Fall 1990, 26; Celestial Seasonings Chamomile tea, box copy © 1987; *RQ*, Summer 1991, 474; Robert Keller, "Haida Indian Land Claims and South Moresby National Park," *The American Review of Canadian Studies*, 20: 7–30, Spring, 1990, 7; *Newsweek*, July 11, 1988, 24.

"A man is known": *RQ*, Spring 1979, 285; Fall 1990, 25; William Law, *Christian Perfection, A Contemporary Version* by Marvin D. Hinten (Wheaton, IL: Tyndale House, 1986), 75; William Law, *A Practical Treatise Upon Christian Perfection* (London: William and John Innys, 1726; J. J. Trebeck, 1902), 269–70.

"A foolish consistency": "Self-Reliance," *The Heart of Emerson's Essays: Selections from His Complete Works* (Boston: Houghton Mifflin, 1933), 103.

34. Emerson-Thoreau: Platt, 286–7; Shenkman 1991, 85–6.

"Build a better mousetrap": Stimpson 1948, 338–9; Seldes 1987, 128. "If a man has good corn": *Journals of Ralph Waldo Emerson* (Boston: Houghton Mifflin, 1912), vol. 8, p. 528.

The Fra, November 1908 in Freeman Champney, *Art and Glory: The Story of Elbert Hubbard* (New York: Crown, 1968), 204. Hubbard's claim of quote: Champney, 204–6; Kenneth Dirlam and Ernest E. Simmons, *Sinners, This is East Aurora* (New York: Vantage Press, 1964), 193–200; Burton Stevenson, "The Mouse Trap," *The Colophon*, December 1934, pages unnumbered; "More About the Mouse-Trap," *The Colophon*, Summer 1935, 71–85; Home Book, 630–1, 2275; "after Emerson students failed to find it," Stevenson, *The Colophon*, 1934, sixth page; Elbert Hubbard, *A Thousand & One Epigrams* (Englewood Cliffs: Prentice-Hall, 1911, 1973), 167; "Mr. Hubbard has a habit," H. T. Morgan in *The Philistine*, July 1912, fifth page (pages unnumbered); "Always credited to Emerson," Ibid.

35. *Borrowings: A Collection of Helpful and Beautiful Thoughts* (New York: Dodge Publishing, 1889), 52; Stevenson, *The Colophon*, 1934, 1935. "The fact that," Stevenson, *The Colophon*, 1935, 85; "one can only wonder," Ibid.

Champney, 205.

36. on Hubbard: Champney, *Art and Glory*, op. cit.; Dirlam and Simmons, *Sinners, This is East Aurora*, op. cit.; Charles F. Hamilton, *As Bees in Honey Drown: Elbert Hubbard and the Roycrofters* (South Brunswick: A. S. Barnes, 1973); Paul McKenna, *A History and Bibliography of the Roycroft Printing Shop* (North Tonawanda, NY: Tona Graphics, 1986); Bruce A. White, *Elbert Hubbard's The Philistine: A Periodical of Protest (1895–1915)* (Lanham, MD: University Press of America, 1989).

Hubbard colleague: Champney 202; Armstrong, *Plain Truth*, January 1982, 1; Edison, MPMFP, 283.

36–37. "Too many people": Hubbard, *A Thousand and One Epigrams*, op. cit., 159; Hubbard, *Roycroft Dictionary and Book of Epigrams* (East Aurora, NY: Roycrofters, 1923), 154; *Elbert Hubbard's Scrap Book* (New York: Wm. H. Wise & Co., 1923), 83; Oscar Wilde, *The Picture of Dorian Gray* (New York: Brentano's, 1890, 1906), 67; *Lady Windermere's Fan*, 1892, III.

37. "Never explain": MPMFP, 728; Platt, 136; Hamilton, *As Bees in Honey Drown*, op. cit., 184; see Disraeli, Chapter four.

"Folks who can": Hubbard, *A Thousand and One Epigrams*, op. cit., 64; Shaw, *Maxims for Revolutionists* in *Man and Superman* (London: Constable, 1931), 213.

"The reward of": *A Thousand and One Epigrams,* op. cit., 82; Emerson, *Essays, Second Series: New England Reformers,* in Stevenson, *The Colophon,* 1934, fifth page.

"Anything that has charms": Hubbard, *Roycroft Dictionary and Book of Epigrams,* op. cit., 41.

"Life is": Hubbard, Ibid., 141; *A Thousand and One Epigrams*, op. cit., 136; O'Malley, *The Literary Digest,* November 5, 1932, 39;

37–38. Sandburg: "When the future generations": Penelope Niven, *Carl Sandburg: A Biography* (New York: Scribner's, 1991), 68; "As a poseur": Harry Golden, *Carl Sandburg* (Cleveland: World, 1961), 59. See also North Callahan, *Carl Sandburg: His Life and Works* (University Park, PA: Pennsylvania State University Press, 1987).

38. Sandburg: Carl Sandburg, *Good Morning, America* (New York: Harcourt, Brace, 1928); *The People, Yes* (New York: Harcourt, Brace, 1936).

Sandburg, *The People, Yes,* op. cit., 43.

James A. Newman letter reprinted in newsletter of Polaris Action, New London, CT, November 1961.

McCall's, October 1966, 26.

"Suppose they gave a war . . .": Guthrie: Jonathan Green, *The Book of Rock Quotes* (New York: Omnibus Press, 1977), 65; Ginsberg: Oxford Modern, 90.

38–39. "Do your own thing.": Safire, *NYT Magazine,* February 15, 1981, March 15, 1981, April 12, 1981; Safire 1984, 118–9; Chaucer, *Canterbury Tales* (New York: Holt, 1928), "The Clerkes Tale," 342, line 652.

39. "Today is": Dederich: Platt, 343; Macmillan, 139; *RQ,* Summer, 1975, 337; *RQ,* Winter, 1978, 184; *RQ,* Winter, 1979, 110.

"Keep on truckin' ": Thomas Marema, "Who is this Crumb?," *NYT Magazine,* October 1, 1972; Green, 706; Rees 1991, 41; Flexner, 312, 382.

"You're either part": Cleaver, Robert Scheer introduction to *Eldridge Cleaver: Post-Prison Writings and Speeches* (Random House, 1969), xxxii; *Newsweek,* September 16, 1968, 30; Gallagher, Reader's Digest Treasury, 236.

40. "We are the people": Von Hoffman, *We Are the People Our Parents Warned Us Against* (New York: Quadrangle, 1967); Rees 1989, 157–8.

"Life is what happens": Macmillan, 325; Harper, 344; Rees 1989, 124; Rees, 91, 23. La Mance: Peter, 305; Barnes & Noble, 210. Saunders: *Reader's Digest,* January 1957, 32. Talmadge: Rowes, 106.

41. Motta: *PDN,* May 8, 1978; *Philadelphia Bulletin,* May 8, 1978; WP, May 8, 1978, June 11, 1978; Sugar, 37; CODP, 171; Platt, 341.

Cook: *RQ,* Winter 1985, 173; CODP, 171; Safire, *NYT Magazine,* February 15, 1987.

Cook in quote collections: Macmillan, 403; Rees 1984, 58; Oxford Modern, 60; Platt, 341.

Fabia Rue Smith and Charles Rayford Smith, *Southern Words and Sayings* (Jackson, MS: Office Supply Company, 1976), 6.

Bethard: interview, May 11, 1992.

Holcomb: interview, October 1, 1991.

Inman, Ingraham: interviews, December 14, 1991.

CHAPTER 4: LET THEM EAT BRIOCHE

43. Strunsky: Simeon Strunsky, *No Mean City* (New York: Dutton, 1944), 274.

43–44. Rousseau: Jean Jacques Rousseau, *Confessions,* Book 6, 254; Bergen Evans, *The Spoor of Spooks* (New York: Knopf, 1954), 63; Home Book, 1571; MPMFP, 274–5. Duchess of Tuscany: Alphonse Karr, *Les Guepes* (1843), in Burnam 1975, 139; *Fabulous Fallacies,* 150. Marie Therese: Louis XVIII, *Relation d'un Voyage a Bruxelles et a Coblentz en 1791* (Paris, 1823) in Oxford, 329; Platt, 253–4; Nesta M. Weber letter to *Times,* April 29, 1959. John Peckham: John Ward letter to *Times,* April 30, 1959.

44. Louis XIV: Bent, 338–42; King, 178–9; Walsh, 627; Voltaire, *The Age of Louis XIV* (New York: Dutton, 1751, 1926, 1961), 257–8; Olivier Bernier, *Louis XIV* (New York: Doubleday, 1987), 97.

44–45. "I disapprove": S. G. Tallentyre, *The Friends of Voltaire* (London: John Murray, 1906), 199; *Reader's Digest,* June 1934, 50. Hall, "I did not intend": *NYT Book Review,* September 1, 1935, 19.

45. "two o'clock": from Las Cases, *Memorial de Ste-Helene* (1823) in Bartlett's, 421; MPMFP, 436. Thoreau: Henry David Thoreau, *Walden* (New York: Holt, Rinehart and Winston, 1854, 1948), 97. Theroux: Paul Theroux, *Mosquito Coast* (Boston: Houghton Mifflin, 1982), 10, 97.

"From the sublime": Bartlett's, 420; Home Book, 1725; MPMFP, 1987; Walsh, 1038; King, 78. Paine: Thomas Paine, *The Age of Reason* (New York: Putnam's, 1795, 1890), 107.

"The English are a nation": Walsh, 1007; CODP, 65–6; Stimpson 1946, 339–40; Bent, 406. Adam Smith, *An Inquiry into the Nature and Causes of the Wealth of Nations* (Edinburgh: Adam and Charles Black, 1838, 1853), 276.

"An army travels": Christopher Hibbert, *Waterloo: Napoleon's Last Campaign* (New York: Mentor, 1969), 36; Oxford, 359; CODP, 6. Frederick the Great: Home Book, 1863.

46. Cambronne: King, 159; Bartlett's, 421; Bartlett's 9th, 810; Oxford, 128; Home Book, 2127; MPMFP, 2251–2; Hoyt's, 844; *Les Miserables,* Book 1, Chapt. 14.

"Up, guards": Bent, 564, 618; Hoyt's, 859; Walsh, 434; Boller and George, 130; Sir William Fraser, *Words on Wellington* (London: John C. Nimmo, 1889), 96–7.

46–47. "The battle of Waterloo": Elizabeth Longford, *Wellington: The Years of the Sword* (New York: Harper & Row, 1969), 16–17; letter to *Times:* Rees 1989, 218; Seldes 1960, xiv; Count Charles de Montalembert, *De L'Avenir Politique de l'Angleterre,* 1856, in Longford, *Wellington,* op. cit., 16; Rees 1989, 218. Fraser, *Words on Wellington,* op. cit., 138.

47. "Blood and iron": Frederic B. M. Hollyday, ed., *Bismarck* (Englewood Cliffs, NJ: Prentice-Hall, 1970), 16–7; Emil Ludwig, *Bismarck: The Story of a Fighter* (Boston: Little, Brown, 1927), 206–7; Louis L. Snyder, *The Blood and Iron Chancellor* (Princeton, NJ: Van Nostrand, 1967) 126–7; Latham, 197; Walsh, 559–60; MPMFP, 2449.

47–48. "If you like laws and sausage": Platt, 190. Talmadge: *The Reader,* November 25, 1977, in Baker, 196. Jim Buchy, *DDN,* September 8, 1991.

48. "one who has missed": Robert Manning, NYT, June 8, 1983; Latham, 208; Mencken, 617.

"peace with honor": Rees 1989, 155; Safire, 1978, 522–4; Bent, 47–8; Latham, 50; Walsh, 879–80; Bartlett's, 727; Coriolanus, III: 2.

49. "That depends": Cerf, 256; Harris, 16; Warren Clements, *Toronto Globe & Mail*, July 30, 1991; Platt, 74; Sir Charles Petrie, *The Four Georges* (Boston: Houghton Mifflin, 1936), 132–3.

Disraeli plagiarism: Robert Blake, *Disraeli* (New York: St. Martin's, 1967), 146, 335.

"I only wish": Ringo, 200; Oxford, 336. "Everything comes": MPMFP, 2440; Pearson, 30. "Yes, I am a Jew": MPMFP, 1269; Home Book, 1011; Harris, 67, 220. "Exhausted volcanoes": Bent, 46–7; Safire, *NYT Magazine*, February 3, 1985; Safire 1990, 161.

49–50. "lies, damned lies": Mark Twain, *Mark Twain's Own Autobiography* (Madison, WI: University of Wisconsin Press, 1924, 1990), 185; Tripp, 185, 612; Orrin Riley, "Lies, Damn Lies, and Disguises," *STATS*, Fall 1991, 8; Home Book, 1112; MPMFP, 802; Bibby, *Quotes, Damned Quotes, And. . . . .* (Edinburgh: John Bibby, 1983, 1986), 29, 50; *Journal of the Royal Statistical Society*, 59: 38–118, 1896, 87; Platt, 333.

50. "Never complain": John Morley, *The Life of William Ewart Gladstone* (New York: Macmillan, 1903, Scholarly Press, St. Clair Shores, MI, 1972), 123. Baldwin: Harold Nicolson, *The War Years, 1939–1945: Volume II of Diaries and Letters* (New York: Atheneum, 1967), 307. Royal Navy: Partridge 1977, 152; John Wayne: Fennell, 90. Henry Ford II: Robert Lacey, *Ford* (Boston: Little, Brown, 1986), 591; Elmore Leonard, *The Switch* (New York: Bantam, 1978), 204.

"The good Lord": J. Hampden Jackson, *Clemenceau and the Third Republic* (New York: Macmillan, 1948), 183; Oxford, 152; Ringo, 229.

"I accuse": Rees 1989, 8.

"War is too important": Jackson, *Clemenceau*, op. cit., 228; Georges Suarez, *La Vie Orgueilleuse de Clemenceau* (Paris: Editions de France, 1930), 172; Platt, 365; John Bailey, *Letters and Diaries* (London: John Murray, 1935), 176; Samuel, 226.

51. "America is the only nation": *Esquire*, January 1980, 7; *The Penguin Dictionary of Modern Humorous Quotations* (New York: Viking, 1986, Penguin, 1987), 14. Bendix, *Saturday Review of Literature*, December 1, 1945, 9.

"Any man": Cerf, 258; Seldes 1985, 157; Benham, 751; *RQ*, Winter 1977, 164.

52. "And you madam": Macmillan, 478; Harris, 173; William Manchester, *The Last Lion* (Boston: Little, Brown, 1983), 810; Fields: Wallace Markfield, *NYT Magazine*, April 24, 1966, 116; Richard J. Anobile, ed., *Drat!: W. C. Fields in His Own Words* (New York: Signet, 1969), 43.

"If I were your husband": Manchester, 34; Elizabeth Langhorne, *Nancy Astor and Her Friends* (New York: Praeger, 1974), 57; Consuelo Vanderbilt Balsan, *Glitter and Gold* (New York: Harper & Brothers, 1952), 204–5. Thayer: April 27, 1971. Lloyd George: Harris 131. Dizzy Dean, Cerf, 305.

"There but for the grace of God": Harris, 174; Rees 1984, 106; Ringo, 194, 279; Boller and George, 96–7.

52–53. "Atlee is a very modest man": Udall, xiii; Ringo, 183. "A sheep": Harris, 164; Rees 1984, 106; Safire 1978, 643; Safire, *NYT Book Review*, December 24, 1978.

53. Churchill on Bartlett's: Winston S. Churchill, *A Roving Commission* (New York: Scribner's, 1930, 1949), 116.

"it has been said": Oxford Modern, 55; Platt, 83.

53–54. "blood, sweat and tears": John Donne, *An Anatomie of the World, The Complete Poetry of John Donne* (New York: New York University Press), 1968, 284; Lord Byron, *The Age of Bronze, The Works of Lord Byron* (New York: Scribner's, 1901), 571; Lord Alfred Douglas, *The Collected Poems of Lord Alfred Douglas* (London: Martin Secker, 1919), 121, 57; Boller and George, 13; Henry James, *The Bostonians* (New York: Modern Library, 1886, 1956), 186; Winston S. Churchill, *The Unknown War* (New York: Scribner's, 1931), 1.

54–55. "iron curtain": Safire 1978, 340; Ignace Feuerlicht, "A New Look at the Iron Curtain," *American Speech,* 30:186–9, 1955. Englishman: Ibid., 186. Abbé de Pradt: Friedrich Henn, *Encounter,* January 1966, 89. Wells: H.G. Wells, *The Food of the Gods* (New York: Dover, 1904), 789. Belgian Queen: Émile Hinzel in *Historie Illustrée de la Guerre du Droit,* vol. II, 407, in Henn, *Encounter,* 89; Bartlett's, 746; Seldes 1985, 123 (citing Bernard Baruch as source). Crile: George Crile, *A Mechanistic View of War and Peace* (New York: Macmillan, 1915), 69. Rozanov: V. V. Rozanov, *Solitairia, The Apocalypse of Our Times,* translated by S. S. Kotelyiansky (New York: Boni & Liveright, 1918, 1927), 148. Snowden: Ethel Snowden, *Through Bolshevik Russia* (London: Cassell, 1920), 32. American magazine article: P. Mohr, *Information About Eastern Questions,* 1921, in Henn, *Encounter,* 89. Goebbels: *Das Reich,* February 23, 1945, in Seldes 1985, 79; Reuters, February 23, 1945, in Allan Fotheringham, *MacLean's,* June 6, 1983, 56. von Koosigk: *Times* of London May 3, 1945. Churchill cable (May 12, 1945): Winston S. Churchill, *Triumph and Tragedy* (Boston: Houghton Mifflin, 1953), 573. *Sunday Empire News* (October 21, 1945), St. Vincent Troubridge, in *American Speech,* 26: 49–50, 1951.

CHAPTER 5: FOUNDING FALSE PHRASES

56. Henry: William Wirt, *Sketches of the Life and Times of Patrick Henry* (Freeport, New York: Books for Libraries Press, 1817, 1836, 1970), 74–85.

57. French journal: "Journal of a French Traveller in the Colonies, 1765, I," *American Historical Review*, 26:726–47, 1921, 745. Freeman: Douglas Southall Freeman, *George Washington: A Biography* (New York: Scribner's, 1951), vol. 3, 136.

57–58. "give me liberty": Wirt, 132–43; Freeman, *George Washington,* op. cit., 404.

58. Boorstin: Daniel Boorstin, *The Americans: The National Experience* (New York: Random House, 1965), 309, 308.

58–59. "Taxation without representation": Boorstin, Ibid., 309; Edward Channing, *A History of the United States* (New York: Macmillan, 1924), 4–5; Samuel Eliot Morison in *Dictionary of American Biography* (New York: Scribner's, 1934), vol. 14, 102.

59. "Where there is liberty": Otis: Bartlett's, 367. Franklin: Mencken, 682; Platt, 201. Paine: Alfred Owen Aldridge, *Man of Reason: The Life of Thomas Paine* (Philadelphia: Lippincott, 1959), 169.

"Eternal vigilance": Platt, 200; Bartlett's, 397; Stimpson 1946, 5–6; Home Book, 1106; MPMFP, 1388.

59–60. "Don't fire": Richard Frothingham, *History of the Siege of Boston and of the Battles of Lexington, Concord and Bunker Hill* (Boston: Little, Brown, 1849, 1903), 140; Bartlett's, 368, 358; Harper, 65; Burnam 1975, 69–70.

60. "There, I guess": William M. Fowler, Jr., *The Baron of Beacon Hill: A Biography of John Hancock* (Boston: Houghton Mifflin, 1980), 213; Barrett Williams, BG, January 21, 1962.

"We must all hang together": P.M. Zall, ed., *Ben Franklin Laughing: Anecdotes from Original Sources by and About Ben Franklin* (Berkeley: University of California Press, 1980), 153–4; Carl Van Doren, *Benjamin Franklin,* op. cit., 551–2; Freeman Hunt, *American Anecdotes* (Boston: Putnam & Hunt, 1830), vol. 1, 97; *The American Joe Miller* (Philadelphia: Carey and Hart, 1839), 181; Jared Sparks, *The Works of Benjamin Franklin* (Boston: Hilliard Gray, 1840), 408.

61. "I only regret": Burnam 1975, 104; Ringo, 315; Lewis, x; Allentown (PA) *Call-Chronicle,* September 15, 1976; George Dudley Seymour, *Captain Nathan Hale, Major John Palsgrave Wyllys, A Digressive History* (New Haven: George Dudley Seymour, 1933), 28; George Dudley Seymour, *Documentary Life of Nathan Hale* (New Haven: George Dudley Seymour, 1941), xxxii, 85–7, 292, 376–82, 402, 409–10, 452–4; Judith Ann Schiff, "Old Yale: Nathan Hale's Many Faces," *Yale,* Summer 1988, 16; Campbell, Maria (Hull), *Revolutionary Services and Civil Life of General William Hull: Prepared from His Manuscripts, by His Daughter* (New York: Appleton, 1848), 38; Addison, *Cato,* IV:4.

61–62. "I have not yet": Platt, 305; Samuel Eliot Morison, *John Paul Jones: A Sailor's Biography* (Boston: Little, Brown, 1959), 236, 240–2; Rush, *The Autobiography of Benjamin Rush* (Princeton: Princeton University Press, 1948), 157; Morison, Ibid., 236.

62–63. "Millions for defense": *The South Carolina Historical and Genealogical Magazine,* vol. 1, 1901, 100–3, 178–9; Bombaugh, 131; Spinrad, 103; Platt, 156; *State Papers and Publick Documents of the United States* (Boston: T. B. Wait and Sons, 1817), vol. 3, 492; Albert J. Beveridge, *The Life of John Marshall* (Boston: Houghton Mifflin, 1916), 349–50.

63. "Don't give up": Harry L. Coles, *The War of 1812* (Chicago: University of Chicago Press, 1965), 86; Bombaugh, 388–9; Home Book, 62; MPMFP, 2091; John White Chadwick, "Mugford's Victory," in Burton Stevenson, *Poems of American History* (Boston: Houghton Mifflin, 1936), 174–5; *Motor-Boating,* October 1965, 72; *Dictionary of American History* (New York: Scribner's, 1940, 1976), vol. 2, 364; Walsh, 1004–5; Platt, 189.

"Damn the torpedoes": A. T. Mahan, *Admiral Farragut* (New York: Greenwood Press, 1895, 1968), 278; Christopher Martin, *Damn the Torpedoes!* (New York: Abelard-Schuman, 1970), 258.

64. "Shoot if you must": Samuel T. Pickard, *Life and Letters of John Greenleaf Whittier* (Boston: Houghton Mifflin, 1894), vol. 2, 454–60; Boller and George, 28–9; Shenkman, 1991, 95–6.

"Hold the Fort": Woods, 153; Lloyd Lewis, *Sherman: Fighting Prophet* (New York: Harcourt, Brace, 1932), 426; Home Book, 65; MPMFP, 869; Rees 1989, 84; Rees 1991, 109–10; Oxford, 88.

65. "War is hell": Sherman, *Memoirs,* op. cit., vol. 2, 126; Basil Liddell Hart, *Sherman: Soldier, Realist, American* (New York: Praeger, 1958), 310; James Merrill, *William Tecumseh Sherman* (New York: Rand McNally, 1971), 238, 259, 298, 379–80; Lloyd Lewis, op. cit., 635–7; *Ohio State Journal,* August 12, 1880.

65–66. Forrest: "I always": James Harrison Wilson, *Under the Old Flag* (New York: Appleton & Co., 1912), 184; "I just took": Basil W. Duke, *Reminiscences of General Basil W. Duke, C.S.A.,* (Garden City, NY: Doubleday, 1911), 345–6; "I got there": Richard Taylor, *Destruction and Reconstruction: Personal Experiences of the Late War* (New York: Longmans, Green, 1955), 244. See also, Donn Piatt, *General George H. Thomas* (Cincinnati: Robert Clarke, 1893), 599, and John Watson Morton, *The Artillery of Nathan Bedford Forrest's Cavalry* (Kennesaw, GA: Continental, 1909, 1962), 198. *Memphis Commercial Appeal,* May 14, 1905. Ralph Selph Henry, *"First With the Most" Forrest* (Indianapolis: Bobbs-Merrill, 1944), 18–9. Confederate General's memoir: Taylor, *Destruction and Reconstruction,* op. cit., 244. "The mostest": *Oxford English Diction-*

ary, second edition, vol. 9, 1117; Rees 1989, 82–3; Rees 1991, 109; *New York Tribune,* May 27, 1918; NYT, May 28, 1918. Foote, PBS, September 25, 1990. Bartlett's, 583.

66–67. "The only good Indian": Edward Sylvester Ellis, *The History of our Country* (Cincinnati: Jones Brothers, 1900), 1483; Michael V. Sheridan, *Personal Memoirs of Philip Henry Sheridan* (New York: Appleton, 1902), 464–5. "If I owned Texas": Stimpson 1946, 398–9; Fadiman, 85; Harper, 231; Morrow, 264. Paul Hutton, *Phil Sheridan and His Army* (Lincoln, NE: University of Nebraska Press, 1985), 180. Cavanaugh: *The Congressional Globe,* May 28, 1868, 2638. "the proverb": Ellis Paxson Oberholtzer, *A History of the United States Since the Civil War* (New York: Macmillan, 1926), 357.

67. "You furnish the pictures": William Randolph Hearst, Jr., with Jack Casserly, *The Hearsts: Father and Son* (New York: Roberts Rinehart, 1991), 38; W. A. Swanberg, *Citizen Hearst* (New York: Scribner's, 1961), 107–8; John K. Winkler, *William Randolph Hearst: A New Appraisal* (New York: Hastings House, 1955), 95–6; James Creelman, *On the Great Highway* (Boston: Lothrop, 1901), 177–178; Joyce Milton, *The Yellow Kids: Foreign Correspondents in the Heyday of Yellow Journalism* (New York: Harper & Row, 1989), xii–xiii; Pauline Kael, *The Citizen Kane Book* (Boston: Little, Brown, 1971, Bantam, 1974), 94; *The New Yorker,* February 27, 1971, 62.

68. "war to end all wars": H. G. Wells, *The War That Will End War* (London: F. & C. Palmer, 1914). Wells discussed claim: *Liberty,* December 29, 1934, 4–7.

"Lafayette": John J. Pershing, *My Experience in the World War* (New York: Frederick A. Stokes, 1931), 93. Bartlett's 14th, 856, 15th, 693.

"Only those": Home Book, 2298d; MPMFP, 1419; *Representative Speeches of General of the Army Douglas MacArthur* (Washington, D.C.: U.S. Government Printing Office, 1964), 3; Theodore Roosevelt, *The Great Adventures* (vol. 19 of *The Works of Theodore Roosevelt,* 1926), 243, in Platt, 214.

68–69. "I shall return": *Representative Speeches,* op. cit., vi; William Manchester, *American Caesar* (Boston: Little, Brown, 1978; Dell, 1979), 311–3; Michael Schaller, *Douglas MacArthur* (Oxford: Oxford, 1989), 62.

69. "In war": *Representative Speeches,* op. cit., 19; Dwight D. Eisenhower, *Letters to Mamie,* John S. D. Eisenhower, ed. (Garden City, NY: Doubleday, 1978), 203; Harper, 578.

"Old soldiers never die": *Representative Speeches,* op. cit., 20; Home Book, 2298h; CODP, 168; Oxford Modern, 82; Platt, 324–5; Rees 1984, 70–1; Rees 1991, 26. Safire: Safire 1978, 482.

70. "eyeball to eyeball," Rusk, *Saturday Evening Post,* December 8, 1962, 16; Safire, *NYT Magazine,* October 21, 1979.

"light": Kennedy, December 12, 1962, in *Public Papers,* December 12, 1962, 870. Navarre: *Time,* September 28, 1953, 22; *RQ,* Fall 1981, 20; *A Supplement to the Oxford English Dictionary,* 1986, 1015; Rees, 1984, 212; Rees 1991, 226–7.

70–71. "A secret plan": Safire, *NYT Magazine,* September 9, 1984; Safire 1988, 219–21; John Chancellor and Walter R. Mears, *The News Business* (New York: Harper & Row, 1983), 30–31; Richard M. Nixon, *RN: The Memoirs of Richard Nixon* (New York: Grossett & Dunlap, 1978), 298.

71. "Guns and butter": Oxford, 229; Home Book, 2298d; Baker, 330; Rees 1984, 228–9; Safire 1978, 282.

Give ulcers: Frost, 137. "Hold it": Bill Adler, ed., *The Johnson Humor* (New York: Simon and Schuster, 1965), 80; Bill Moyers, interview, June 15, 1977.

CHAPTER 6: LIP-SYNC POLITICS

72. Safire 1978, xii.

72–73. Schroeder: Patricia Schroeder, interview, February 17, 1992; Dan Buck, interview, December 7, 1990; *Congressional Record,* August 2, 1983; NYT, August 9, 1983; *People,* August 22, 1983, 88; "Teflon candidate," *Public Opinion,* April/May 1984, 17; "Teflon coated," NYT (editorial), March 1, 1987; Bush: *Denver Post, Rocky Mountain News,* May 5, 1984.

73. Schroeder comment, interview, February 17, 1992.

73–74. "It's not what he doesn't know": NYT, October 13, 1984, October 18, 1984. Copelands, 779. *The Complete Works of Artemus Ward (Charles Farrar Browne)* (New York: G. W. Dillingham, 1901), 25; *The Complete Works of Josh Billings (Henry W. Shaw)* (New York: G. W. Dillingham, 1876); Home Book 1964, 1055. Hubbard: NYT, October 18, 1984.

74. "Where's the beef?": Clifford Freeman: NYT, February 11, 1984; Beckel-Mondale, Peter Goldman and Tony Fuller, *The Quest for the Presidency 1984* (New York: Bantam, 1984), 152. Kerrey-Hart: *New York Newsday,* October 8, 1991.

75. Shaffer: Samuel Shaffer, *On and Off the Floor* (New York: Newsweek Books, 1980), 14–5.

Dirksen: Ibid., 18.

Stevenson: John Kenneth Galbraith, *A Life in Our Times* (Boston: Houghton Mifflin, 1981), 288, 290; John Bartlow Martin, *Adlai Stevenson and the World* (Garden City, NY: Doubleday, 1977), 22.

Harris, 242–4.

75–76. "If they will stop": Porter McKeever, *Adlai Stevenson: His Life and Legacy* (New York: Morrow, 1989), 251. Hearst: John K. Winkler, *William Randolph Hearst,* op. cit., 150. Depew: Platt, 261; Harris, 244.

76. "There are no gains": Spinrad, 20; Baker, 87; Platt, 19. Franklin: Newcomb, 292.

"An editor": Reston, *NYT Book Review,* September 25, 1977; Harris, 238; Laurence J. Peter, *Human Behavior,* May 1978, 68. Kihss: Sidney Schanberg, NYT, January 1, 1985; Hubbard, *1001 Epigrams,* op. cit., 21.

"A politician": Rees 1989, 161. "Brinkmanship": Morris, 88. "Quality of life": Safire 1978, 584–5.

"would rather light": Miller, 278–9; Platt, 89; Morris, 57–58.

76–77. "No woman has ever": Luce: Lewis, ix; Ringo, 218; Ringo, 218. Dooley: Winkler, *William Randolph Hearst,* op. cit., 12. Mencken, 852.

77. Biden: NYT, September 12, 1987. Disraeli: Robert Blake, *Disraeli,* op. cit., 146, 335.

Kinnock: Rees 1989, 163–4, citing *Time,* December 28, 1987, about Johnson, *Sunday Today,* May 5, 1987, about Kinnock, *Observer Magazine,* March 20, 1988, about Tutu.

Udall: DDN, April 20, 1991; Udall, 191–2.

77–78. Truman: Simpson 1988, 42; Simpson 1957, 180; *Saturday Evening Post,* November 4, 1899, 356. Saxbe: *Current Biography,* 1974, 347.

78. Kennedy: Bill Adler, *The Robert F. Kennedy Wit* (New York: Berkeley, 1968), 104. Darrow: Clarence Darrow, *The Story of My Life* (New York: Scribner's, 1932), 13.

Burford: Platt, 368.

Buchanan-Leno: *The Tonight Show,* February 19, 1992; DDN, February 21, 1992; *Newsweek,* February 24, 1992, 21. Leno-Quayle: *The Tonight Show,* June 23, 1992; DDN, June 25, 1992.

78–79. Babbitt: *Newsweek,* June 13, 1988, 30; Judith Daniels letter to *Newsweek,* July 11, 1988, 10; O'Reilly, *GQ,* November 1984, 298.

79. Richards: Ann Richards with Peter Knobler, *Straight From the Heart* (New York: Simon and Schuster, 1989), 26. Booth: NYT, July 3, 1988, July 26, 1988; Morris: NYT, April 19, 1960, April 1, 1966.

"Ginger Rogers": Richards, *Straight from the Heart,* op. cit., 24. Whittlesey: Anne W. Schaef, *Meditations for Women Who Do Too Much* (San Francisco: Harper & Row, 1990), May 2.

Solarz: NYT January 23, 1982; Richard W. Wallach letter, NYT, February 2, 1992. Johnson: James Boswell, *The Life of Samuel Johnson* (London: Navarre Society, 1924), 403. Gray aide: PI, December 2, 1990. Kennedy-Dante: Platt, 230.

80. "Every man": Latham, 14–5; Stimpson, 1948, 261–2; Home Book, 1605; MPMFP, 1878; CODP, 68.

80–81. "Your people": Clinton Rossiter, *Alexander Hamilton and the Constitution* (New York: Harcourt, Brace and World, 1964), 162. Tuchman: Morris, 574. Theophilus Parsons, Jr., *Memoir of Theophilus Parsons* (Boston: Ticknor & Fields, 1859, Da Capo Press, 1970), 110; Shenkman 1989, 172; William Ander Smith, "Henry Adams, Alexander Hamilton, and the American People as a 'Great Beast,'" *The New England Quarterly,* June 1975, 216–30. Henry Adams, *History of the United States of America During the First Administration of Thomas Jefferson* (New York: Scribner's, 1891), 85, 109. Machiavelli-Pope, et al.: Bartlett's, 108, 154, 339; Mencken, 901–2; Home Book, 1484; MPMFP, 1775; Adams letter, Smith, *New England Quarterly,* op. cit., 230.

81. "Rum, Romanism": Woods, 57; Matthew Josephson, *The Politicos* (New York: Harcourt, Brace and World, 1938), 369; Oberholtzer, *A History of the United States,* op. cit., 206.

81–82. "Public office": William C. Hudson, *Random Recollections of an Old Political Reporter* (New York: Cupples & Leon, 1911), 175–83. Clay, Calhoun: Home Book, 1550. Johnson: Harnsberger, 263.

82–83. "Smoke-filled room": Woods, 100; Washington *Evening Star,* June 14, 1920; Mark Sullivan, *Our Times* (New York: Scribner's, 1935), vol. 6, 37–8. "I found him sunning": Jonathan Daniels, *The Time Between the Wars* (Garden City, NY: Doubleday, 1966), 63. Sullivan, *Our Times,* op. cit., 38. See also: Wesley M. Bagby, *The Road to Normalcy: The Presidential Campaign and Election of 1920* (Baltimore: Johns Hopkins Press, 1962), 87–89; Ray Baker Harris, *Warren G. Harding: An Account of his Nomination for the Presidency by the Republican Convention of 1920* (Washington, D.C., 1957), 16–7; Francis Russell, *The Shadow of Blooming Grove* (New York: McGraw-Hill, 1968), 341–2.

83–84. "Are you aware": *Time,* April 17, 1950, 27–8; NYT, February 24, 1983; Ringo, 152; Eric Burns, *TV Guide,* March 19, 1988, 30–2; Shaffer, *On and Off the Floor,* op. cit., 108; Michael Dorman, *Dirty Politics* (New York: Delacorte, 1979), 73. Buckley, et al.: NYT, February 24, 1983.

84. "Where fraternities": Edwin McDowell, *Barry Goldwater: Portrait of an Arizonan* (Chicago: Henry Regnery, 1964), 160. See also Boller, 357.

84–85. "The Vice-Presidency": *Time,* February 1, 1963, 17; Sidey interview, January 3, 1977; O. C. Fisher, *Cactus Jack* (Waco, TX: Texian Press, 1982), 118.

85. "Jerry Ford": Richard Reeves, *A Ford, Not a Lincoln* (New York: Harcourt Brace Jovanovich, 1975), 25; Shaffer, *On and Off the Floor,* op. cit., 265.

"Inoperative": NYT, April 18, 1973; Safire, 1978, 331–2; Carl Bernstein and Bob Woodward, *All the President's Men* (New York: Simon and Schuster, 1974), 290–2.

85–86. "If you've got them": Morrow, 72; Shenkman and Reiger, 1982, 242; Colson letter, March 17, 1992; Steven Brill, *The Teamsters* (New York: Simon & Schuster, 1978), 393–4; Rivers: Udall, 167.

86. "The Big Enchilada": Safire 1978, 48; Steve Allen letter, *Newsweek,* December 11, 1978, 11. "When the going gets tough": see Knute Rockne, Chapter 10. "Deep six": Safire 1978, 161.

"Extremism": Hess: *Playboy,* July 1976, 60. Goldwater: Platt, 114. Paine: Thomas Paine, *Rights of Man,* 1791, in Seldes 1987, 166, and Bartlett's, 385.

86–87. Keating: Morrow, 169; Udall, 236; Harris, 228; Lance Morrow, *The Chief* (New York: Random House, 1984), 11–2.

87. Darrow: Irving Stone, *Clarence Darrow for the Defense* (Garden City, NY: Doubleday, Doran, 1941), 169. Ford: Richard Reeves, *A Ford not a Lincoln,* op. cit., 120. Barry: Dave Barry, *Dave Barry Turns 40* (New York: Crown, 1990), dedication.

87–88. Buck: interview, December 7, 1990; February 13, 1992.

CHAPTER 7: ALL THE PRESIDENT'S MISQUOTES

89–90. "The only thing necessary": *RQ,* Fall 1980, 16, Spring 1981, 237, Spring 1987, 291; Seldes 1985, 60; Seldes 1960, 329; Bartlett's 14th, 454; Bartlett's 15th, ix; Safire, *NYT Magazine,* March 9, 1980, April 5, 1981; Safire 1980, 224–6; Seldes 1985, 60; Platt, 109. Ted Kennedy: PI, October 20, 1979.

90. "I'll hitch my wagon": Theodore C. Sorensen, *Kennedy* (New York: Harper & Row, 1965, Bantam, 1966), 71.

90–91. "The new frontier": Harnsberger, 105; David Wise in Lester Tanzer, ed., *The Kennedy Circle* (Washington, D.C.: Luce, 1961), 41. Alf Landon, *America at the Crossroads* (New York: Dodge Publishing, 1936), 13; Henry Wallace, *New Frontiers* (New York: Reynal & Hitchcock, 1934); Safire 1978, 456–7.

91. "Ask not": Harnsberger, 66. Holmes: May 30, 1884 speech, Keene, NH, before John Sedgwick Post No. 4, Grand Army of the Republic, in *Speeches by Oliver Wendell Holmes* (Boston: Little, Brown, 1900), 2–3. Harding: *Ohio* February 1989, 11; Morris, 28. Sorensen, op. cit., 240; Arthur Schlesinger, Jr., *A Thousand Days* (Boston: Houghton Mifflin, 1965), 4.

91–92. "Victory has a hundred fathers": Schlesinger, *A Thousand Days,* op. cit., 289–90. *The Desert Fox:* Paul Hoffman to Safire 1978, 764. Ciano: Count Galeazzo Ciano, *The Ciano Diaries* (Garden City, NY: Garden City Publishing, 1947), 521. Inflationary spiral: Macmillan, 550; Safire 1978, 764, *NYT Magazine,* April 1, 1990; Frost, 56; Jeff Greenfield, *NYT Book Review,* May 1, 1977; *Newsweek,* March 11, 1991, 42. *Parade,* August 18, 1991.

92. "Washington is a city": William Manchester, *Portrait of a President* (Boston: Little, Brown, 1967), 200; Arthur Schlesinger, Jr., *A Thousand Days,* op. cit., 673. 1961 speech: "Remarks to the Trustees and Advisory Committee of the National Cultural Center," November 14, 1961, *Public Papers of the Presidents of the United States,* John F. Kennedy, 1961, 719.

"You see things": John F. Kennedy *Public Papers,* 1963, 537; Shaw, "Back to Methuselah," 1922, part 1, act 1. Edward Kennedy on Robert Kennedy: NYT, June 9, 1968; W. P. Kinsella, *Shoeless Joe* (Boston: Houghton Mifflin, 1982, Ballantine, 1983), frontispiece.

93. "Peace, commerce": Harnsberger, 90; Platt, 121; Safire 1978, 204; Woods, 16.

"That government": Boller and George, 56, citing Buckley column of November 11, 1987. Henry David Thoreau, "Civil Disobedience," *The Portable Thoreau* (New York: Viking, 1947, 1975), 109.

O'Sullivan: *The United States Magazine and Democratic Review,* October 1837, 6; Oxford, 365; Platt, 146; Bartlett's, 552.

"Few die," Bailey, 43; Thomas V. DiBacco, WSJ, January 17, 1989; MPMFP, 1714; Walsh, 366.

94. "John Marshall": Marquis James, *Andrew Jackson: Portrait of a President* (Indianapolis: Bobbs-Merrill, 1937), 304–5; Robert V. Remini, *Andrew Jackson and the Course of American Freedom* (New York: Harper & Row, 1981), 276–7; Horace Greeley, *The American Conflict* (Hartford, CT: O. D. Case, 1864), vol. 1, 106.

"One man": NYT, October 11, 1987. Kennedy: Platt, 172. Knox, et al.: Oxford, 305; Macmillan, 234; Bailey, 92; Hoyt's 319; Home Book, 1236; MPMFP, 1505; Platt, 217.

94–95. "Elevate": Macmillan, 292. *E pluribus":* Shenkman 1988, 33–4; John William Ward, *Andrew Jackson: Symbol for an Age* (New York: Oxford, 1955), 84–6.

95. Lincoln: Boller and George, 77–91; Shenkman 1988, 173; Reinhard H. Luthin, *The Real Abraham Lincoln* (Englewood Cliffs, NJ: Prentice-Hall, 1960), 400–401; Fred Kerner, ed., *A Treasury of Lincoln Quotations* (Garden City, NY: Doubleday, 1965), vii–viii; David Donald, *Lincoln Reconsidered* (New York: Knopf, 1972); Albert A. Woldman, "Lincoln Never Said That," *Harper's,* May 1950, 70–4; DDN, September 12, 1991. Lincoln estimates half spurious: David Homer Bates, *Lincoln Stories* (New York: William Edwin Rudge, 1926), 12; Harris, 94.

95–96. "You can fool": Clinton: *Time,* December 27, 1976, 26; Oxford 314; Harper 351. Bloomington: Home Book, 421; MPMFP, 534; Emanuel Hertz, *Lincoln Talks* (New York: Viking, 1939), 138. 1862: Mencken, 902. 1863: Evans, 159. Roy P. Basler, ed., *The Collected Works of Abraham Lincoln* (New Brunswick, NJ: Rutgers University Press, 1953), 81; Woldman, op. cit., 74. Alexander K. McClure, *Abe Lincoln's Yarns and Stories* (Chicago: Thompson and Thomas, 1901), 184.

96. "Tell me what brand": Burnam 1975, 98; Bates, *Lincoln Stories,* op. cit., 50 Oxford, 223.

96–97. "You cannot": Platt, xiv; Tiffany's, *Newsweek,* March 8, 1976; Woldman, 70–71; *Congressional Record,* March 18, 1964, 5579–80; Lee Metcalf and Vic Reinemer, *Overcharge* (New York: David McKay, 1967), 121–2; Morris Kominsky, *The Hoaxers* (Boston: Branden Press, 1970), 18–26; Woldman, *Harper's,* op. cit., 702. *Time,* January 30, 1950, 58.

97. "Government of the people": Woods, 41; Bent, 609–10; Walsh, 425–6; Bombaugh, 176–7; Spinrad, 118–9; Seldes 1987, 245; Home Book, 431; MPMFP, 549; William H. Herndon and Jesse W. Weik, *Abraham Lincoln* (New York: Appleton, 1892), vol. 2, 65; Robert E. Collins, *Theodore Parker: American Transcendentalist* (Metuchen, NJ: Scarecrow Press, 1973), 2–3.

"With malice": Bent, 610; MPMFP, 1506.

"He reminds me": Home Book, 1028; George Horner, ed., *The Great Americana Scrap Book* (New York: Crown, 1985), 172. Barkley: Udall, 236. Taft, *Liberty,* Summer, 1971, 12, 55. Rosten: Leo Rosten, *Hooray for Yiddish* (New York: Simon & Schuster, 1982), 85. Ward: Harper, 307; *The Complete Works of Artemus Ward,* op. cit., 115–6; Gerald R. Ford, *Humor and the Presidency* (New York: Arbor House, 1987), 119.

"I remember a good story": Harris, 94.

98. "Here I stand": Safire, *NYT Magazine,* August 6, 1988; Safire 1991, 132–5. "A statesman thinks," Clarke: *Newsweek,* September 19, 1977, 47. "last best hope": Harnsberger, 136; Safire, *NYT Magazine,* March 15, 1981; Safire 1982, 207–8; November 27, 1988.

Roosevelt: Safire 1988, 268; Gamaliel Bradford, *The Quick and the Dead* (Boston: Houghton-Mifflin, 1931), 31. "Weasel word": Frost, 59; Stewart Chaplin, "The Stained Glass Political Platform," *Century,* June 1900 in Evans, 742. "Muckraker": Baker, 70; Safire 1978, 434; Ringo, 175; Mathews, vol. 2, 1094.

99. spinal similes: Max Lerner, ed., *The Mind and Faith of Justice Holmes* (Boston: Little, Brown, 1943), xxxii; Edmund Morris, *The Rise of Theodore Roosevelt* (Coward, McCann & Geoghegan, 1979; Ballantine, 1980), 610; Harry Thurston Peck, *Twenty Years of the Republic* (New York: Dodd, Mead, 1907), 642. Grant-Garfield: Frost, 93.

"Square deal," Woods, 239; Mathews, vol. 2, 1624; Mark Twain, *Life on the Mississippi* (New York: Heritage, 1944), 301.

"Speak softly": *Minneapolis Tribune,* September 3, 1901. Chicago: *Presidential Addresses and State Papers,* I, 265–6, in Albert Bushnell Hart and Herbert Ronald Ferleger, ed., *Theodore Roosevelt Cyclopedia* (Oyster Bay, NY: Theodore Roosevelt Association, 1989), 42; Platt, 123; NYT, April 4, 1903 in Oxford Modern, 183. Letter to friend: Henry F. Pringle, *Theodore Roosevelt: A Biography* (New York: Harcourt, Brace, 1931), 214. Sandburg, *The People, Yes,* op. cit., 17.

99–100. Coolidge: John Hiram McKee, *Coolidge Wit and Wisdom* (New York: Frederick A. Stokes, 1933); Claude M. Fuess, *Calvin Coolidge: The Man From Vermont* (Hamden, CT: Archon Books, 1939, 1965), 475–8; Ashley Montagu and Edward Darling, *The Prevalence of Nonsense* (New York: Harper & Row, 1967), 212–3; Donald R. McCoy, *The Quiet President* (Lawrence, KS: University Press of Kansas, 1967, 1988), 295–6; Shenkman 1988, 44.

100. "The business of America": Oxford, 162; NYT, January 18, 1925; Fuess, *Calvin Coolidge,* op. cit., 358; Bartlett's, 736.

"They hired the money": Woods, 246; Fuess, *Calvin Coolidge,* op. cit., 333; Jules Abels, *In the Time of Silent Cal* (New York: Putnam's, 1969), 40–1.

"You lose": Udall, 9; Ishbel Ross, *Grace Coolidge and Her Era* (New York: Dodd, Mead, 1962), 67; Edward Connery Lathem, ed., *Meet Calvin Coolidge: The Man Behind the Myth* (Brattleboro, VT: Stephen Greene, 1960), 159.

101. "He was against it": Harper, 509; Lathem, *Meet Calvin Coolidge,* op. cit., 151.

"Tell Mrs. Coolidge": Michael S. Gazzaniga, *Mind Matters* (Boston: Houghton Mifflin, 1988), 171.

"When more and more people": Fadiman, 214; Baker, 57; Shenkman 1988, 43; Edward Bennett Williams introduction to Ford, *Humor and the Presidency,* op. cit., 7; Stanley Walker, *City Editor* (New York: Frederick A. Stokes, 1934), 131. Thurber: William L. Shirer, *20th Century Journey* (New York: Simon & Schuster, 1976), 224–5.

"Rugged individualism": Herbert Hoover, *The Challenge to Liberty* (New York: Scribner's, 1934), 54; Bartlett's, 750; MPMFP, 1238; Harper, 295.

102. "A noble experiment": Herbert Hoover, *The Memoirs of Herbert Hoover: The Cabinet and the Presidency, 1920–1933* (New York: Macmillan, 1952), 201–2; Eugene Lyons, *Herbert Hoover: A Biography* (Garden City, NY: Doubleday, 1948, 1964), 181; Woods, 248; MPMFP, 728; Shenkman 1991, 125.

"A chicken": Woods, 104–5; Bailey, 376; Safire 1978, 110; Seldes 1960, 142; Latham, 125.

"Prosperity": MPMFP, 1902; Richard Norton Smith, *An Uncommon Man: The Triumph of Herbert Hoover* (New York: Simon & Schuster, 1984), 126; Boller and George, 48; Edward Angly, *Oh Yeah?* (New York: Viking, 1932), 17.

102–103. "A New Deal": Safire 1978, 100, 449–51; Safire, *NYT Magazine,* October 7, 1984; Safire 1988, 209; Safire 1990, 54; Raymond Moley, *After Seven Years* (New York: Harper & Brothers, 1939), 23–7; Samuel I. Rosenman, *Working With Roosevelt* (London: Rupert Hart-Davis, 1952), 77–8; MPMFP, 498; Home Book, 2298–8a.

103–104. "The only thing": Home Book, 655; MPMFP, 783–4; Bartlett's, 164, 179, 421; Morris, 416; Safire 1978, 471–2; Rosenman, *Working With Roosevelt,* op. cit., 93–5.

104. "I see": Harnsberger, 255; Safire 1978, 489; Leo Rosten, *The Power of Positive Nonsense* (New York: McGraw-Hill, 1977), 110–11; Wells, *In the Days of the Comet* (New York: Airmont, 1966), 37.

"Rather die": NYT, June 20, 1941; Harnsberger, 101. Ibarruri: Dolores Ibarruri, *They Shall Not Pass: The Autobiography of La Pasionaria* (New York: International Publishers, 1966), 195; Seldes 1960, xlviii; Seldes, 1985, 199. Zapata: Bartlett's, 759; John Gunther, *Inside Latin America* (New York: Harper & Brothers, 1941), 63; Leigh White, *The Long Balkan Night* (New York: Scribner's, 1944), 390. Ford: *Public Papers,* July 4, 1976, 645.

Reagan: Elizabeth Drew, *The New Yorker,* October 29, 1984, 140, 143; NYT, September 9, 1985; Paul D. Erickson, *Reagan Speaks* (New York: New York University Press, 1985), 38–50; Michael Paul Rogin, *Ronald Reagan: The*

Movie (Berkeley, CA: University of California Press, 1987), 7–9, 14–7, 33; Lou Cannon, *President Reagan: The Role of a Lifetime* (New York: Simon & Schuster, 1991), 123, 129.

104–105. "I paid": Drew, *The New Yorker,* October 29, 1984, 140, 143; Rogin, *Ronald Reagan,* op. cit., 7; Cannon, *President Reagan,* op. cit., 67–8, 123, "Nightline," ABC-TV, May 27, 1992.

105. "A recession": Reagan: Harper, 203; NYT, October 2, 1986. Truman: Morrow, 292; Macmillan, 583–4; Beck: Simpson 1957, 26.

"If not us": Reagan: Alcoa ad, NYT, October 22, 1981; Hillel: two letters to Safire 1990, 71; R. Travers Herford, ed., *The Ethics of the Talmud: Sayings of the Fathers* (New York: Schocken Books, 1962), 34.

"There is no greater happiness:" *Newsweek,* December 21, 1981, 26; Rogin, *Ronald Reagan,* op. cit., 33; Rowes, 50; Lorraine L. Koeppen letter to *People,* December 8, 1980, 6.

105–106. "Honey, I forgot to duck": Reagan: *Time,* April 13, 1981, 30. Dempsey: Cerf, 314; Sugar, 55; Oxford Modern, 67; Red Smith, NYT, April 1, 1981.

"Go ahead": Reagan: NYT, March 14, 1985. Eastwood: *Playboy,* May 1984, 145; Fennel, 210.

"Where do we find such men?": Erickson, *Reagan Speaks,* op. cit., 38; Rogin, *Ronald Reagan,* op. cit., 7; Rees 1989, 136; Rees 1991, 240.

"There is nothing better": *Time,* December 28, 1987, 52; January 18, 1988, 7; CODP, 165; Home Book, 929; MPMFP, 1988; Boller and George, 108.

107. "A thousand points": Peggy Noonan, *What I Saw at the Revolution* (New York: Random House, 1990), 312–3; *People,* February 26, 1990, 84; Lewis, *The Magician's Nephew* (New York: Macmillan, 1955, Collier, 1970), 99; Wolfe, *The Web and the Rock* (New York: Grosset & Dunlap, 1939), 169, 45, 169; Noonan, *What I Saw at the Revolution,* op. cit., 313.

107–108. "A kinder, gentler": Noonan, *What I Saw at the Revolution,* op. cit., 304; Darrow, *The Story of My Life,* op. cit., 68; Safire, *NYT Magazine,* March 12, 1989. Chaplin: videotape of *The Great Dictator;* Gregory Najarian letter to NYT, May 1, 1989; Crews, *A Childhood: The Biography of a Place* (New York: Harper & Row, 1978), 49. Cuomo, Orbison, Presley: WSJ, January 19, 1989.

108. "Read my lips": NYT, November 22, 1988. "Opera," Michael Kramer, *New York,* April 7, 1980, 13. "Ninety percent": Safire, *NYT Magazine,* August 13, 1989; Thomas Peters and Robert Waterman, *In Search of Excellence* (New York: Harper & Row, 1982), 119; DDN, January 12, 1992; Lax, interview, November 13, 1991; Allen-Safire, *NYT Magazine,* August 13, 1989.

CHAPTER 8: THE TWAIN SYNDROME

109. Cerf, x.

Twain: LAT, August 6, 1991; DDN, August 6, 1991; *ABC World News Tonight,* October 22, 1991; Hirst interview, December 16, 1991; January 29, 1992.

109–110. "So I became a newspaperman": Platt, 237. "The only way for a newspaperman": Bill Adler, ed., *The Washington Wits* (New York: Macmillan, 1967), 166; Mencken, 939. "For every problem": Studds: *ABC World News Tonight,* September 26, 1991; H. L. Mencken, *A Mencken Chrestomathy* (New York: Knopf, 1944), 443; Platt, 326–7.

110. Bradley: Mark Crispin Miller, *Boxed In* (Chicago: Northwestern University Press, 1988), 112–3; Safire: Safire 1991, xi; Quayle: NYT, June 18, 1992.

Hirst: *ABC World News Tonight,* October 22, 1991.

"To cease smoking": *Reader's Digest,* December 1945, 26; Hirst, op. cit.

"When I was a boy": *Reader's Digest,* September 1937, 22; Platt, interview, December 5, 1990; Platt, xiv.

111. "The coldest winter": Caen, NYT, September 26, 1975; *RQ,* Winter 1988, 148; Robert Pack Browning, *Bancroftiana,* November 1981, 10.

"The man who does not read": *New York Post,* April 6, 1990; *RQ,* Summer 1978, 340.

111–112. "The reports of my death": Hirst, interviews, op. cit.; Hirst letter, January 30, 1992; Frank Marshall White, "Mark Twain as a Newspaper Reporter," *Outlook,* December 24, 1910, 966–7; *New York Journal,* June 2, 1897; Twain typescript, April 3, 1906, in Mark Twain Papers; revision, undated, ibid.; Mark Twain, "Chapters from My Autobiography," *North American Review,* September 21, 1906, 460. Longhand note: *Outlook,* op. cit., 965; *The Rotarian,* August, 1945; *Mark Twain Quarterly,* Spring-Summer 1947, cover.

112. "The finest Congress": Platt, 57.

"Whenever I feel": *ABC World News Tonight,* October 22, 1991; *Newsweek,* November 17, 1989, 77; *Reader's Digest,* January 1938, 80; Ashmore, *Unseasonable Truths: The Life of Robert Maynard Hutchins* (Boston: Little, Brown, 1989), 114.

"Wagner's music": Mark Twain, *Mark Twain's Autobiography* (New York: Harper & Brothers, 1924), 338.

112–113. Hirst: interview, December 20, 1992.

113. "Even paranoids": *People,* September 11, 1989, 99; Udall, 224. "I'm not afraid of dying": Peter, 234; Gerald Gardner, *I Coulda Been a Contender* (New York: Warner, 1992), 169, back jacket.

Mizner: Addison Mizner, *The Many Mizners* (New York: Sears, 1932); Edward Dean Sullivan, *The Fabulous Wilson Mizner* (New York: Henkle, 1935); Jim Tully, *Esquire,* July 1938, 45, 176–7, 179; Alva Johnston, *The Legendary Mizners* (New York: Farrar, Straus and Young, 1953); Sidney Phillips, *Diners' Club,* December 1963, 56–7, 60; John Burke, *Rogue's Progress* (New York: Putnam's, 1975).

Mencken: Burke, Ibid., viii; Loos, *A Girl Like I* (New York: Viking, 1966), 22; Burke, *Rogue's Progress,* op. cit., 281.

113–114. Mizner comments: Bartlett's, 757; Fadiman, 994–5; Green, 561; Morris, 389; Sullivan, *The Fabulous Wilson Mizner,* op. cit., 53, 268–9; Johnston, *The Legendary Mizners,* op. cit., 66–7; Tully, *Esquire,* op. cit., 176.

114. Mizner on suckers: Burke, *Rogue's Progress,* op. cit., 124–5; Johnston, *The Legendary Mizners,* op. cit., 208–9.

"Hello, sucker!": Sullivan, *The Fabulous Wilson Mizner,* op. cit., 144; Glenn Shirley, *Hello, Sucker!: The Story of Texas Guinan* (Austin, TX: Eakin Press, 1989), 47.

"Never give a sucker": Mizner: Tully, *Esquire,* op. cit., 45; Johnston, *The Legendary Mizners,* op. cit., 209; *The New Yorker,* January 25, 1947, 19; Fields: Nicholas Yanni, *W. C. Fields* (New York: Pyramid, 1974), 113; Oxford Modern, 79; *Collier's,* November 28, 1925, 26; Helen Hayes, *Collier's,* September 22, 1951, 80. Albee: Bartlett's 14th, 842; Bartlett's 15th, 683; Fadiman, 833; Joe Laurie, Jr., *Vaudeville: From the Honky-Tonks to the Palace* (New York: Henry Holt, 1953), 342.

Addison Mizner: Addison Mizner, *The Many Mizners,* op. cit., 265.

115. "just some mouse": Gary Nuhn, DDN, October 23, 1991; Steve Gietschier, *Sporting News,* April 20, 1992.

"if you steal": Allan Fotheringham, *MacLean's,* June 6, 1983, 56; Burke, *Rogue's Progress,* op. cit., 127; Cerf, 232.

"Be nice to people": Winchell: Larry Fields, PDN, May 21, 1979. Durante, Rowes, 22; Fadiman, 995. Mizner: Bartlett's, 75; Partridge and Beale, 10.

"Living in Hollywood": Loos, *A Girl Like I,* op. cit., 21. Walker: Fadiman, 240; Macmillan, 128; Johnston, *The Legendary Mizners,* op. cit., 67.

"Life's a tough proposition": Harper, 346; Hendrickson, 333; S. J. Perelman, *NYT Magazine,* April 23, 1978.

115–116. Sullivan, *The Fabulous Wilson Mizner,* op. cit., 143; Tully, *Esquire,* 45, 176.

116. "The only difference": Liberace: Rowes, 50. Brothers: Bennett Cerf, *The Sound of Laughter* (Garden City, NY: Doubleday, 1970), in Dickson 1980, 20. Franklin: Home Book, 33; Newcomb, 265.

"There's more old drunkards": Van Doren, *Benjamin Franklin,* op. cit., 110; MPMFP, 596–7. Willie Nelson: "I Gotta Get Drunk," words and music by Willie Nelson, © 1983, Tree Publishing.

Allen: Steve Allen, *Mark It and Strike It: An Autobiography* (New York: Holt, Rinehart and Winston, 1960), 341. *Punch* editor: Bates, *Lincoln Stories,* op. cit., 12. Berle: Fadiman, 835.

117. "I may vomit," Johnston, *The Legendary Mizners,* op. cit., 67.

Woollcott: Samuel Hopkins Adams, *A. Woollcott: His Life and His World* (New York: Reynal & Hitchcock, 1945); Edwin P. Hoyt, *Alexander Woollcott: The Man Who Came to Dinner* (New York: Abelard-Schuman, 1968); Howard Teichmann, *Smart Aleck* (New York: Morrow, 1976). Hoyt, *Alexander Woollcott,* op. cit., 196.

"This is the way": Woollcott: David A. France letter to *People,* February 28, 1977. Kaufman: *People,* February 7, 1977, 32. Gibbs: Cerf, 27; Fadiman, 903. Case: Fadiman, 903. Shaw: Wagner, 85. Fleming: Macmillan, 585.

117–118. "All the things": Teichmann, *Smart Aleck,* op. cit., 221; *Reader's Digest,* December 1933, 109; Platt, 163. Fields: Tony Vellela, *Circus,* March 16, 1978, 45; Schieffer, *TV Guide,* August 17, 1991, 24.

118–119. "Let's get out": Woollcott: Fadiman, 255; Hendrickson, 182; Macmillan, 15; Bartlett's 14th, 999; Bartlett's 15th, 812. Teichmann, *Smart Aleck,* op. cit., 107. Cerf, 132. Nathaniel Benchley: *Robert Benchley* (New York: McGraw-Hill, 1955), 146; Teichmann, *Smart Aleck,* op. cit., 107. Benchley film: Fennell, 67. Smith: LAT, August 21, 1985. Oxford Modern, 225.

119. "There is less": NYT, January 4, 1922; Lee Israel, *Miss Tallulah Bankhead* (New York: Putnam's, 1972, Dell, 1973), 63; Tallulah Bankhead, *Tallulah: My Autobiography* (New York: Harper & Brothers, 1952), 82.

119–120. Parker: Jim Murray, LAT, September 23, 1973. Kaufman: Scott Meredith, *George S. Kaufman and His Friends* (Garden City, NY: Doubleday, 1974), 139.

120. Parker denial: Hubbard Keavey, *Dallas Morning News,* December 7, 1941.

"Pearls before swine": Robert E. Drennan, ed., *The Algonquin Wits* (New York: Citadel, 1968), 113; DDN, July 12, 1990; Donald J. Quigley letter to NYT, February 4, 1989; John Keats: *You Might as Well Live* (New York:

Simon & Schuster, 1970), 48–9. Woollcott story: Hoyt, *Alexander Woollcott,* op. cit., 42.

Alexander Woollcott, *While Rome Burns* (New York: Viking, 1935), 142–52; Dorothy Parker, "A Valentine for Mr. Woollcott," Cleveland Amory and Frederic Bradlee, ed., *Vanity Fair: Selections from America's Most Memorable Magazine* (New York: Viking, 1960), 290–1.

"MEN": Woollcott, *While Rome Burns,* op. cit., 144; Parker denial: Saul Pett, *New York Herald Tribune,* October 13, 1963; Parker letter, Nathaniel Benchley, *Robert Benchley,* op. cit., 145.

120–121. "Runs the gamut": Woollcott, *While Rome Burns,* op. cit., 147; Katharine Hepburn, *Me: Stories of My Life* (Knopf/Random House Large Print, 1991), 231; Garry Carey, *Katharine Hepburn* (Thorndike, Maine: Thorndike Press, 1983), 103.

121. "Excuse my dust": Woollcott, *While Rome Burns,* op. cit., 146; *Vanity Fair,* June 1925, 51. Ephron: Nora Ephron, *Crazy Salad* (New York: Knopf, 1975, Bantam, 1976), 141.

"How can they tell?": Cerf, 261; Fadiman, 1004; Udall, 9. Tully, *Esquire,* op. cit., 175; Alva Johnston, *The Legendary Mizners,* op. cit., 65; Ringo, 193.

121–122. Rogers: Homer Croy, *Our Will Rogers* (New York: Duell, Sloan and Pearce, 1953); Paula McSpadden Love, ed., *The Will Rogers Book* (Indianapolis: Bobbs-Merrill, 1961); Donald Day, *Will Rogers: A Biography* (New York: David McKay, 1962); Richard M. Ketchum, *Will Rogers: His Life and Times* (New York: American Heritage, 1973); Peter C. Rollins, *Will Rogers: A Bio-Bibliography* (Westport, CT: Greenwood Press, 1984).

122. "Buy land": *New York,* June 13, 1977, 109. "There is nothing": Love, *The Will Rogers Book,* op. cit., 67.

122–123. "I've never met": Croy, *Our Will Rogers,* op. cit., 286–8; *Saturday Evening Post,* November 6, 1926, 231; Day, *Will Rogers,* op. cit., 189–90; Rollins, *Will Rogers,* op. cit., 52; BG, June 16, 1930. Croy: Croy, *Our Will Rogers,* op. cit., Foreword.

123. Marx-Kaufman: NYT, April 16, 1988; Malcolm Goldstein, *George S. Kaufman: His Life, His Theater* (New York: Oxford, 1979), 109

123–124. "I don't want to belong": Arthur Marx, *Life with Groucho* (New York: Simon & Schuster, 1954), 45. Zeppo: Rees 1984, 24; Sheekman: introduction to Groucho Marx, *The Groucho Letters* (New York: Simon & Schuster, 1967), 8. Groucho: Groucho Marx, *Groucho and Me* (Bernard Geis, 1959, Dell, 1960), 239–40; Rees 1984, 24.

124. "Time wounds all heels": Groucho: Macmillan, 572; Green, 526. Cerf: Fadiman, 1009. Ace: Goodman Ace, *The Fine Art of Hypochondria* (Garden City, NY: Doubleday, 1966), 63. Fields: Morris, 576. Brecher: Oxford Modern, 38. Case: Frank Case, *Tales of a Wayward Inn* (New York: Frederick A. Stokes, 1938), 232.

"I've been around": Max Wilk, *The Wit and Wisdom of Hollywood* (New York: Atheneum, 1971), 51; Levant: Oscar Levant, *The Memoirs of an Amnesiac* (New York: Putnam's, 1965), 192. Harris: Jules Witcover, *Marathon* (New York: Viking, 1977), 146.

CHAPTER 9: SAY IT AGAIN, SAM

125–126. Goldwyn: Alva Johnston, *The Great Goldwyn* (New York: Random House, 1937, Arno Press, 1978); Arthur Marx, *Goldwyn: A Biography of the Man Behind the Myth* (New York: Norton, 1976); Carol Easton, *The Search for Sam Goldwyn* (New York: Morrow, 1976); A. Scott Berg, *Goldwyn: A Biography* (New York: Knopf, 1989); Arthur Mayer, *Merely Colossal* (New York: Simon & Schuster, 1953), 9–15, 170, 249; Norman Zierold, *The Moguls* (New York: Coward-McCann, 1969), 119–29; Wagner, 106–14.

126. *Random House Dictionary* (New York: Random House, 1967), 608.

Goldwyn-reporter, Earl Sparling, *New York Post*, July 25, 1939. Staffers: Carl Rollyson, *Lillian Hellman: Her Legend and Her Legacy* (New York: St. Martin's, 1988), 77; Philip French, *The Movie Moguls* (Chicago: Henry Regnery, 1969), 46; Marx, *Goldwyn*, op. cit., 9–10.

"blanket check": Marx, ibid., 298. "mucus of a good picture": Mayer, *Merely Colossal*, op. cit., 10.

126–127. Goldwyn embarrassed: *Reader's Digest* incident: Marx, Goldwyn, op. cit., 296–8. Grumbled: Loudon Wainwright, *Life,* February 16, 1959, 116. Wife concurred: *Toronto Globe & Mail*, September 24, 1959.

127. "Include me out": *Variety*, February 6, 1974, 6; *New York Post*, April 23, 1976; Marx, *Goldwyn*, op. cit., 9. Own epitaph: Wagner, 107.

127–128. "A verbal contract": Kanin, *Hollywood*, op. cit., 299; Zierold, *The Moguls,* op. cit., 128.

128. "I can answer": Zierold, Ibid., 127; Johnston, *The Great Goldwyn*, op. cit., 27–8. Chaplin: Kanin, *Hollywood*, op. cit., 298.

"I read part": Johnston, *The Great Goldwyn*, op. cit., 28. "Anyone who sees": Hellman: Kanin, *Hollywood*, op. cit., 299; Marilyn and Hy Gardner, *Glad You Asked That!* (New York: Ace, 1976), 53. See psychiatrist: *New York Post*, November 22, 1946; *Reader's Digest*, December 1948, 122.

128–129. "We'll make her": Mayer, *Merely Colossal,* op. cit., 9; NYT, October 30, 1986. Marx, *Goldwyn,* op. cit., 210.

129. "Too blood and thirsty": Marx, ibid., 322. Thurber: see chapter 6.

"What won't they": Berg, *Goldwyn,* op. cit., 396; Marx, *Goldwyn,* op. cit., 112. Johnston, *The Great Goldwyn,* op. cit., 28.

129–130. *People,* November 23, 1981, 140; April 29, 1985, 130.

130. "If you have a message": Goldwyn: NYT, March 25, 1982; *Mother Jones,* September–October 1977, 61; Melinda Corey and George Ochoa, *The Man in Lincoln's Nose* (New York: Simon & Schuster, 1990), 169. Warner: Rees 1981, 60. Cohn: Colombo, 113. Bogart: Boller and Davis, 339. Brando: Rowes, 220. Kaufman: James R. Gaines, *Wit's End* (New York: Harcourt Brace Jovanovich, 1977), 47. Hemingway: Rowes, 307. Shaw: Rex Reed, *People are Crazy Here* (New York: Delacorte, 1974; Dell, 1975), 257.

"Never let that bastard": Goldwyn, Warner, Zukor: Rowes, 228. Cohan: Johnston, *The Great Goldwyn,* op. cit., 29; Cerf 38; vaudeville: Tanzer, *The Kennedy Circle,* op. cit., xv.

"I don't have ulcers": Goldwyn: Jonathon Green, *Morrow's International Dictionary of Contemporary Quotations* (New York: Morrow, 1982), 309. Cohn: Ringo, 266; Macmillan 272; French, *The Movie Moguls,* op. cit., 40. Sarnoff: "Empire of the Air," PBS, January 29, 1992; *Newsweek,* January 27, 1992, 61. Koch: NYT January 20, 1984 in Simpson 1987, 31. Lombardi: Tom Weir, *USA Today,* August 16, 1990. Fitch: Sports Illustrated, *They Said It* (New York: Oxmoor House, 1990), 60. Novelty sign: Spinrad, 94.

131. "I have a foolproof device": Cohn: *Newsweek,* October 27, 1980, 123; Colombo, 113; French, *The Movie Moguls,* op. cit., 57. Hewitt: NYT, April 25, 1989, April 29, 1989.

"It only proves": Skelton: Bob Thomas, *King Cohn* (New York: Putnam's, 1967, Bantam, 1968), xvii; PI, September 28, 1989; Boller and Davis, *Hollywood Anecdotes,* op. cit., 69; French, *The Movie Moguls,* op. cit., 1; Wagner, op. cit., 114. Lahr: John Lahr, *Notes on a Cowardly Lion* (New York: Knopf, 1969, Ballantine, 1970), 210; Ringo, 275. "The reason so many people": Macmillan, 285; Ringo, 266.

"I've been rich": Tucker: Bartlett's, 789; Morris, 465; NYDN, February 10, 1966. Lewis: Rowes, 21; Edwin McDowell, *NYT Book Review,* June 27, 1982; Patrick O'Connor, interview, July 7, 1990. Tucker-Lewis performance ads, Joe E. Lewis archives, Lincoln Center Theater Collection.

"From birth": NYDN, August 5, 1979; Bartlett's, 788–9. Norris: Gee, 116.

132. "Life begins": Macmillan, 11; CODP, 132; Rees 1984, 55–6; Rees 1991, 22–3.

"Just know your lines": *People,* July 17, 1978, 118; Harper, 550; Macmillan, 3; Rees 1984, 18. Coward: Ibid.

"Toto, I have a feeling": videotape of *The Wizard of Oz.*

"What we've got here": videotape of *Cool Hand Luke*; Haun, 95.

132–133. "Me Tarzan, you Jane": Weissmuller: *Photoplay,* June 1932, 119; exact words: Burroughs v. Metro-Goldwyn-Mayer 683 F.2d 610, (2nd Cir. 1982); Safire, *NYT Magazine,* April 28, 1985.

133–134. "The poor people": Grizzard, *If I Ever Go Back to Georgia I'm Gonna Nail My Feet to the Ground* (New York: Villard, 1990), 96.

134. Rocky V: WNYW-Channel 5 news (New York City), December 14, 1990; DDN, December 18, 1990.

"To be on the wire": videotape of *All That Jazz;* Fennell, 192. Wallenda: PI, October 27, 1987. Caracciola: *Car and Driver,* November 1985, 127.

"Dying is easy": *Time,* September 27, 1982, 71; Kean: NYT, November 14, 1982. Gwenn: *Time,* January 30, 1984, 79; NYT, November 14, 1982. See also Dale Thomajan, *Film Comment,* March–April, 1990, 68.

"He has every characteristic": Fennell, 143; Harris, 60.

"Are we having fun yet?" Fennell, 206; Bill Griffith, *Zippy Stories* (Berkeley, CA: And/Or Press, 1981), cover; Justin Kaplan letter, July 24, 1990.

135. "I want to be alone": Haun, 7; PDN, April 16, 1990; *USA Today,* April 16, 1990; *People,* April 30, 1990, 93; Alexander Walker, *Sex in the Movies* (Baltimore: Penguin, 1966), 99–100. Told friend: John Bainbridge, *Life,* January 24, 1955, 113; Fennell, 19.

"Come with me": Harry Purvis, *TV Guide,* December 30, 1978; *The Morning Call* (Allentown, PA), August 29, 1978; *Time,* September 4, 1978, 71; *NBC Nightly News,* August 27, 1978; Burnam 1980, 47; Larry Swindell, *Charles Boyer* (Garden City, NY: Doubleday, 1983), 108.

"Why don't you come up": videotape of *She Done Him Wrong;* George Eells and Stanley Musgrove, *Mae West: A Biography* (New York: Morrow, 1982), 112.

"No man who hates": see Chapter 1.

"Never give a sucker": Fields-sucker: Donald Deschner, *The Films of W. C. Fields* (New York: Citadel Press, 1966), 158.

136. "On the whole": actual words on vault, PI, January 29, 1979; Burnam, 123. More popular version, Cleveland Amory and Frederic Bradlee, ed., *Vanity Fair,* June 1925, 51.

Hired ghosts: Florabel Muir, NYDN, January 12, 1970. Cerf, 179.

"It's not a fit night": Fields's denial: Ronald J. Fields, ed., *W. C. Fields by Himself* (Englewood Cliffs, NJ: Prentice-Hall, 1973, Warner, 1974), 94.

Robinson: *Sight and Sound,* Summer 1967, 128.

137. "Judy!": Purvis, *TV Guide,* op. cit., 28–9; Grant comment: Hy Gardner, Philadelphia *Evening Bulletin,* August 24, 1969.

"Old Cary Grant fine": Geoffrey Wansell, *Haunted Idol: The Story of the Real Cary Grant* (New York: Morrow, 1984), 310.

"You dirty rat!": PI, March 15, 1974; *PI TV Week,* March 17, 1974, 3; Michael Freedland, *Cagney* (New York: Stein & Day, 1975), 240–1. *Blonde Crazy:* Macmillan, 284; Rees 1991, 67.

137–138. "All right, you guys!": James Cagney, *Cagney by Cagney* (Garden City, NY: Doubleday, 1976), 74. Keyes: *PI TV Week,* March 17, 1974, 3. To Gorshin: Doug Warren with James Cagney, *Cagney* (New York: St. Martin's, 1983), 198.

138. "Drop the gun": Burnam 1975, 255; Ezra Goodman, *Bogey: The Good-Bad Guy* (New York: Lyle Stuart, 1965), 31; Safire, *NYT Magazine,* July 1, 1990; Rees 1984, 178; Rees 1991, 119.

"Tennis anyone?": Burnam 1975, 255; Goodman, *Bogey,* op. cit., 31; Safire, *NYT Magazine,* July 1, 1990. Bartlett's 14th, 1046; Bartlett's 15th, 843. Oxford, 199.

138–139. "Play it again": Howard Koch, *Casablanca: Script and Legend* (Woodstock, NY: Overlook Press, 1973), 87, 95; Rees 1984, 184; Safire 1980, 231; Koch, *Casablanca,* op. cit., 17. "The Spoilers": Purvis, *TV Guide,* op. cit., 28; Allen, *Life,* March 21, 1969, 65.

139. "Did you ever wonder": CBS News, *60 Minutes,* September 13, 1989, transcript, vol. XXI, #52, 6.

"Beam me up": Oxford Modern, 182; Rees 1991, 149.

139–140. "I laughed all the way": Joseph Laffan Morse, ed., *The Unicorn Book of 1954* (New York: Unicorn Books, 1955), 306; Simpson 1988, 212; Morris, 344. Perdue: *People,* August 30, 1982, 71. Tavern owner: *Newsweek,* January 7, 1980, 70.

140. "WIOU": *DDN TV Week,* January 6, 1991, 4. Anderson fable: *People,* June 20, 1988, 21.

CHAPTER 10: SAY IT AIN'T SO!

142–143. "Nice guys": Frank Graham, *New York Journal-American,* July 16, 1946; Red Barber interview, February 14, 1992; *Baseball Digest,* September 1946, 59–60. See also: Frank Graham, Jr., *A Farewell to Heroes* (New York: Viking, 1981), 207–9.

143–144. Durocher denies: Marilyn and Hy Gardner, *Glad You Asked That!* op. cit., 20. Durocher assents: Leo Durocher, *Nice Guys Finish Last* (New York: Simon & Schuster, 1975), 14. Late 1970s: NYT, May 21, 1978. English collection: Green, 268.

144–145. Fullerton, *New York Evening World,* September 30, 1920.

145. Oliver Gramling, *AP: The Story of the News* (New York: Farrar and Rinehart, 1940), 292. *Chicago Herald,* September 29, 1920.

Jackson denial: Donald S. Gropman, *Say it Ain't So, Joe!* (Boston: Little, Brown, 1979), 191–2.

145–146. "Win one": Jerry Brondfield, *Rockne* (New York: Random House, 1976), 97, 219–223; NYDN, November 12, 1928, in Francis Wallace, *Knute Rockne* (Garden City, NY: Doubleday, 1960), 212–7. Rockne magazine article: *Collier's,* November 22, 1930, 64.

146. *Knute Rockne, All-American,* 1940, NYT, October 27, 1980; Rees 1991, 242; Fennell, 57.

Philadelphia lawyer: *PI Today,* October 1, 1978.

"When the going gets tough": Martin Gross, *Nostalgia Quiz Book #3* (New York: Bonanza Books, 1975), 104, 274; CODP, 96; Oxford Modern, 120; Safire 1978, 575; Brondfield interview, June 10, 1977.

146–147. "Show me a good loser": Brondfield, *Rockne,* op. cit., 102; June 10, 1977 interview. Nixon: *RN,* op. cit., 19–20; Carter: David Broder, *Morning Call* (Allentown, PA), October 27, 1976. Jimmy Carter *Why Not the Best?* (Nashville, TN: Broadman Press, 1975), 112.

147. "The bigger they are": Sullivan: Albert Payson Terhune, *American Magazine,* June, 1926, 19. Corbett: MPMFP, 749; Maria Leach, ed., *Funk & Wagnalls Standard Dictionary of Folklore, Mythology and Legend* (New York: Harper & Row, 1949, 1972), 916. Fitzsimmons: Oxford Modern, 81; Ringo, 46; Lee Green, *Sportswit* (New York: Harper & Row, 1984), 57; Spinrad, 215; Fadiman, 271; Morris, 61. Fitzsimmons popularized: *Brooklyn Daily Eagle,* August 11, 1900. Terhune, *American Magazine,* op. cit.; English proverb: CODP, 18.

147–148. "We was robbed!" Bartlett's, 836. Gunboat Smith: Peter Heller, *"In This Corner . . . !"* (New York: Simon & Schuster, 1973) 44–5. Jacobs obituary:

NYT, April 25, 1940. New York newspapers, *Daily Mirror,* June 22, 1932; *Times,* June 22, 1932; *Evening Post,* June 22, 1932; *American,* June 22, 1932.

148–149. "I should of stood": Lardner: *Strong Cigars and Lovely Women* (New York: Funk & Wagnalls, 1951), 60; Bartlett's 12th, 1001; Bartlett's 13th, 975. Morris, 524. Bruccoli to Safire 1988, 43. Murray-Smith, LAT, November 9, 1989.

149. Lardner, *Strong Cigars and Lovely Women,* op. cit., 61.

"We'll win": Roger Wilkins, NYT, November 13, 1977, George J. Friedman letter, November 27, 1977, Arthur J. Susskind letter, December 11, 1977; Joe Louis with Edna and Art Rust, Jr., *Joe Louis: My Life* (New York: Harcourt Brace Jovanovich, 1978), 174; Barney Nagler, *Brown Bomber* (New York: World Publishing, 1972), 130–1; Joe Louis Barrow, Jr., and Barbara Munder, *Joe Louis* (New York: McGraw-Hill, 1988), 139; Chris Mead, *Champion* (New York: Scribner's, 1985), 218; Gerald Astor, *And a Credit to His Race* (New York: Saturday Review Press, 1974), 219. Lincoln: MPMFP, 983.

"I am the greatest": Ali comments: Colman McCarthy, PI, September 22, 1978. See also Lee Green, *Sportswit,* op. cit., 64–65; Rees 1984, 221–2. Hauser interview, December 7, 1991. Wilfrid Sheed, *Muhammad Ali* (New York: New American Library, 1976), 70, 72; Lewis, vii.

"Float like a butterfly": Sheed, *Muhammad Ali,* op. cit., 57; Lewis, vii; Harper, 533; *Time,* February 27, 1978, 74; Hauser interview, December 7, 1991.

150. "Don't look back": *Collier's,* June 13, 1953, 55. "Someone": Morris, 187. "They": Ford, *Humor and the Presidency,* op. cit., 9, 146. "Like they say": USAT, October 11, 1990. "If you look back": *Sporting News,* April 6, 1992.

"You could": *Saturday Evening Post,* April 5, 1941, 9, 114; Dickson 1991, 427; Lee Green, *Sportswit,* op. cit., 65; Safire, NYT *Magazine,* March 2, 1986.

"I'd like to thank": Joe Garagiola, *It's Anybody's Ballgame* (Chicago: Contemporary, 1988, Jove, 1989), 191; Powers in Dickson 1991, 43.

150–151. "How the hell": Dickson 1991, 44.

151. "I really didn't say": *Sports Ilustrated,* March 17, 1986, 18. Garagiola: *It's Anybody's Ballgame,* op. cit., 190; Rosenthal, NYT *Magazine,* September 15, 1991.

"It ain't over": Yogi Berra with Tom Horton, *Yogi: It Ain't Over . . .* (New York: McGraw-Hill, 1989), 5.

151–152. "You can observe": NYT, October 25, 1963; Berra, *Yogi,* op. cit., 76.

152. "It's déjà vu": Berra, *Yogi,* op. cit., 15; to Safire, *NYT Magazine,* February 15, 1989.

"A wrong mistake": Berra, *Yogi,* op. cit., 8; Pepe, *The Wit and Wisdom of Yogi Berra,* op. cit., 40, xv.

152–153. "Baseball is 90 percent mental": David Ring letter to *Sports Illustrated,* May 14, 1979, 114. Ozark: Sugar, 3. Wohlford: *Sporting News,* October 1, 1977, 4; *Sports Illustrated,* October 24, 1977, 16. Berra, *Yogi,* op. cit., 7.

153. "Always go": Berra denial: *Yogi,* op. cit., 15–16; to Safire, *NYT Magazine,* February 15, 1989. Day: Clarence Day, *Life With Father* (New York: Washington Square Press, 1935, 1962), 164.

"Nobody ever goes there": Murray Chass, NYT, February 13, 1984; Roy Blount, *Sports Illustrated,* April 2, 1984, 92; Carmen Berra, Safire, *NYT Magazine,* February 15, 1987; Roy Blount, *Sports Illustrated,* op. cit., 92; Pepe, *Wit and Wisdom,* op. cit., 37; Garagiola, *It's Anybody's Ballgame,* op. cit., 190. Parker: Blount, *Sports Illustrated,* op. cit., 92. John McNulty, *New Yorker,* February 10, 1943, 13.

"The future": Jon Talton, DDN, November 11, 1990; Schwarzkopf in Rosenthal, *NYT Magazine,* op. cit. Clarke: Paul Dickson, *The Future File* (New York: Rawson, 1977), vii.

Dr. Zhivago: Dickson 1991, 42.

"When you reach": Murray Chass, NYT, June 24, 1990.

154. "Football isn't": Lombardi: James Michener, *Sports in America* (New York: Random House, 1976, Fawcett Crest, 1977), 520. Daugherty: Sugar, 80; Sports Illustrated, *They Said It,* op. cit., 56. Ditka: Melvin Durslag, *TV Guide,* November 8, 1986, 45.

"Winning isn't everything": Sanders: Joel Sayre, *Sports Illustrated,* December 26, 1955, 29; Platt, 373. Kuharich: NYT, January 29, 1981. Tatum: Stephen D. Ward in Ralph Slovenko and James A. Knight, ed., *Motivations in Play, Games and Sports* (Springfield, IL: Charles Thomas, 1967), 312. Veeck: *NYT Magazine,* October 18, 1964, 28; Simpson 1964, 467.

155. Lombardi profile: Marshall Smith, *Life,* December 7, 1962, 52; Jerry Kramer *Instant Replay* (New York: New American Library, 1968; Signet, 1969), 50. Former player: Joe Murphy letter to NYT, January 9, 1977; "the *will* to win: Ibid.; Robert Riger, *Esquire,* November 1962, 178. "I have been quoted": *Vince Lombardi on Football* (New York: Van Nostrand Reinhold, 1973, 1981), 4.

Algren: H. E. F. Donahue, *Conversations with Algren* (New York: Hill and Wang, 1964), 154.

CHAPTER 11: THE LITERARY LIFT

156. "Immature poets": T. S. Eliot, "Philip Massinger," in *Sacred Wood* (New York: Barnes & Noble, 1920), 125.

"A good composer": Igor Stravinsky in Peter Yates, *Twentieth Century Music* (New York: Minerva Press, 1967), 41.

156–157. "Never play cards": Nelson Algren, *A Walk on the Wild Side* (New York: Farrar, Straus and Giroux, 1956, Fawcett Crest, 1968), 243. Subsequent interview: H. E. F. Donahue, *Conversations with Algren*, op. cit., viii. Bettina Drew, *Nelson Algren: A Life on the Wild Side* (New York: Putnam's, 1989). Drew interview, December 4, 1991. Peltz interview, December 12, 1991.

157. Byron: Stephens, 100.

157–158. Fitzgerald-Hemingway: "The Rich Boy," in F. Scott Fitzgerald, *Babylon Revisited and Other Stories* (New York: Scribner's, 1960), 152. Hemingway, "The Snows of Kilamanjaro," *Esquire*, August 1936, 200. F. Scott Fitzgerald, *The Crack-Up*, Edmund Wilson, ed. (New York: New Directions, 1945), 125. Hemingway-Perkins-Colum: Matthew J. Bruccoli, *Some Sort of Epic Grandeur: The Life of F. Scott Fitzgerald* (New York: Harcourt Brace Jovanovich, 1981), 411–13; John Kuehl and Jackson R. Bryer, ed., *Dear Scott/Dear Max* (New York: Scribner's, 1971), 230–2. Hemingway, *The Snows of Kilamanjaro* (New York: Scribner's, 1927, 1936), 23. King: Larry L. King, *None but a Blockhead* (New York: Viking, 1985), 242.

158–159. "You are a lost generation": James R. Mellow, *A Charmed Circle,* (New York: Praeger, 1974), 273–4; Hemingway, *A Moveable Feast* (New York: Scribner's, 1964), 29–30; Gertrude Stein, *Everybody's Autobiography* (New York: Cooper Square, 1937, 1971), 52–3.

159. "rather have her room": Morris, 87; MPMFP, 386.

160. "Mad, bad": Bartlett's, 454; Macmillan, 89; Ringo, 61. Waugh: *Time,* February 12, 1979, 96. Richler: Mordecai Richler, *Joshua Then and Now* (New York: Knopf, 1980), 241, 376–7; *Time*, February 16, 1980, 81.

"You pays your money": *Huckleberry Finn* (New York: Harper & Row, 1965), 170. *Punch* cartoon: CODP, 175; Safire 1991, 359.

"Mean streets": Scorsese, 1973; Chandler, "The Simple Art of Murder," *Atlantic Monthly*, December 1944, 59. Morrison: Arthur Morrison, *Tales of Mean Streets* (London: Methuen, 1894), in Rees 1989, 136, Rees 1991, 57.

"there's a thin man": *Coming Up for Air* (New York: Harcourt, Brace, 1939, 1950), 23; Connolly, *The Unquiet Grave* (New York: Viking, 1945, 1957), 61.

160–161. "At 50": *People,* June 16, 1980, 78. Orwell: *In Front of Your Nose 1945–1950: The Collected Essays, Journalism and Letters of George Orwell* (New York: Harcourt, Brace & World, 1968), vol. 4, 515. Lincoln: Fadiman, 688; Daniel Goleman and Jonathan Freedman, *What Psychology Knows That Everyone Should* (Lexington, MA: Lewis, 1981), 50; Schlesinger, *Saturday Review,* December 1980, 67. Stanton: W. H. Auden and Louis Kronenberger, *The Viking Book of Aphorisms* (New York: Viking, 1962), 391. West: Joseph Weintraub, ed., *The Wit and Wisdom of Mae West* (New York: Putnam's, 1967), 85. Chanel: *Ladies' Home Journal,* September 1956, 69. Camus: Albert Camus, *The Fall* (New York: Vintage, 1956), 57. Just: Ward Just, *The American Ambassador* (Boston: Houghton Mifflin, 1987), 52.

162. Wilde: Robert H. Sherard, *Oscar Wilde* (New York: Haskell House, 1905, 1970); Leonard Cresswell Ingleby, *Oscar Wilde* (New York: D. Appleton, 1908); Hesketh Pearson, *Lives of the Wits* (New York: Harper & Row, 1962); Alvin Redman, *The Wit and Humor of Oscar Wilde* (New York: Dover, 1952, 1959); Richard Ellmann, *Oscar Wilde* (New York: Knopf, 1988).

Frost: John Savage letter to *Playboy,* July 1978, 16; "Life is never fair": *An Ideal Husband* in Redman, *Wit and Humor,* op. cit., 65. "Beautiful people": John Lennon and Paul McCartney, "Baby You're a Rich Man," 1967. Wilde-Boulton: Bartlett's, 914.

Whistler-Wilde: Redman, *Wit and Humor,* op. cit., 52; Hesketh Pearson, *The Man Whistler* (New York: Harper & Brothers, 1952), 162–70.

"Good Americans": Platt, 17; MPMFP, 1745; Richard Hanser, *NYT Magazine,* August 10, 1980; Wilde, *The Picture of Dorian Gray* (London: Bodley Head, 1925), 44; *A Woman of No Importance,* Act I, in *The Complete Works of Oscar Wilde* (London: Hamlyn, 1963).

163. "Please don't shoot": "Impressions of America" (1882), in *The Works of Oscar Wilde* (New York: Lamb, 1909), 259; Lloyd Lewis and Henry Justin Smith, *Oscar Wilde Discovers America* (New York: Harcourt, Brace, 1936), 316; Ellman, *Oscar Wilde,* op. cit., 204; MPMFP, 1788; Oxford, 7.

"I can resist everything": *Lady Windermere's Fan,* Act I, *Oscar Wilde's Plays, Prose Writings and Poems* (New York: Dutton, 1930, 1966); attributed to others: Peter, ix.

"Experience": *The Picture of Dorian Gray* (New York: Brentano's, 1906), 85; *Lady Windermere's Fan,* Act III. Other attributions: Leo Rosten, *The Power of Positive Nonsense,* op. cit., 108–9; J. Chalmers Da Costa, *The Trials and Triumphs of the Surgeon* (Philadelphia: Dorrance, 1944), 42; Macmillan, 369.

"Nowadays people know": Wilde, *The Picture of Dorian Gray,* op. cit., 67; *Lady Windermere's Fan,* Act III. Hubbard: Elbert Hubbard, *A Thousand and*

One Epigrams, op. cit., 159; *Roycroft Dictionary and Book of Epigrams,* op. cit., 154.

164. "In this world": *Lady Windermere's Fan,* Act III. Shaw, *Man and Superman,* Act IV; Hubbard, *Roycroft Dictionary,* op. cit., 157. Kristol: George Will, *Newsweek,* November 28, 1977, 132. Huxley: Thomas Huxley, "Address on University Education," September 26, 1876, *Essays* (New York: Macmillan, 1929), 283; Platt, 127. Smith: Oxford Modern, 202. Wilde: *An Ideal Husband,* in Redman, *Wit and Wisdom,* op. cit., 69.

"We have really": *The Canterville Ghost, The Complete Works of Oscar Wilde* (New York: Wm. H. Wise, 1927), 91; Rees 1989, 45–6. "America is": see Clemenceau, Chapter 4.

164–165. Shaw: Hesketh Pearson, *G.B.S.: A Full Length Portrait* (New York: Harper & Brothers, 1942); St. John Ervine, *Bernard Shaw: His Life, Work and Friends* (London: Constable, 1956); Michael Holyrod, *Bernard Shaw* (New York: Vintage, 1991).

165. Shaw: *Man and Superman,* Act II. Lincoln: Caroline Thomas Harnsberger, *The Lincoln Treasury* (Chicago: Wilcox and Follett, 1950), 29. Hertz, *Lincoln Talks,* op. cit., 596. Davis-Shaw: MPMFP, 54. "If I find in a book": Holyrod, *Bernard Shaw,* op. cit., vol. 2, 334.

"The world is a comedy": Burnam 1975, 259; Oxford 2nd, 563; Bartlett's, 363.

"I have defined": Pearson, *G.B.S.,* 366. "Oh, all Americans": Joseph P. Lash, *Helen and Teacher: The Story of Helen Keller and Anne Sullivan Macy* (New York: Delacorte, 1980), 612–4; Pearson, *G.B.S.,* op. cit., 366; Ervine, *Bernard Shaw,* op. cit., 532; Holyrod, *Bernard Shaw,* op. cit., vol. 3, 308.

"Youth is a wonderful thing": Lewis and Faye Copeland, *10,000 Jokes, Toasts and Stories,* op. cit., 555; *Reader's Digest,* April 1940, 84. Weintraub: Platt, 392.

"England and America": *Reader's Digest,* November 1942, 100. Platt, 105–6. Wilde: *The Canterville Ghost,* op. cit., 91.

166. "But suppose": Duncan: Copeland, *10,000 Jokes,* op. cit., 560; NYT June 8, 1982; July 23, 1982; DDN, July 12, 1990. Swiss woman: Hesketh Pearson: *Lives of the Wits,* op. cit., 265.

"Who are we": Cerf, 121. Woollcott: Teichmann, *Smart Aleck,* op. cit., 229. Pearson: Hesketh Pearson, *Lives of the Wits,* op. cit., 255–6; *G.B.S.,* op. cit., 167.

"The trouble, Mr. Goldwyn": Zierold, *The Moguls,* op. cit., 128; NYT, September 27, 1936; Macmillan, 236. See also *Film Comment,* March–April, 1990, 68; Cerf, 121. Dietz: Arthur Mayer, *Merely Colossal,* op. cit., 10; Max Wilk, *The Wit and Wisdom of Hollywood,* op. cit., 287.

166–167. "Messages": Rex Reed, *People are Crazy Here,* op. cit., 257. Kennedys: see Chapter 7. Fraser: Shaw, *Back to Methuselah,* Part V; Rees 1984, 41. "All professions": Shaw, *The Doctor's Dilemma,* Act I. Boulding: Roland Marchand, *Advertising the American Dream* (Berkeley, CA: University of California Press, 1985), 48.

167. "You can't go home": David Herbert Donald, *Look Homeward: A Life of Thomas Wolfe* (Boston: Little, Brown, 1987), 434.

"Stranger in a strange land": Bartlett's, 9, 75; MPMFP, 2224. "For whom": Donne, *The Complete Poetry and Selected Prose* (New York: Modern Library, 1952), 441; Platt, 30.

"Gone with the wind": *The Poems of Ernest Dowson* (Philadelphia, PA: University of Pennsylvania Press, 1962), 58.

168. "The right stuff": Ian Hay, *The Right Stuff* (Boston: Houghton Mifflin, 1910); Rees 1989, 187; Rees 1991, 187.

"The best and the brightest": Elizabeth Webber and Mike Feinsilber, *Grand Allusions* (Washington, D.C.: Farragut, 1990), 39–40. Heber: Wilson, 89; Dickens, Kipling: Elizabeth Weber and Mike Feinsilber, *Grand Allusions,* op. cit., 39–40.

"The cold war": Safire 1978, 127–9; Platt, 48–9; NYT, April 17, 1947; Bernard Baruch, *The Public Years* (New York: Holt, Rinehart and Winston, 1960), 388; Home Book, 2298h; Bartlett's, 729. Bernstein: Siracusa to Safire, Safire 1986, 68. Manuel: Adda B. Bozeman, *Politics and Culture in International History* (Princeton, NJ: Princeton University Press, 1960), 426; Safire 1986, 69–70.

168–169. "There's no such thing": Friedman *There's No Such Thing as a Free Lunch* (LaSalle, IL: Open Court, 1975); Safire, *NYT Magazine,* March 13, 1988, September 3, 1989; Safire 1991, 229. Oxford Modern, v, 100; Heinlein, *The Moon is a Harsh Mistress* (New York: Putnam's, 1966, Ace, 1987), 129. Crane, *The Sophisticated Investor* (New York: Simon & Schuster, 1959) in Dickson 1978, 33. Morrow: RQ, Winter 1976, 163. History of free lunch: John Lardner, *The World of John Lardner* (New York: Simon & Schuster, 1961), 196, 213–4; Flexner: Safire 1978, 245; RQ, Fall 1981, 20. San Francisco publication: Mathews, 659; Lloyd Lewis and Henry Justin Smith, op. cit., 187; *The Philistine,* July 1895, 46–51. Hessen: John Eatwell, Murray Milgate and Peter Newman, ed., *The New Palgrave Dictionary of Economics* (London: Macmillan, 1987), vol. 2, 420–1.

CHAPTER 12: MISQUOTE U.

170–172. "Mark Hopkins": Carroll A. Wilson, *The Colophon,* Spring 1938, 194–208.

173. "Sometimes a cigar": Peter Gay, *Freud: A Life For Our Time* (New York: Norton, 1988), 169–70; Elisabeth Young-Bruehl, *Anna Freud* (New York: Summit, 1988). Alan Elms interview, December 14, 1991.

173–174. "Love and work": Erikson, *Childhood and Society* (New York: Norton, 1950, 1963), 265. Seldes 1960, 620. Macmillan, 385; Reader's Digest Treasury, 188; Simpson 1964, 1988, 135. Theodore Reik, *Of Love and Lust* (New York: Farrar, Straus and Cudahy, 1957), 194. Platt, 163. Tolstoy: Henri Troyat (Garden City, NY: Doubleday, 1965, 1967), 158; Cindy Hazen and Philip R. Shaver, "Love and Work: An Attachment-Theoretical Perspective," *Journal of Personality and Social Psychology,* 59:270–80, 1990.

174. "But still": Oxford, 220; Giuseppe Baretti, *The Italian Library, Containing An Account of the Lives and Works of the Most Valuable Authors of Italy* (London: A. Millar, 1757), 52; Abbe Irailh, *Querelles litteraires* (1761), vol. 3, 49 in Bartlett's, 183; MPMFP, 657; Morris Rosenblum, "They Never Said It," *American Mercury,* April 1946, 494. See also Bent, 241–2; King, 36; Walsh, 252; Colin A. Ronan, *Galileo* (New York: Putnam's, 1974), 220.

174–175. "If I have seen": Robert K. Merton, *On the Shoulders of Giants* (New York: Free Press, 1965, Harcourt Brace Jovanovich, 1985), 3–9, 12–3, 32–4, 40–1, 73–9, 177–96, 200–1, 209–11, 218, 246–61, 267–9.

175. "Survival": Herbert Spencer, *The Principles of Biology* (New York: D. Appleton, 1865, 1898), vol. 2, 444; Charles Darwin, *The Origins of Species* (Chicago: Britannica, 1859, 1952), 32.

175–176. "There is no hitching post": Einstein-Seldes 1985, 119. "God does not play dice": Seldes 1985, 120; Oxford Modern, 72; Max Born, *The Born-Einstein Letters,* Irene Born, trans. (New York: Walker, 1971), 91. See also, Banesh Hoffman, *Albert Einstein: Creator and Rebel* (New York: Viking, 1972), 193.

176. "If only I had known": Morrow, 98; Macmillan, 180; Harper, 292; *New Statesman,* April 16, 1965, 601; NYT, July 2, 1979, Otto Nathan letter, July 11, 1979. Einstein letter to *The Reporter,* November 18, 1954, 8.

"Vote early": Curley: *Time,* March 5, 1979, 6. Miles: Bartlett's, 590; Home Book, 2278. Van Buren: James Morgan, *Our Presidents* (New York: Macmillan, 1924), 30; MPMFP, 2438; Bailey, 120. Billings: *The Complete Works of Josh Billings,* op. cit., 253.

177. "Nobody ever": Macmillan, 587; Harper, 480; Bailey, 371; *Time,* February 16, 1970, 84; *Newsweek,* March 5, 1973, 46; *The Bulletin* (Philadelphia), December 24, 1978; Tom Fox, PI, July 19, 1979. Bartlett's, 772; Seldes 1985, 283; CT, September 19, 1926; Oxford Modern, 150.

"If fascism comes": Arthur Schlesinger, Jr., *The Politics of Upheaval* (Boston: Houghton Mifflin, 1960), 67, 664–5; Boller and George, 94–5; Shenkman 1988, 178.

177–178. "Less is more.": Macmillan, 27; Reader's Digest Treasury, 22; Peter Blake, *The Master Builders* (New York: Knopf, 1960), 169; Arthur Drexler, *ludwig mies van der rohe* (New York: George Braziller, 1960), 31; David Spaeth, *Ludwig Mies van der Rohe: An Annotated Bibliography and Chronology* (New York: Garland, 1979), 8. Browning, *Andrea del Sarto* in *Browning's Poetical Works* (London: Oxford, 1940), 433; Robert W. Kent, *Money Talks* (New York: Pocket Books, 1981), 312; Safire 1991, 264. Franz Schulze, *Mies van der Rohe: A Critical Biography* (Chicago: University of Chicago, 1985); Schulze interview, April 21, 1992.

178. "God is in": PI, January 13, 1980; *PC Computing*, November 1988, 4. Schulze, *Mies van der Rohe,* op. cit., 281; interview; David Spaeth, *Mies van der Rohe* (New York: Rizzoli, 1985); Spaeth interview, February 25, 1992.

"When I hear": Seldes 1985, 214; Oxford Modern, 114; Rees 1984, 228; Boller and George, 36; Peter Bloch letter to NYT, April 12, 1981; Thomas Vinciguerra letter to NYT, September 17, 1987; NYT, May 28, 1933.

"Typing": Capote-Kerouac: Peter Lewis, *The Fifties* (New York: J.B. Lippincott, 1978), 175; George Will, *Newsweek*, July 4, 1988, 64.

179. "Easy writing": Hemingway: Morris, 606. Johnson: Stephens, 29. Sheridan: Home Book, 2254; MPMFP, 2654.

"Read over": Berger, 88–9; Jon Winokour, *Writers on Writing* (Philadelphia: Running Press, 1987), 78; James Boswell, *The Life of Samuel Johnson*, op. cit., 74. Mark Twain, *Pudd'nhead Wilson* (New York: Harper & Brothers, 1894, 1922), 83.

179–180. "Writing is easy": Smith: Peter Axthelm, *Newsweek*, May 17, 1976, 75; James Charlton, *The Writer's Quotation Book* (Wainscott, NY: Pushcart Press, 1980), 55; Donald Hall, *NYT Book Review,* July 18, 1982; *Time,* July 16, 1982, 61. Fowler: Charlton, *The Writer's Quotation Book*, op. cit., 1986, 41; Winokour, *Writers on Writing*, op. cit., 78; Harper, 624. Wolfe: Gene Olson, *Sweet Agony* (Grants Pass, OR: Windyridge Press, 1972), 18. Smith: Lady Holland, *A Memoir of the Reverend Sydney Smith* (London: Longman, Brown, Green and Longmans, 1855), vol. 1, 258; Ringo 141; Home Book, 2254.

180. "Bad money": Raymond de Roover, *Greshan on Foreign Exchange* (Cambridge, MA: Harvard University Press, 1949), 91–3.

"If you have to ask": NYT, June 14, 1982; *Block Island Times,* August 3, 1991; Rees 1989, 75–6; Frederick Lewis Allen, *The Great Pierpont Morgan* (New

York: Harper & Brothers, 1949), 192; Edwin P. Hoyt, Jr., *The House of Morgan* (New York: Dodd, Mead, 1966), 271. Other wealthy men: BG, August 23, 1991. Getty: Macmillan, 605; Rees 1989, 76; Robert Lenzner, *The Great Getty* (New York: Crown, 1985), in Simpson 1988, 96; Clifton Chadwick to Dickson 1980, 68. Hunt, Harry Hurt III, *Texas Rich* (New York: Norton, 1981) in *Publishers Weekly,* April 10, 1981, 63.

180–181. "Under capitalism": Gorbachev: DDN January 4, 1992. Galbraith: Christopher Lehmann-Haupt review of John Kenneth Galbraith, *A Life in Our Times* (Boston: Houghton Mifflin, 1981), NYT, May 1, 1981.

181. "Religion . . . is the opium": Safire, *NYT Magazine,* February 21, 1980; Safire 1991, 189.

"Workers of the world": Bartlett's, 205; Burnam 1980, 205.

Lenin: Kominsky, *The Hoaxers,* op. cit.; Boller and George, 63–77; NYT, January 22, 1983; Abraham Brumberg, *New Republic,* August 29, 1960, 15–6.

181–182. "The capitalists": Safire, *NYT Magazine,* April 12, 1987; Platt, 51; Boller and George, 64. Barry Goldwater, *With No Apologies* (New York: Morrow, 1979), 86.

182. "The best way to destroy": John Maynard Keynes, *The Economic Consequences of the Peace* (Harcourt, Brace and Howe, 1920), 235; Platt, 229.

"Promises": NYT, January 22, 1983; Platt, 290; CODP, 184; Kominsky, *The Hoaxers,* op. cit., 27–35.

183. "The United States": *RQ,* Spring 1987, 292; Kominsky, *The Hoaxers,* op. cit., 35–42.

"Useful idiots": Safire, *NYT Magazine,* April 12, 1987; Safire 1991, 49–51; Boller and George, 76.

"the love of money": Burnam, 159; Magill, 599–600.

"pride goeth": Rees 1989, 166; Burnam 198.

"The lion shall lie down" Pearson, 20.

"Can the leopard": Pearson, 20; MPMFP, 1673.

"Let us eat": Pearson, 20; Bartlett's, 27, 30, 43.

184. "God helps those": 1991 survey: George Barna, *What Americans Believe* (Ventura, CA: Regal Books, 1991), 80; *News-Gazette* (Champaign–Urbana, IL), September 13, 1991. Aesop: Bartlett's, 66. Howell: Newcomb, 294. Sidney: Hoyt's, 319. Franklin: MPMFP, 979.

"Cleanliness": *The Works of John Wesley* (Grand Rapids: Zondervan, 1872, 1958), vol. 7, 16; Bartlett's, 346; Walsh, 167; Bombaugh, 177–8; Burnam, 47; Boller and George, 7; MPMFP, 361.

184–185. "God, give us": Platt, 276. "It may have been spooking": *RQ*, Spring 1978, 290. Subsequent comment: Richard Wightman Fox, *Reinhold Niebuhr: A Biography* (New York: Pantheon, 1985), 291. Mowbray: *RQ*, Winter 1978, 183–4.

185. "Go placidly . . .": Fred D. Cavinder, "Desiderata," *TWA Ambassador*, August 1973, 14–5, in Platt xiv, 212. Rees 1984, 48. Rees 1989, 16. Court ruling: Robert Bell v. PRO ARTS, INC., 366 F. Supp. 474 (N.D. Ohio 1973).

"Burn your bra": Rees 1984, 215; Rees 1991, 214. Judith Hole and Ellen Levine, *Rebirth of Feminism* (New York: Quadrangle, 1971), 123, 136, 229–30.

186. "Sisterhood": Robin Morgan, ed., *sisterhood is powerful* (New York: Random House, 1970), xvi–xvii; Bartlett's, 914; Oxford Modern, 155. Brownmiller, Amatniek: Hole and Levine, *Rebirth of Feminism,* op. cit., 179, 118; Colette Price letter to *NYT Book Review,* May 3, 1981.

"The only man": *Time,* March 26, 1973, 61, December 18, 1978, 43; Golda Meir, *My Life* (New York: Putnam's, 1975), 114; Meir interview, Oriana Fallaci, *Ms.,* April 1973, 100. Flora Larsson, *My Best Men are Women* (New York: The Salvation Army, 1974), 73. Goldwyn: *Life,* February 16, 1959, 116. Barbara Castle: Macmillan, 449.

186–187. "Call me Madam": George Martin, *Madam Secretary* (Boston: Houghton Mifflin, 1976, 16–7; Eleanor Roosevelt and Lorena Hickock, *Ladies of Courage* (New York: Putnam's, 1954), 190; Rees 1991, 62–3.

187. "Close your eyes": Macmillan 369; Partridge 1977, 35; Partridge and Beale, 50–1; Rees 1984, 251–2; Rees 1989, 42.

"Love is two minutes": Macmillan, 516; Rees 1989, 130.

187–188. "That was the most fun": Haun, 300; Rees 1991, 135; Mencken, 717; William Cole and Louis Phillips, *Sex: The Most Fun You Can Have Without Laughing . . . and Other Quotations* (New York: St. Martin's, 1990).

CHAPTER 13: COULD YOU LOOK IT UP?

189–190. Bond-Mencken: Jeff Prugh, LAT, June 16, 1978; *Village Voice,* July 31, 1978; Julian Bond letter to *Rolling Stone,* September 7, 1978.

190. Hirst: interview, December 16, 1991.

191. Johnston: Alva Johnston, *The Great Goldwyn,* op. cit., 28; A. Scott Berg, *Goldwyn: A Biography,* op. cit., 396.

H. Allen Smith, *Lost in the Horse Latitudes,* op. cit., 191–2.

Darwin: Oxford 2nd, xvi–xvii.

Ted Williams: Dan Buck interview, February 13, 1992.

Hume-Macaulay: Mencken, 996.

192. Eliot: *The Sacred Wood,* op. cit., 123–9.

Trilling: Robert Benton and Gloria Steinem, "The Student Prince, Or How to Seize Power Though an Undergraduate," *Esquire,* September 1962, 85; James Charlton, *The Writer's Quotation Book,* op. cit., 1985, 58; *The Penguin Dictionary of Modern Humorous Quotations,* op. cit., 192; Oxford Modern, 218; Simpson 1988, 316; Tripp, 474.

Anderson: *RQ,* Summer 1987, 413.

193. Voltaire: *The Complete Works of Voltaire* (Oxford: The Voltaire Foundation, 1976), vol. 120, 18; King, 61. Leo Rosten, *The Power of Positive Nonsense,* op. cit., 101; Seldes 1985, 434; Rees 1989, 181. Norbert Guterman, *The Anchor Book of French Quotations* (New York: Doubleday, 1963), 189.

193–194. Shadegg: Stephen Shadegg, *Barry Goldwater: Freedom Is His Flight Plan* (New York: McFadden, 1963), 171.

194. Burger: WSJ, January 31, 1986.

"The Lord prefers": Seldes 1960, xiii; Boller, 330–1; Boller and George, 84; Shenkman 1988, 173–4; Oxford, 315; James Morgan, *Our Presidents,* op. cit., 149. John Hay, *Letters of John Hay and Extracts From Diary* (Washington, D.C., 1908), vol. 1, 142–3; Platt, 252

194–195. "Everybody talks": *Hartford Courant,* August 24, 1897. Warner attribution: *Hartford Daily Courant,* January 5, 1945; Bartlett's, 603; Morris, 209; Harper, 250; Richard Hanser, *NYT Magazine,* August 10, 1980; WSJ, January 7, 1988. Burnam, 78. Clark: Home Book, 2128. Robert Underwood Johnson, *Remembered Yesterdays* (Boston: Little, Brown, 1923), 322; Platt, 370–1.

195. "Nuts!": Harper, 261; Rees 1989, 148; Rees 1991, 42. Maxey interview, December 13, 1976.

Attali: Jacques Attali, *Stories of Time,* in Jean-Louis Servan-Schreiber, *The Art of Time* (Reading, MA: Addison-Wesley, 1988), 130. Lewis Mumford, *Technics and Civilization* (New York: Harcourt, Brace, 1934), 14.

196. Voltaire: Barnes & Noble, xiv; Platt, 389.

Trudeau: *People,* July 20, 1981, 7.

Pearson: Pearson, 10.

197. Thurow: speech to National Press Club, May 28, 1992. "Play up!": R. Z. Sheppard, *Time,* March 13, 1978, 92; *Time,* April 3, 1978.

"The miracle is not": Lawrence Eisenberg, *TV Guide,* November 8, 1986, 19. Middle East expert: Barry Rubin, NYT, December 18, 1984; Leon Aron letter to NYT, January 1, 1985.

Fadiman: Macmillan, 467.

Bouton-Cannon: *Washington Star,* November 5, 1977; Sugar, 99. Burton-Churchill: Melinda Corey and George Ochoa, *The Man in Lincoln's Nose,* op. cit., 121; Bartlett's, 743.

197–198. Leno: Jay Leno speech to National Press Club, broadcast December 12, 1991, WYSO (Yellow Springs, OH).

198. Rosenblum: Morris Rosenblum, *American Mercury,* April 1946, 493.

The following indexes are designed to help readers locate quotations whose wording or attribution is discussed in the text. In the first, each such quotation is indexed by its key words. In the second, quotations are indexed by the names of those to whom they have been attributed (correctly or incorrectly). Quotations or people referred to in passing in the text are not indexed.

Key Word Index

curse: rather light candle than c. darkness, 76

curtain: iron c., 54–55

damn: d. torpedoes, full speed ahead, 63

dancing: d. is a contact sport, 154

dangerous: mad, bad, d. to know, 160

darkness: rather light a candle than curse d., 76

daughters: marry d. when can, 31

day
make my d., 106
today first d. of rest of life, 39

dead
only good Indian a d. Indian, 66–67
survivors envy d., 24

deal
new d. for American people, 102–103
square d., 99

death
give me liberty or d., 57–58
reports of my d. exaggerated, 111–112, 140
defend to d. your right to say it, 44–45

deathbed: no one on d. ever said wish spent more time on business, 20–21

decision: John Marshall has made his d., 94

deed: the reward of a good d. is to have done it, 37

deep: d. six, 86

defeat: victory has hundred/thousand fathers, d. an orphan, 91–92

defend: d. to death your right to say it, 44–45

defense
extremism in d. of liberty no vice, 86
millions for d., not one cent for tribute, 62–63

degeneration: from barbarism to d. without civilization, 51

déjà vu: d. all over again, 152

democracy: d. worst form of government, 53

Democrats: if they stop telling lies about D., 75–76

depression: recession when neighbor loses job, d. when you lose yours, 5, 105

destruction: pride goeth before d./fall, 182

details: God in the d., 178

device: foolproof d. for judging picture, 131

die
eat, drink, be merry, for tomorrow d., 183
few d., none resign, 93
good Americans, when d., go to Paris, 162
guards d., never surrender, 46
old soldiers never d., 69
only those fit to live not afraid to d., 68
rather d. on feet than live on knees, 104

difference: d. between men and boys is price of toys, 116

dime: don't care if pictures don't make a d., 127

disapprove: d. of what you say, defend your right to say it, 44–45

discretion: better part of valor is d., 4

distressed: no woman has so comforted d., 76–77

do
d. your own thing, 38–39
folks who can d., who can't chin/teach, 37

doc: never play cards with man called d., 156–157

Dr. Zhivago: D. Z. again; what's the matter now, 153

doctors: more old drunkards than old d., 116

dog
has every characteristic of d. except loyalty, 134
in this business, it's d. eat d., 127

dogs: any man who hates d. and children, 1–2, 135–136

don't
d. fire until see whites of eyes, 59–60
d. give up ship, 63
d. look a gift horse in mouth, 3
d. look back, something might be gaining, 150
d. throw stones at neighbors, 32

door
no greater happiness for man than approaching d., 105
world will beat path to your d., 34–35

Doris Day: I knew D. D. before a virgin, 124

Dorothy Parker: everything I've

said be credited to D. P., 120

down
d. these mean streets, 160
meet on way d., 115

dream: I d. things and say "Why not", 92

drink
eat, d., be merry, 183
if I were your husband, I'd d. it, 52

drinks: tell me what brand Grant d., 96

drives: bad money d. out good, 180

drop
d. the gun, Louie, 138
just open vein and bleed, 179–180

drunkards: more old d. than old doctors, 116

dry: get out of wet clothes and into d. martini, 118–119

duck: forgot to d., 105–106

dull: d. people always formal, 116

dumb: Jerry Ford so d., 85

dust: excuse my d., 121

dying
d. easy, comedy hard, 134
not afraid of d., 113

Earl Long: poor people of Louisiana have three friends: Jesus, Sears, and E. L., 133–134

early: vote e. and vote often, 176

earth
every part of e. sacred to my people, 18–19
do not inherit e. from ancestors, borrow from children, 32–33
last best hope of e., 98

earthquake: story starts with e. works to a climax, 125

easiest: to cease smoking the e. thing, 110

easy
dying e., comedy hard, 134
e. writing makes hard reading, 179
writing e., just sit at typewriter, open vein, 179–180

eat
can't have your cake and e. it, 3
e., drink, be merry, 183
let them e. cake/brioche, 43–44
never e. at place called Mom's, 156–157

pains: no gains without p., 30, 76

paper: verbal contract isn't worth p. written on, 127–128

paranoids: even p. have real enemies, 113

parents
from birth to 18, girl needs good p., 131
p. obey their children, 26
reminds me of man who killed p., then pleaded for mercy because orphan, 97
we are people our p. warned us about, 40

Paris: good Americans when die go to Paris, 162

part
one p. mush, two parts Eleanor, 15
either p. of problem or solution, 39–40

passage: read over compositions, wherever meet with a p. think fine, strike out, 179

passion: man in p. rides mad horse, 31

pays: p. your money, takes your choice, 160

peace
go placidly amid noise, remember p. in silence, 185
p., commerce, honest friendship for all nations, 93
p. with honor, 48

pearls: p. before swine, 120

people
can fool all p. some of time, 95–96
dull p. always formal, 116
every part of earth sacred to my p., 18–19
give p. what want to see, they'll come out, 131
government of p., by p., for p., 97
greatest pleasure is doing what p. say you cannot, 27
if p. don't want to come, nothing stop them, 25
lord prefers common-looking p., 194
a new deal for American p., 102–103
poor p. of Louisiana have three friends, 133–134
religion is opium of the p., 181

we are p. our parents warned about, 40
when more p. thrown out of work, unemployment results, 101
worst tempered p. I've met, 113
your p. a great beast, 80–81

percent: 80 p. of success just showing up, 108

person: steal from one p., it's plagiarism, 115

personality: from 35 to 55, needs a good p., 131

perspiration: genius 99% p., 36

Philadelphia: rather be in P., 136

physical: baseball 90% mental, other half p., 152–153

pianist: please don't shoot p., 163

pickle: weaned on p., 22–23

picture
foolproof device for judging p., 131
mucus of a good p., 126
one p. worth a thousand words, 27–28
to hell with cost, if a good p. we'll make it, 125

pictures
don't care if p. don't make dime, 127
you furnish p., I'll furnish war, 67

pie: promises like p. crusts, to be broken, 182

piss: vice-presidency isn't worth pitcher of warm p./spit, 84–85

pitcher: vice-presidency isn't worth p. of warm spit/piss, 84–85

place: hottest p. in hell reserved, 79

plagiarism: if steal from one person, it's p., 115

plan: a secret p. to end the war, 70–71

plans: life what happens while making other p., 40

play
can't anyone p. this game, 17
p. it again, Sam, 138–139
p. up! p.! and p. the game!, 197

playing: battle of Waterloo won on p. fields of Eton, 46–47

playthings: old boys have p., 116

please: p. don't shoot pianist, 163

pleasure: greatest p. in life doing what people say cannot, 27

poets: immature p. imitate, mature p. steal, 156, 192

points: thousand p. of light, 107

politician
only way for newspaperman to look at p. is *down*, 109
p. approaches every subject with open mouth, 76
statesman thinks of future generations, p. of coming election, 98

politics: p. is applesauce, 122

poor
been rich and p., 131
p. George born with silver foot in mouth, 78–79
p. people of Louisiana have three friends, 133–134

poorhouse: only nation go to p. in automobile, 122

post: no hitching p. in universe, 175–176

pot: chicken in every p., 102

pound: ounce of prevention worth p. of cure, 30

powerful: sisterhood is p., 186

praise: a man known by p. gives, 33

pregnant: if men could get p., abortion be a sacrament, 22

presidency: Teflon p., 72–73

president
Eisenhower proved don't need a p., 86–87
Roosevelt proved could be p. for life, 86–87
Truman proved anybody could be p., 86–87

pressure: grace under p., 6

prevention: ounce of p. worth pound of cure, 30

price
eternal vigilance p. of liberty, 59
every man has p., 80
only difference between men and boys is p. of toys, 116
p. of everything, value of nothing, 36–37

pride: p. goeth before fall/destruction, 182

priests: mine [ancestors] were p. in temple of Solomon, 49

principles: depends whether embrace your p. or your mistress, 49

problem
for every p. a solution

us: have met enemy and he is
    u., 14
useful: u. idiots of West, 183

valor: better part of v.
    discretion, 4
value: price of everything, v. of
    nothing, 36–37
vast: v. wasteland, 23
vein: just open v. and bleed
    drop by drop, 179–180
verbal: v. contract isn't worth
    paper written on, 127–128
vice: extremism no v., 86
vice-presidency: v.-p. isn't
    worth pitcher of warm
    spit/piss, 84–85
victory
    in war no substitute for v.,
    69
    v. has hundred/thousand
    fathers, 91–92
Viet Cong: no V. C. called me
    nigger, 7–8
views: v. on birth control
    distorted by fact was
    seventh, 78
virgin: been around so long,
    knew Doris Day before v.,
    124
vigilance: eternal v. price of
    liberty, 59
virtue: moderation in the
    pursuit of justice no v., 86
volcanoes: exhausted v., 49
vomit: I may v., 117
vote: v. early and v. often, 176
votes: as long as I count v.,
    24–25

Wagner's: W. music better
    than sounds, 112–113
wait: everything comes if man
    only w., 49
waiting: to be on wire life, rest
    w., 134
walk
    Jerry Ford so dumb can't
    w./fart and chew gum at
    same time, 85
    w. over my own
    grandmother, 24
war
    in w. no substitute for
    victory, 69
    never lost a w., never won a
    conference, 122
    a secret plan to end w.,
    70–71
    suppose gave a w., nobody
    came, 38
    w. is hell, 65
    w. to end wars, 68

w. too important to be left to
    military/generals, 50–51
you furnish pictures, I'll
    furnish w., 67
warned: we are people our
    parents w. about, 40
warts: w. and all, 98
Washington
    known all over W. as
    shameless extrovert, 83–84
    W. a city of Northern
    charm, Southern
    efficiency, 92
wasteland: vast w., 23
watching: can observe a lot by
    w., 151–152
watchmaker: if only known,
    should have become a w.,
    176
Waterloo: battle of W. won on
    playing fields of Eton,
    46–47
Watson: elementary, my dear
    W., 2, 7
wear: if shoe fits, w. it, 3
weak: cannot strengthen w. by
    weakening strong, 96–97
weaned: w. on pickle, 22–23
weather: everybody talks about
    w., nobody does anything
    about it, 194–195
wedding: little man on w.
    cake, 22
well: living w. best revenge, 27
west
    go w. young man, 21–22
    useful idiots of W., 183
Western Union: if have
    message, send by W.U.,
    130
wet: get out of w. clothes, into
    dry martini, 118–119
what
    w. we've got here is failure
    to communicate, 132
    w. won't they think of next,
    129
what's: w. good for General
    Motors good for country,
    8–9
wheat: an editor separates w.
    from chaff and prints
    chaff, 76
when: if not now, w., 105
where
    w. do we find such men,
    106
    w. fraternities not allowed,
    communism flourishes, 84
    w. liberty, there is my
    country, 59
where's: w. the beef, 74
whites: don't fire until see w.
    of eyes, 59–60

who
    if not us, w.?, 105
    w. are we two against so
    many?, 166
why
    w. don't you come up and
    see me sometime, 135
    w. so it does, 26
    you see things and you say
    "Why?", 92
will: at 20 w. reigns, 32
win
    we'll w. because God's on
    our side, 149
    w. one for the Gipper,
    145–146
wind: gone with the w., 167
windows: don't throw stones if
    w. glass, 32
winning: w. isn't everything, 2,
    154–155
winter: coldest w. ever spent
    summer in San Francisco,
    5, 111
wire: to be on w. life, rest
    waiting, 134
wisdom: God give us w. to
    distinguish one from
    other, 184–185
wise: a word to w. enough, 30
wish: w. could be sure of
    anything as opponent is of
    everything, 49
wit: at 20 will reigns, at 30 w.,
    32
with: w. malice toward none,
    w. charity for all, 97
woman
    hell hath no fury like w.
    scorned, 2–3
    never sleep with w. whose
    troubles worse than own,
    156–157
    no w. has so comforted
    distressed or distressed
    comfortable, 76–77
wonder
    ever w. why, 139
    for first six months w. how
    got here, 77–78
word
    never trust man has only one
    way to spell w., 110
    when I hear w. culture,
    reach for gun, 178
    w. to wise enough, 30
words
    answer in two w. "Im
    possible", 128
    one picture worth thousand
    w., 27–28
work
    when more people thrown

Name Index